NO-EXCUSES INNOVATION

NO-EXCUSES

INNOVATION

STRATEGIES FOR SMALL- AND MEDIUM-SIZED
MATURE ENTERPRISES

BRUCE A. VOJAK AND
WALTER B. HERBST

STANFORD BUSINESS BOOKS
An Imprint of Stanford University Press
Stanford, California

Stanford University Press
Stanford, California

Special discounts for bulk quantities of Stanford Business Books
are available to corporations, professional associations, and other
organizations. For details and discount information, contact the special
sales department of Stanford University Press. Tel: (650) 725-0820, Fax:
(650) 725-3457

Printed in the United States of America on acid-free, archival-quality paper

Library of Congress Cataloging-in-Publication Data

Names: Vojak, Bruce A., author. | Herbst, Walter B., author.
Title: No-excuses innovation : strategies for small- and medium-sized
    mature enterprises / Bruce A. Vojak and Walter B. Herbst.
Description: Stanford, California : Stanford Business Books, an imprint of
    Stanford University Press, 2022. | Includes bibliographical references
    and index.
Identifiers: LCCN 2021061491 (print) | LCCN 2021061492 (ebook) | ISBN
    9781503627581 (cloth) | ISBN 9781503633469 (ebook)
Subjects: LCSH: Small business—Technological innovations. | Small
    business—Management.
Classification: LCC HD2341 .V65 2022 (print) | LCC HD2341 (ebook) |
    DDC 338.6/42—dc23/eng/20211227
LC record available at https://lccn.loc.gov/2021061491
LC ebook record available at https://lccn.loc.gov/2021061492

Cover design: Tandem Design
Cover image: Ceramic bladed box cutter for "Slice" by Herbst Produkt

"The future is purchased by the present."

—Samuel Johnson[1]

Contents

Preface and Acknowledgments

"Everybody has a plan until they get punched in the mouth."
—Mike Tyson, former undisputed world
heavyweight boxing champion[1]

Over the past decade, we have had the good fortune and pleasure to engage together on various innovation topics. Our complementary expertise, experiences, observations, perspectives, and personalities always have yielded fruitful discussions, providing even more for each of us to consider.

While various themes have ebbed and flowed, for some time now, the innovation needs of small- and medium-sized mature enterprises (SMMEs) have dominated our thinking. Both of us see the same pattern. A handful of SMMEs "get it." They know what to do, embrace it, and make it happen. At the other end of the spectrum, many SMMEs don't "get it." Whether consumed with or satisfied by current business, they are not inclined toward innovation and seemingly not convincible. And then there are those SMMEs—likely appearing at least as often as those that get it—touting innovation capability with expertise that is nowhere to be found.

At some level, we could easily walk away from all this. Yet we are concerned. SMMEs play a significant role in total employment and thus a substantial role in local, regional, and national economies. When SMMEs succeed by their innovativeness or are brought down by that of others— metaphorically punching or getting punched in the mouth à la Mike

Tyson—it has an impact on the lives of individuals and the survival of firms. And when SMMEs flourish, falter, or fail, localities and regions often follow suit.

What makes the situation more challenging for SMMEs is that they are relatively neglected in the innovation literature. Further, it is difficult enough for large and mature companies' executives, innovation managers, and innovation practitioners to keep up with the countless innovation blogs, podcasts, articles, and books released annually. Imagine now the broader and often more urgent set of responsibilities typically carried by their SMME counterparts. Without clear and straightforward means to bring those in SMMEs up to speed and make them conversant on innovation as an investment opportunity, innovation often gets ignored.

Our motivation, then, is two-fold: to help SMMEs—their owners, boards, CEOs, executive leaders, and employees—survive and thrive in business and, as a result, to support local, regional, and national economies. We believe that SMMEs, and thus economies, can flourish over time if they practice innovation and do so wisely.

WHAT WE MEAN BY AN SMME

So what do we mean by a mature company? We begin by recognizing that all companies are on an S-curve (see Figure P.1). At some point, every company, product, service, or business model that survives will, in looking in the mirror, hit an inflection point (B) in growth and, without intervention, eventually reach maturity (C). Yet since companies only recognize this inflection point and maturity in hindsight, they will not realize that they have reached them until it is too late. Therefore, we address our book to all small- and medium-sized companies that have moved beyond the emergence phase (A).

Then what do we mean by small- and medium-sized enterprises? We take a broad view for industrialized economies, including businesses with annual revenue up to several hundred million dollars. We readily acknowledge that this definition is not very specific. For example, it does not address potential questions about whether these are privately held or public companies or whether a founder or later-generation family member runs the company. We are not overly concerned with such distinctions. Our

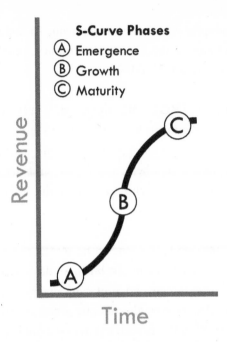

S-Curve Phases
- Ⓐ Emergence
- Ⓑ Growth
- Ⓒ Maturity

FIGURE P.1. The three primary S-curve phases.

message is more holistic, pertinent to all companies in this size range since their unique challenges are more fundamental than these differences.

In contrast to large companies, SMMEs are on their own to win or lose in the marketplace. They may lack the relative economies of scale and scope, available to large companies, to understand and invest in innovation. Often they are in a position of sustained disadvantage with no perceived path of renewal. A significant number of these companies focus more on optimizing existing business rather than renewal. Many are "milking" their business, even if they do not explicitly acknowledge it. Without attending to renewal, even SMMEs in a current position of competitive advantage will eventually fail.

As a potentially unexpected example to illustrate our definition's breadth and the opportunity innovation provides, consider the Oakland Athletics baseball team. This franchise reported total annual revenue of $225 million in 2019.[2] Because of extreme internal pressure to limit Major League Baseball's highest cost, player salaries, in the 1990s the franchise renewed the basis of competition in its more than hundred-year-old industry by being an early adopter of sabermetrics, applying statistics to sports. The "Moneyball"[3] team and its success offer an initial glimpse of the type of potential we seek to share with SMMEs.

OUR INTENDED AUDIENCE AND HOW THEY WILL BENEFIT

Having defined what we mean by an SMME, we consider our primary audience to consist of four categories of people working in or with SMMEs—owners, board members, and CEOs; presidents or GMs and their leadership teams; those who are skilled and inclined toward innovating; and those who are skilled and inclined toward optimizing the existing business.

In addition to those working in and with SMMEs, there are others who may have an interest as well—including business, design, engineering, and marketing students; government and think-tank analysts and decision makers who address local and regional economic needs; and academic educators and researchers. We address each group in the following.

Owners, Board Members, and CEOs—Those with Strategic, but Not Operating Responsibility

- The question for you is simple: Do you invest in innovation or not? This book will help clarify your options for investment and help you make informed decisions.
- It will help you to know what to look for and what questions to ask.
- For those who run your company, it also will identify a suite of low-investment, low-risk, high-value methodologies, processes, and tools to deploy.
- And perhaps most important, it will help you understand who to trust with this critical investment.

Presidents or GMs and Their Leadership Teams—Senior Executives with Operating Responsibility

- This book will help clarify what you can do, how you do it, and why it is essential to keep doing it to make innovation happen.

- It will provide insight into how you can most effectively strategically lead innovation in your company.
- It also will help you articulate an innovation message to both owners and company employees.
- As for owners, board members, and CEOs, it will help you understand who to invest in to make innovation happen.

Those Who Are Skilled and Inclined Toward Innovating—Organizationally Anywhere Within the SMME

- This book will help define what to do, how to do it, and why it is essential to keep doing it to make innovation happen. It also will provide a broader context for your contributions.
- It will provide insight into how you can innovate even more effectively.
- It also will help you articulate an innovation message to executive leaders and owners who are often either not sufficiently aware of or disinclined toward such opportunities. Further, it will help you evaluate and articulate a strong case for your most promising innovative insights.
- It will help you help those around you understand how you innovate and validate why you work and innovate the way you do, providing them insight into how to better collaborate with you or manage you more effectively.
- Finally, it will help you realize whether your company will ever embrace real innovation or not, with the latter placing the company's existence and your job at risk. If your employer is averse to or incapable of exploring or succeeding at renewal, knowing so will help you consider your career options before the inevitable occurs.

Those Who Are Skilled and Inclined Toward Optimizing the Existing Business—Organizationally Anywhere Within the SMME

- This book will help clarify how to implement innovation in SMMEs most successfully.

- Regardless of whether you are in production, design, engineering, finance, sales, marketing, human resources, or some other function, it will help you understand and collaborate with those around you who innovate most effectively. Doing so will increase the likelihood of your company and your job surviving and thriving through difficult times.

- Finally, it will help you realize whether your company will ever embrace real innovation or not, with the latter placing the company's existence and your job at risk. If your employer is averse to or incapable of exploring or succeeding at renewal, knowing so will help you consider your career options before the inevitable occurs. We especially emphasize this with those not directly charged with innovation because as goes your employer, so goes your job.

In Addition to Those Working in and with SMMEs, Others May Have an Interest

- Business, design, engineering, and marketing students—and perhaps others, such as those studying finance, human resources, and operations: this book, particularly the stories herein, provide a comprehensive overview of what innovation can look like in an SMME.

- Government and think-tank analysts and decision makers who address local and regional economic needs: this book, grounded in real-life examples, will help you evaluate which types of programs (such as tax incentives and funds for workforce training), within the context of local and regional constraints, best align with what naturally produces innovation success in SMMEs.

- Academic educators and researchers: this book will provide many stories illustrating how the innovation that leads to renewal works in practice within an SMME.

A WORD ABOUT WHAT THIS BOOK IS AND IS NOT

Our book is for professionals, industry people. It is for those working in and with SMMEs that require renewal, and thus innovation, to survive and thrive. Importantly, this pool includes those who may not yet realize their need.

It is holistic in scope, not focusing on just one aspect of innovation. Many in our audience lack the time and foundation to explore even portions of the vast innovation literature on their own. Instead, this book brings together salient innovation topics into a new whole that provides the reader with a comprehensive view, not one that they must piece together after first identifying the necessary components. In this way, it saves the reader the time, effort, and preexisting insight required to form a working understanding.

This book is a guidebook. It is a guidebook built on our personal experience with SMMEs and our grasp of both the professional and academic literature. We intend this to be a high-utility book, designed as the go-to, jump-start guide for those who otherwise might feel trapped or not know where or how to begin. Similarly, it will be useful also for recent hires in a company that already invests wisely and executes renewal successfully.

We do not intend it to be a traditional textbook, although workshop leaders and academic instructors could benefit by using it to supplement instruction. As a guidebook, it will be seasoned by our experiences working with SMMEs in a way unlike the more traditional, arms-length coverage contained in a textbook.

Finally, because of its guidebook nature, we intentionally write in a conversational style, just as we might speak with clients—clients with whom we have a trusting, respectful, long-standing working relationship. Therefore, where necessary, we don't pull punches. In this, we seek to challenge readers who might otherwise be uncomfortable embracing innovation or might do so ineffectively when it comes to renewal.

We do this for you.

ACKNOWLEDGMENTS

First, we are indebted to those who generously shared their stories and their successes and failures, and who are identified and profiled in this book.

Their contributions bring to life the "how-to" concepts of renewal in ways not otherwise possible. We list them in order of appearance.

- Jason Arends, president of Wes-Tech Automation Solutions, John Veleris, chairman of JVA Partners (Wes-Tech's owner), and George Garifalis, partner at JVA Partners, for sharing their industry-changing experience with NOVUS.
- TJ Scimone, CEO of Slice, for his insight on methods that have proven invaluable in finding the right products that can fulfill an unmet, unarticulated, and under-met need.
- Nick Arab, co-founder and CEO of Pattern Bioscience, for sharing his story and the value of emotion in the design of the Pattern medical diagnostic system in helping to ensure value for end users.
- Bracken Darrell, CEO of Logitech, for his clarity of the usage of design and the three different stages organizations need to develop for long-term goals.
- Nancy Dawes, proven Serial Innovator, for sharing her experiences as an exemplar innovator who had a significant impact on a company the size of Procter & Gamble.
- Steve McShane, founder and CEO, Kevin Bertness, Jason Ruban, Will Sampson, Todd Stukenberg, and indirectly all of Bruce's other Midtronics colleagues, for sharing their multiple yet seamless perspectives, both broadly and deeply illustrating what it looks like when an SMME survives and thrives by insightfully pursuing an innovation strategy over time.

Further, we are indebted to a handful of immediate colleagues with whom we worked out, over time, some of the key ideas we share here.

- Abbie Griffin and Ray Price, for their lively, insightful, and long-term collaboration with Bruce leading to new insights on a people- rather than process-view of innovation, resulting in our joint authorship of *Serial Innovators: How Individuals Create and Deliver Breakthrough Innovations in Mature Firms* (2012).

- Professor Warren Haug, PhD, who brought OGSMT strategy to the MPD program at Northwestern University on the basis of his years of success as Senior VP of R&D at Procter & Gamble for Laundry.
- Scot Herbst for his ongoing reviews and guidance, ensuring accuracy in reflecting optimum phase-gate methodology for delivering the right products on the basis of proven structure.
- Professor Jim Wicks, whose leadership in teaching innovation management at Northwestern University and his concentration on models of objective-based planning gave clarity to innovation structure within an organization. His guidance in understanding types of innovators and alignment of talent to the portfolio and to products has been invaluable.
- Steve Wille, whose proven insight and skill at helping production operators innovate helped inform Bruce's understanding of the potential that exists with them and how best to unleash it.

We also thank the many others, both colleagues and SMME clients, who worked through a wide variety of innovation-related topics with us over time—those who shared their insights, questions, enthusiasm, doubts, and feelings about aspects of renewal. This group includes Matt Banach, Brad Barbera, Jeff Beavers, Marc Blackman, Andy Blake, Tom Carmazzi, Frank Chambers, Don Clark, Ken Davis, Mark Dawes, Rick Delawder, Christian Eitel, Mary Rose Hennessy, Matthew Hollingshaus, Ted Lind, "Mac" McCauley, John Metselaar, Francene Pelmon, Mike Pop, Bob Rath, Ken Serwinski, Frank Sexton, Rita Shor, and Dave Wilcox. We are indebted to each of you.

We wrote this book hoping that it will help you, and others like you, achieve the results you desire, with fewer difficulties than what some of you have encountered already, to the benefit of all.

In closing, we express our sincere gratitude to Steve Catalano and Cindy Lim, of Stanford University Press, whose deep insight and unceasing support made this book a reality.

NO-EXCUSES INNOVATION

Introduction

"Success breeds complacency. Complacency breeds failure. Only the paranoid survive."

—attributed to Andrew S. Grove, co-founder
and former CEO of Intel[1]

It's simple. Whether we are talking about a product, process, service, or business model, SMMEs ultimately have three strategic options as they progress toward maturity: extend maturity, exit, or renew (see Figure I.1).

That's it. Anything else is a variation on these themes.

The most-pursued SMME strategy is to extend maturity, with the weakest companies attempting to do so only by optimizing production while the most capable also invest in incremental product innovation. If you seek only to extend maturity without already exploring opportunities to renew, your competitive position is tenuous at best. Whether at the hand of existing participants in your industry, new entrants, or those bringing entirely new substitute concepts to the market, your days are numbered. Struggling to compete, you will drain the business financially, ultimately facing decline leading to an exit. It is only a matter of when you will either run the company into insolvency or sell it.

Having considered this, are you pleased with your strategy at maturity? Are you pleased with the strength with which you seek to extend maturity? Are you pleased with your attempts, if any, to renew your business? In the

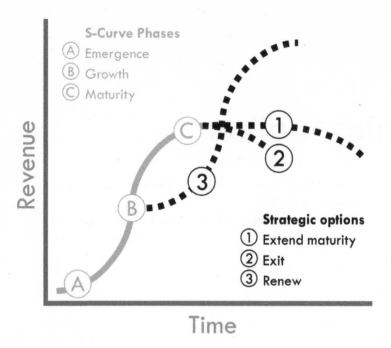

FIGURE I.1. The three strategic options available to SMMEs as they progress toward maturity.

quiet of your thoughts, can you truthfully say that you gave all that was appropriately required with an honest and appropriately sustained effort?

If your answer to this last question is "no," trust that we understand. Strategic success requires a growth mindset. An increasingly aggressive growth mindset is needed the more you move from incremental innovation, characteristic of extending maturity, to the breakthrough innovation characteristic of renewal. There is something different about SMMEs that have attempted and succeeded at innovation. They not only establish a robust capability to extend maturity but, most important, maintain a healthy tension between extending maturity and renewal. While it is easier and cleaner to ignore renewal, ultimately it is deadly. Those that have attempted and succeeded at innovation get it. You see it in the patterns of their behavior.

WES-TECH AUTOMATION SOLUTIONS

2016 brought a rare and significant opportunity for Wes-Tech Automation Solutions, an automated production project for an emerging electric vehicle manufacturer that, for the purposes of this book, we'll call NOVUS.[2] The nature of NOVUS's challenge and how Wes-Tech embraced it illustrate how one SMME attempted and succeeded at renewal.[3]

The Custom Automation Systems Industry

The custom automation systems industry, in which Wes-Tech participates, provides various solutions (including assembly and test systems, manufacturing systems, robotic integration, and material-handling conveyors) to multiple industries (ranging from automotive to manufacturing to consumer products to medical to defense).

Competitors within this industry work with two simple business models—providing "made to design" or "made to specification" solutions—or some portfolio combination of the two depending on the mix of customer demand.

With the made-to-design business model, customers know precisely what they want in an automated system and choose to outsource implementation. Here, the customer provides a request for quotation containing the exact design to the supplier; in response, the supplier provides a cost-competitive price quote. This often is the case when the customer is performing maintenance on or updating existing capability. The customer and supplier infrequently interact throughout the engagement, at most to negotiate the project scope and price, preliminary system acceptance, and ultimately final system acceptance. While not without technical contribution by the supplier, such projects are relatively straightforward to deliver.

With the made-to-specification business model, customers know what they want to accomplish but wish to outsource how to achieve the objective. Here, the customer outsources both design and implementation of the custom automation system. This situation often exists when the customer has familiarity with automation systems yet requires the contributions of a supplier with broader expertise gained across time and industries. In these cases, the customer submits a request for proposal framing the problem and providing performance specifications; in response, the supplier provides a price quote and a proposal beginning with an automated system design and ending with implementation. Similar to made-to-design solutions, customer and supplier set specifications early, and infrequently interact throughout the engagement.

The difference between these two business models lies in whether the customer or the supplier designs the automated system. The similarity is that expertise to address the problem is firmly grasped by one or the other.

Finally, to frame Wes-Tech's story, the custom automation systems industry is characterized by often-unarticulated assumptions and expectations regarding such things as delivery time, problem definition, and the nature of the customer-supplier relationship. While variation exists, new participants in this industry, whether customer or supplier, historically have not questioned these patterns.

NOVUS's Challenge to Suppliers

In 2016, NOVUS approached vendors in the custom automation systems industry with requirements to mass produce its next-generation, volume production electric vehicle, NOVISSIMA.

The NOVISSIMA represented a challenge unlike anything previously encountered by Wes-Tech and the custom automation systems industry. While many individuals within NOVUS possessed significant manufacturing expertise and experience, the company lacked a collective capability in automated assembly familiar to those established in the automotive industry. Further, NOVUS's previous experience with fragile body components was limited to hand assembly. How these parts would behave in a high-volume automated assembly line was unknown. Finally, the company defined a time frame for completion that was extremely aggressive by any standard within the custom automation systems industry.

Compounding these issues was that NOVUS had to establish coordination of its production capability across multiple suppliers in the custom automation systems industry. Unlike standard industry practice, a problem experienced by one supplier on the NOVUS NOVISSIMA project might easily have an impact on countless others. Such situations would cause a ripple effect across the production floor, with requirements changing in real time. Ultimately, NOVUS and all its suppliers needed to gain insight into working together, almost as one, to solve the challenges associated with manufacturing this unique project.

These characteristics collectively define an often-confusing environment, one that is volatile, uncertain, complex, and ambiguous, referred to as VUCA.[4] Notably, NOVUS sought to remove "silos" between suppliers, just as it does internally. Further, NOVUS provided estimates and problems that needed to be solved, rather than specific requirements, for many of their needs. A project such as this runs counter to standard practices in the custom automation systems industry in which either customer or supplier possesses design confidence. In contrast, this project's progress and success were initially stymied more by what NOVUS, Wes-Tech, and other suppliers collectively did not know than by what anyone knew.

Because of this request's novel and extreme features, it represented a significant diversion and challenge. NOVUS required a new design service paradigm from their suppliers, a new business model that differed from current business models, providing made-to-design or made-to-specification solutions. Only those suppliers who possessed the proven capabilities necessary to overcome these challenges and work within this new business model could meet NOVUS's needs.

Wes-Tech's Response

Having no direct experience with a project as novel and extreme as this, and with no time to explore existing processes and paradigms from other industries before embarking on it, the Wes-Tech team responded intuitively, relying on its belief in its existing people and proven capabilities. Wes-Tech's owners, John Veleris (chairman of JVA Partners[5]) and George Garifalis (partner at JVA Partners), with Wes-Tech's president, Jason Arends, saw this as a significant and unique opportunity to lead their industry by collaborating with NOVUS to renew it. Further, they understood that they could accomplish these goals while minimizing risk and cost, as Wes-Tech had a lead customer with which they could work.

The standard industry practice, in which a customer project is delegated to a single project engineer to develop a quote followed by team implementation, had to be abandoned due to ongoing client changes and, within the context of this project, an appropriate lack of direction. Changes to industry standard practice included Wes-Tech forming a small core team of the company's top technical and business experts meeting daily via conference call with NOVUS and NOVUS's other suppliers. The Wes-Tech team did so to immerse themselves in understanding NOVUS's needs, operating culture, and style, and the technical challenges that had to be addressed collaboratively with NOVUS and the other suppliers in real time.

Like NOVUS, Wes-Tech had to return to first principles to move quickly, innovate on the fly, and essentially do the impossible. Wes-Tech leveraged its existing skill in being a customer-centric learning organization to respond to NOVUS's needs. Yet while all this was necessary, the core team still needed to dedicate itself to the type of 24/7 availability required to meet NOVUS's aggressive timeline.

While Wes-Tech was building upon its proven capabilities, unplanned (positive) patterns of behavior, process, and business practice emerged. These practices were consistent with those observed in the software industry and in startups, where such projects are more often the norm and upon which NOVUS based its developing company culture.

As the core team members observed, the NOVUS project represented something of a once-in-a-career opportunity to participate in such a unique customer project that could have a significant and lasting impact on the custom automation systems industry. In response, the entire Wes-Tech team, out of necessity, brought their "A game" to this project to develop new ways of operating to deliver on it.

And the outcome?

Wes-Tech's contribution not only passed acceptance testing but also was explicitly recognized by NOVUS as highly successful. Further, NOVUS posted 2020 robust financial performance reports that bolstered share prices.

Most important for this book, Wes-Tech renewed itself and its industry. It established itself as a new service paradigm provider to a new market—knowledgeable in how to price, specify, and deliver on such projects, accepting and embracing volatility, uncertainty, complexity, and ambiguity rather than dreading and hiding from them. In early 2022, as we finalize the story shared here, Wes-Tech continues work on other engagements with this and other clients seeking precisely the type of design services described here. And more is on the horizon.

Why Wes-Tech Succeeded at Renewal, and Why It Should Matter to You

Wes-Tech's success raises the question as to why it worked for them and what implications are worth noting for SMMEs as a group.

Before engaging with NOVUS, Wes-Tech had successfully designed, implemented, and delivered hundreds of technically innovative custom automated assembly and testing systems in various industries. Each project could be categorized as providing either a made-to-design or made-to-specification solution. Each of these systems was unique, as Wes-Tech designed and built each to meet that customer's specific assembly component parts and production requirements. This type of work is internally complex, requiring the collaborative involvement of several engineering disciplines such as application design, mechanical, electrical, industrial controls, robotic programming, machine-building trades, and project management to plan and coordinate the complexity of hundreds of interdisciplinary work activities. Further, such work requires broad and deep customer insight.

Even without Wes-Tech's demonstration of success with NOVUS, they had an enviable track record. Yet in this situation, the Wes-Tech team went above and beyond by working within this new, more engaged business model. What was unique about Wes-Tech's ability to scope the work and deliver such a highly complex project as NOVUS's? Why was the company able to manage the diverse project complexity and uncertainty and convert it to a deliverable predictably and consistently?

Answering these questions involves identifying Wes-Tech's proven capabilities, each of which depends entirely on the company's people:

- Owners like John and George, leaders like Jason, and numerous employees who understand and embrace the reality that a company must renew to survive and thrive—and, as illustrated in this story, not only accept the reality but run toward it.

- The insight that the cost and risk of renewal can, and should, be managed effectively—in this case, by working with a paying customer.
- Mastery of a suite of perspectives, skills, methodologies, processes, and tools to innovatively address customer needs. For this story, this means the ability to work intimately with both their customer and other suppliers—so intimately that Wes-Tech could assume a more significant leadership role than imagined in standard industry practice by dedicating a cross-functional team to the project 24/7.
- The courage to take on a project of this magnitude, both in size and unique character, and do so in a way that served all.

Admittedly, this story highlights specific capabilities and does not illustrate each of the topics we cover in this book. Yet when considered as a whole, the stories we share present a comprehensive view of what it means to "get it" when it comes to innovation in an SMME.

THE CHALLENGE OF INNOVATING IN SMMES AND WHAT TO DO ABOUT IT

Wes-Tech's story is typical of those SMMEs that "get it," investing in and succeeding at innovation and renewal, in this case by developing the comprehensive set of skills to work within this new-to-industry business model. Yet such companies are few and for various reasons. First, many owners are unwilling to reinvest profits or make an additional investment—in this case, in the diverse, deep set of talent necessary to succeed—as a means of securing future options for growth and renewal. They prefer cash today over long-term viability. Others, often subsequent-generation owners of family businesses, are unfamiliar with, and thus unwilling to take on, what they understand as the risk associated with innovation. They might want to see the company survive and be handed to the next generation but are unsure how to proceed. Still others have made such investments in the past and failed. They see innovation, at best, as a financial roll of the dice.

On one hand, investment in innovation represents an opportunity for SMMEs to renew, to survive and thrive. On the other, innovation is often considered sufficiently difficult, expensive, and risky, so many are unwilling to develop the skills and capabilities necessary to succeed.

The purpose of this book is to help you understand the following:

- The critical importance of innovation investment as well as the weaknesses of typical excuses not to pursue such investment (Chapter 1)
- How design thinking significantly improves the likelihood of successful innovation investment and how SMMEs effectively pursue it (Chapter 2)
- That there is an important, often neglected emotional component in nearly all consumption, an element that can be addressed not only with the product but also the service, packaging, and after-service sensitivity in follow-up (Chapter 3)
- The importance of innovation processes and tools such as phase-gate, lean innovation, open innovation, 2x2 matrices, and roadmaps, as well as how they are effectively deployed in SMMEs (Chapter 4)
- How talented individuals make innovation happen in SMMEs and how best to manage them (Chapter 5)
- The importance of a simple strategic perspective to ensure that you focus innovation on the most impactful opportunities (Chapter 6)
- When you bring all this together, what it looks like when an SMME "gets it" when it comes to innovation that leads to renewal (Chapter 7)

We emphasize six major themes and insights in our book.

1. *Renew to survive and thrive*: First and foremost, innovation that renews is the lifeblood of any SMME. It is how, as Andy Grove suggested, the paranoid survive and, for that matter, thrive. SMMEs without renewal are on the path to failure. Further, we believe that all—SMME owners, board members, CEOs, presidents or GMs and their leadership teams, innovators, and all other employees—

should be prepared, as appropriate for their role, to thoughtfully articulate the case for as well as consider and evaluate innovation investment opportunities.

2. *Manageable risk*: Second, there are low-risk ways to explore opportunities to renew, from proven methods to hiring the right people. We wish for our readers a growing ability to accept a reasonable amount of uncertainty while expecting serendipity. We want our readers to realize that the real risk is not to innovate: it is to *not* innovate.

3. *Reasonable cost*: Third, we address the fallacies held within many SMMEs that innovation is too expensive, too time-consuming, or only for startups or large, mature companies. From design thinking to lean innovation to open innovation to hiring the right people, we share simple, commonsense approaches that are financially responsible and accessible to all. As with risk, innovation is most costly if not undertaken.

4. *Proven methods*: Fourth, we prepare our readers by concisely exposing them to established perspectives, skills, methodologies, processes, and tools that, when employed collectively, make innovation happen—and do so in a way that is not unnecessarily risky or expensive.

5. *Personal courage*: Fifth, we want each reader to take with them the understanding that innovation is up to them. All individuals in an SMME should be prepared, and should possess the prudent courage and integrity, to contribute to making innovation happen, as they are best suited for the benefit of all. Such courage may mean that owners, board members, CEOs, and those in executive leadership address the challenges of a culture that has ossified in its inability to embrace innovation. At the same time, those deeper within the organization must not assume that someone else is responsible for renewal.

6. *People*: Sixth, and finally, successful innovation is about people, several categories of people: SMME owners, board members, CEOs, presidents or GMs and their leadership teams, innovators, and all other employees, and—most important—your custom-

ers. This means hiring and effectively managing the right people, those who "get it" when it comes to innovation and act on that understanding. And it means simultaneously focusing on what your customers really need and returning financial rewards to those who invest.

It's a tall order. But, as we illustrate with multiple examples and stories, it is not beyond your reach. As we discussed while writing this book, "After reading this book, those owning, advising, leading, and working in SMMEs will have no excuse when it comes to innovation." We are confident that our book can help you and your colleagues survive and thrive in ways not previously imagined.

CHAPTER 1

The Case for Innovation

"I've pissed away a million dollars on an innovation project in the past, with nothing to show for it."

—an anonymous, justifiably frustrated owner
and CEO of an SMME

PRELIMINARY QUESTIONS AND INTRODUCTORY THOUGHTS

- Does my company invest in innovation?
- If it does invest in innovation, why? If it does not, why not?
- Am I satisfied with my company's investment in innovation? Why?
- What can my company reasonably expect from investing in innovation?

Nearly all innovation books assume an audience that is inclined to innovate. Our experience is that many are either unfamiliar with or question the value of such an investment. Therefore, we dedicate Chapter 1 to making the business case for innovation. In particular, we focus primarily on the kind of innovation that renews the SMME, enabling it to not only survive but also thrive. In the process, we address the risk and cost of not pursuing such an investment. And we conclude the chapter by expanding on one of this book's major themes: the people who make innovation happen.

WHY INVEST IN INNOVATION?

If you own, advise, or lead an even moderately successful SMME, you know how to extend maturity (see Figure I.1). You know how to optimize production. You also very likely implement incremental innovation to optimize your product portfolio. You do both to maintain profitability and fend off ultimate decline and failure.

But how effective are you at incremental innovation? And what about renewing your business by going beyond the incremental to breakthrough innovation? Why invest in innovation? What if you do? What if you don't? Do you care? Should you care?

Our Concern on Your Behalf

Let's begin with a simple example to illustrate our concern.

A hundred or more years ago, if you wanted to peel a carrot, you would have used a knife (Figure 1.1). If, like us, you were not very good at it, your peels would be too deep or too shallow, and rarely would you finish without the chance of hurting yourself. In the first part of the twentieth century, it became apparent to some insightful and industrious individuals that there was a better way, the safety peeler. The sale of these dedicated peelers surged, as they addressed the need not only for safety but also for reproducibly shallow and uniform peels. As evidenced by issued patents, competitors within the industry explored various configurations at first. Further, as time went on, designs were simplified and modified, reducing fabrication and material costs.

In 1990, Sam Farber upended the peeler industry by introducing the ergonomic peeler. You now could peel to your heart's content without your hand becoming fatigued by gripping the steel-handled peeler. While many continued to eke out an existence fabricating the now-commodity safety peeler, Farber's company (OXO) grew rapidly, defining an entirely new basis of competition.[1]

At roughly the same time, Mike Yurosek began processing full-sized carrots into prepeeled "baby carrots" sold in a plastic bag.[2] At this point, you might have moved your peeler to a less prominent place in the kitchen although you found yourself consuming more carrots and with greater frequency than ever. Yurosek's holistic understanding of the end-user's needs,

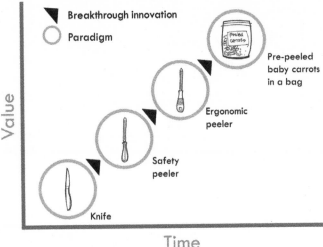

FIGURE 1.1. The progression of peeling carrots over time. Note that each subsequent breakthrough innovation provides a stepwise increase in value to customers, as well as to the company that creates and delivers it to the market.

rather than the manufacture of specialized knives, both reduced waste and freed one from even the thought of having to peel a carrot unless you chose to do so.

After brief consideration of this simple illustration, we can generalize it with the illustration of Figure 1.2. Each of the four product types depicted in Figure 1.1 represents a paradigm within which competition remains generally constant, with companies pursuing incremental innovation such as optimizing performance, simplifying manufacturing, and reducing cost. Yet once someone recognizes an opportunity and successfully implements a breakthrough innovation that changes the basis of competition, they move the industry into a new paradigm, renewing the industry.

So who and where would you have liked to have been as this industry progressed and morphed over time? Optimizing production to squeeze fractions of pennies out of products that cost a dollar? Employing incremental innovation to improve performance or lower cost within the paradigm, the existing basis of competition? Perhaps creating breakthrough

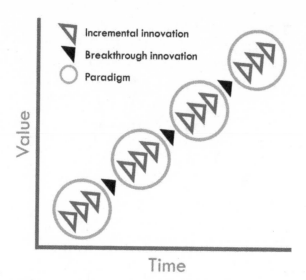

FIGURE 1.2. The general progression of any industry over time.

innovation to redefine and renew the basis of competition and reap the associated reward? Or maybe some intermediate—more bold than incremental, while more modest than breakthrough (yet still critical and lucrative)—success of the type we also illustrate throughout this book?

Extending Maturity

Extending maturity is characterized by continuous improvement within the paradigm, the existing basis of competition. At best, it results in moderate and relatively short-lived financial success in the marketplace until competitors up the ante. At worst, it keeps you from going out of business then and there.

Think implementing lean manufacturing, six sigma quality, and supply-chain management to realize new efficiencies. These tools of optimization are the bread and butter of contemporary SMME management, and in the best cases, they yield profitability, but for a limited time.

Think expanding, with existing products, into new geographic regions or new-to-company or new-to-world segments. Think implementing new product and process development processes to incrementally improve features (such as adding whiteners and scents to laundry detergent at one end of the spectrum, removing dyes and perfumes at the other) to existing products. Again, you are competing within an existing paradigm, as illustrated in Figure 1.2.

Think acquisition to achieve economies of scale. Adding new customers and capacity, particularly capacity that you can improve upon by applying any of your operating expertise, enables you to spread fixed costs over a larger volume, assuming the market will support this capacity. And by doing so, you are seeking to optimize within the existing paradigm.

Think acquisition to achieve economies of scope. Adding complementary products, particularly products that rely on your engineering, operations, or sales and marketing teams' expertise—products that also enable you to spread fixed costs over more substantial volumes, again assuming the market will support this capacity. Adding to strategically critical areas where you currently lack competency enables you to spread fixed costs over larger volumes and better serve or access existing or potential customers. Further, strategically acquiring an organization with a specific core competency that could take years to replicate can propel you into a competitive position not currently available to your company.

Much of the expertise required to extend maturity, particularly optimizing production, already exists in most companies. If not, seasoned executives know how to hire for it. Deploying it to extend maturity for a time is a matter of prioritizing investment on the basis of anticipated financial return. However, optimizing production and implementing simple incremental innovation are insufficient to renew the enterprise or sustain even modest, commodity-like profitability over time.

Collectively, these activities extend maturity for a while. They are relatively low-risk investments that yield low- to modest-profit, short-duration business success. To survive, you must pursue such investments continuously, variously, and vigorously to extend maturity. When implemented effectively, the resulting improvements, at best, ensure that the company might survive to fight another day. While not renewing the basis of competition, the activities to extend maturity repeatedly prop up declining margins and provide brief periods of revenue gain, both of which bring real, though not sustained, value to the company.

Only pursuing activities to extend maturity leaves your company vulnerable. You will be susceptible to attack by existing competitors, customers, suppliers, new entrants, and substitutes. Eventually, as others redefine the nature of competition their actions will lead to your decline and, ultimately, exit.

Renewing the Enterprise

Renewal achieved through breakthrough innovation is another story.

Representing a spectrum from incremental to breakthrough, innovation is characterized by appearances of increasingly unanticipated new products, processes, services, or business models; an ongoing impact in the marketplace; and provision of a longer-term financial return.

At the extreme, renewal by way of breakthrough innovation redefines the nature of competition.

Think Apple and its relentless progression of paradigm-breaking new product concepts. Think P&G and its portfolio of "billion-dollar brands," some of which, such as Olay®, were near extinction before renewal. Think Toyota and the Prius, followed by Toyota's launching hybrid-electric technology across its entire fleet of product offerings. Think Uber and Lyft implementing a business model that eliminates the need for a massive investment in a physical inventory of cars, instead making use of those belonging to others. Think of the countless SMMEs that, while less well-known, have survived and thrived by renewing their offerings, some of which we will discuss in this book.

In contrast to optimizing production or product portfolios, breakthrough innovation occurs in an environment increasingly characterized by volatility, uncertainty, complexity, and ambiguity. Yet it yields higher-profit, longer-duration business success than what optimization alone can provide. The most impactful innovation delights customers. It returns sizeable and sustainable financial returns to owners, stuns competitors, and allows companies that successfully practice it to survive and thrive. If it were easy, someone else would already have done it. And at the extreme, breakthrough innovation changes the paradigm within which competition occurs.

When implemented effectively, breakthrough innovation has a significant impact on a company's financial performance. As opposed to merely prolonging stagnant sales or propping up declining margins—which is possible through optimization, as it extends maturity for a time—the best innovation yields renewal and resets the cycle.

The company that succeeds with breakthrough innovation realizes competitive advantage and returns to revenue growth and healthy margins, with such financial performance available over a much longer time frame than what is possible by merely extending maturity by optimizing the enterprise.

Extending Maturity and Renewal Must Coexist

The breakthrough innovation necessary to renew your company is best pursued in combination with the optimization and incremental innovation required to extend maturity. These investments are complementary, with extending maturity representing the pursuit of survival in the near term and renewal representing the pursuit of a thriving future.

Such organizations[3] and the individuals[4] who lead them are called ambidextrous since they can simultaneously work in two very different, complementary ways. They grasp the importance of not only sustaining their core business but also exploring new opportunities—opportunities that might even destroy their existing business, as long as they do it before someone else does. They resist the very real temptation of only addressing the most current needs.

Focus on extending maturity or on pursuing renewal—without the other—leaves the company vulnerable to competitive threats. Yet such coexistence is challenging for many to consider, let alone maintain. For SMMEs, it requires a commitment to renewal, as it is too easy to ignore while chasing apparently easier, near-term results by optimizing within the current paradigm, the existing basis of competition.

Core Capabilities and SMME Categories of Competitiveness

In the end, when discussing innovation, we identify four primary "core capabilities" that can exist in any company (found in the rows of Table 1.1):

- Production optimization (for example, implementing tools such as lean six sigma)

- Incremental innovation (for example, launching slightly different new products in existing markets or existing products in new markets)
- Platform innovation (for example, establishing a defensible base that enables rapid conversion and growth)
- Breakthrough innovation (for example, launching product concepts that redefine the basis of competition)

While sixteen combinations of these core capabilities are possible, the five commonly observed in SMMEs appear as the columns of Table 1.1. These range from a complete inability to sustain profitable operation, as even production optimization is at best weak, to expertise in all four core capabilities. These span the spectrum from those that "don't get it" to those that "get it."

As a first step, you can assess your business's ability to survive and thrive financially over time by evaluating the existence or strength of each of these four core capabilities and, as a result, identify which of these five SMME "categories of competitiveness" your business operates within. As a next step, you can explore the implications of what you observe.

So what are the financial implications of each of the five SMME categories of competitiveness?

1. *Exit*: These companies exhibit no real innovation behaviors or success, regardless of whether or not they are investing in innovation or say they are. Similarly, they are falling behind the competition relative to their production optimization capability, again, whether or not they are investing in it. As a result, they are on the fast track to negative cash flow, assuming that they are part of a reasonably competent industry and competitive landscape.

2. *Weak Extend*: These companies invest in, and are able to optimize, production within the current paradigm yet do not possess a proven capability to launch incremental innovations. As with those destined to exit, these companies may be investing in innovation—or what they believe is innovation—yet have nothing to show for it. Meanwhile, some companies in this category are clear

TABLE 1.1. The four core capabilities and the five SMME categories of competitiveness.

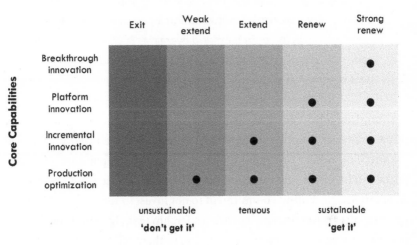

about their intentionally not investing in innovation. All those in this category may buy time with their production optimization capabilities. Yet they are destined eventually to be eclipsed by more competent industry participants within a reasonably competitive landscape because they lack any actual innovation capability.

3. *Extend*: These companies optimize production and regularly launch successful incremental innovations. They will fare better than those in the first two categories, yet they are vulnerable to new platforms or breakthrough innovations launched by more proficient competitors. A competitor's new platform will hasten this business's financial trend toward zero-margin commodity status. A competitor's breakthrough innovation may drive enterprises such as this out of business.

4. *Renew*: In addition to the capabilities of those in the Extend category, these companies possess the ability to launch new platforms to successfully drive the direction of the industry within which they compete and reap such investment's financial benefits. However,

they remain vulnerable to a breakthrough move taken by a more capable competitor.

5. *Strong Renew.* These companies have proven themselves in all four capabilities (product optimization, incremental innovation, platform innovation, and breakthrough innovation). They drive the industry both in the near term and over time. Such enterprises can generate a significant financial return over time and do so with the least associated risk.

An unfortunately interesting characteristic of many companies in the first three categories (Exit, Weak Extend, and Extend) is their denial of a need for anything other than the most basic innovation capability. Yet when pushed to live with such a choice, they often hesitate, stepping back from an otherwise clear all-in commitment to not invest in renewal. To illustrate just this, after observing one client's leadership team ignoring suggestions over time to explore renewal and listening to them tell him that things like "Something new might not appear for fifty years" and "There's nothing new here," Bruce probed their underlying feelings. He asked if they would support releasing him from any noncompete commitments, allowing him to pursue new platforms and breakthroughs in their industry independent of the client. Since they saw no need to invest in an innovation capability that might lead to renewal, Bruce reasoned that the leadership team should not see this as a threat. What he heard was fascinating, things like "That would be a conflict of interest!" Most important, however, was that there was no willingness to give him that release. This behavior suggests that their words that "innovation investment that leads to renewal isn't warranted" were betrayed by their behavior. And trust that this was an outstanding team, both individually and collectively. It's just that they were unable or unwilling to take that (as we will discuss throughout this book, low-risk, low-investment) next step toward exploring renewal.

The challenge that many face when considering the financial implications of the five SMME categories of competitiveness is that they may never have experienced either a platform innovation or breakthrough innovation in their industry. They only know the prosperity that requires, at most, incremental innovation. They primarily know about end-user or customer needs by passively tracking orders and order trends, perhaps shielded by mediators such as distributors and sales representatives, rather than by way of a deep, holistic understanding of end-user or customer requirements.

If this is your experience, I encourage you to consider, as examples, what digital transformation has done to the retail industry by Amazon, to taxi drivers by Uber, and to journalism by the now vast array of online news outlets. Our point here is not to limit us to considering a specific disruptive technology but to understand that something entirely unanticipated can hit your industry or company.

Are you prepared for such a shock, such a "punch in the mouth"? Do you buy insurance to manage risk in other parts of your business yet ignore your responsibility to manage risk of the type discussed here? Are you comfortable with your choices? Should you be comfortable with them?

Beyond the Financial Argument

And while the financial argument alone should suffice, other factors support innovation investment. We believe that a truly innovative enterprise is an increasingly important means of attracting, developing, and retaining the best next generation of employees, especially future leaders. This includes a culture that accepts appropriate risk-taking, as we begin to explore in earnest in Chapter 2, while recognizing that risk will, at times, inevitably result in failure.

We are concerned for your company's future when innovation is nonexistent, only given lip service, or delegated to a part of the organization separate from the core rather than an integrated part of your business.

THE CASE AGAINST INNOVATION

A handful of recurring arguments emerge as you consider why some companies do not pursue renewal through innovation. Thoughtful reflection on each will help you craft your position on innovation. Ten of the most common counterarguments heard from those in SMMEs are listed here, after which we consider and respond to each:

1. It reduces profit.
2. Innovation doesn't provide our desired return on investment.

3. We're already innovating.
4. We'll deal with it when the time comes.
5. We're not big enough to support innovation.
6. We're not ready for innovation.
7. We don't have the financial resources.
8. There are no opportunities for innovation in our industry.
9. I'm not comfortable with the risk.
10. We don't know how to innovate.

It Reduces Profit

Well, yes, it just might reduce profit—but only for a while if done well, as you establish an innovation capability. Over time you can expect financial sustainability and profitability unmatched by those who do not pursue it. You will have survived beyond the current competitive landscape and moved into new, more profitable paradigms. Further, by adding the right people with the right expertise (discussed in Chapter 5), you might find that even your near-term profitability can improve.

Innovation is all about increasing the net present value of your business. If you are serious about financial and operational sustainability, the argument that it reduces profits does not hold.

Innovation Doesn't Provide Our Desired Return on Investment

Similar to the complaint that innovation reduces profits, this argument suggests that, while perhaps profitable, innovation is less lucrative than other investment options. It's all a matter of near-term versus long-term perspective and of how well you implement innovation. As we lay out for you in the rest of this book, there are proven ways to minimize investment, reduce risk, and increase potential return. If followed, this argument, like the previous one, does not hold over time.

We're Already Innovating

Perhaps the most awkward to address, we regularly hear this as pushback. Often expressed defensively, this argument points to small, incremental, admittedly successful changes made within the existing paradigm. While we would not tell SMMEs to stop making such investments where warranted, they miss the point. Making matters worse, some rely only on recipe-like processes, entirely missing the true nature of what innovation is, as if they could conjure up innovation the way fast-food chains make hamburgers.

Many keep using that word, innovation. We do not think it means what they think it means.

We'll Deal with It When the Time Comes

This argument comes in two forms.

Many suggest that they have intentionally chosen not to innovate, opting instead to be a "fast follower" in response to changes in the marketplace. While a valid strategy, what we find in practice is that virtually none who espouse this position have prepared to be a fast follower. Companies that falsely claim this strategy do not sufficiently and carefully track industry trends, consumer wants and needs, competitive behaviors, the patent literature, customer or supplier offerings, or entirely unexpected substitutes. These companies will be caught flat-footed. Further, even if they do pick up on a significant change in their industry, they are insufficiently agile—having never truly practiced or developed the art of being a "fast follower" while giving it lip service—to catch up.

A variation on being a "fast follower" is to be a "scrambler." While less frequently observed and seen most often in smaller SMMEs, these companies typically offer one primary product or service. Only when their product or service enters a period of rapid revenue decline do they begin to look for other needs to serve. This situation differs from the fast follower. These enterprises are willing to implement more significant pivots, often standing up what appears to be an entirely new business on an existing manufacturing skill base.

To their credit, both positions acknowledge that innovation is a "pay me now or pay me later" proposition. Yet if you are not prepared to follow through on what you need to do when "later" becomes "now," you are in denial.

We're Not Big Enough to Support Innovation

Advocates base this argument on a misunderstanding of the type and magnitude of investment—financial and human resources—required to succeed at innovation. There are many ways to structure an innovation capability to maintain investment at a reasonable level. As discussed later in this book, implementing design thinking, open innovation, and allocating individuals to fractional innovation assignments are three such approaches.

We're Not Ready for Innovation

This argument is most often posed by SMMEs that do not have their operational house in order. Perhaps not yet finished or satisfied with their lean six sigma or other such implementation, they see innovation as a next-step, sequential investment. As a result, they choose to wait. This position is indicative of an owner, board, CEO, and president or GM and their leadership team that have neglected investment in the company's core business over time. Further, it suggests a perspective that innovation is a luxury, something perhaps to be added later. It misses the point that optimization and renewal of the enterprise are both necessary. Finally, it suggests a flawed mindset that innovation must be expensive, time-consuming, and risky.

What makes this perspective even worse is that every month the company waits to invest in innovation—should they ultimately even decide to do so—is one more month that the company further ossifies in its inability to embrace innovation. This situation arises because they further establish, strengthen, and encourage a self-protecting production optimization culture. Every month they wait is another step toward condemning current shareholders to lost value and employees to eventual unemployment.

Adding to this, at the time of writing, Bruce has never seen a company that said it "wasn't ready for innovation" eventually become ready. These companies either focus increasingly on short-term financial wins at the expense of a future or they never quite get ahead of—or, for that matter, even catch up with—the competition when it comes to operational excellence, as you can't expect competitors to stand still while you play catch-up.

We Don't Have the Financial Resources

Similar to the argument that the company is not ready for innovation, this position reveals underlying perspectives and realities. If the company is not profitable, as opposed to choosing to not invest in innovation, either the market they serve is not sustainable, they do not have their operational house in order, or both. We are talking about a severely neglected company. Ironically, if the market they serve is no longer sustainable, innovation is precisely what might have kept them from this situation in the first place.

Further, this argument—as do a few others we already have covered—raises the question of owner cash withdrawals and employee compensation across the board. We accept that some wish to milk a business financially. It is a valid strategic decision. However, such a decision may not imply that financial resources are not available. Instead, it may mean that innovation investment has been declined as unattractive. If this is the case, we encourage you to consider the impact on employees who do not benefit from such payments, particularly the less mobile, those counting on employment.

There Are No Opportunities for Innovation in Our Industry

With no disrespect intended, tell this to the medallion-holding cab drivers displaced by the likes of Uber and Lyft.

Even if you ultimately learn that few opportunities exist for your company, it will guide you into other investment directions with added confidence. When implemented in a low-cost, low-risk manner, an innovation investment provides your enterprise with the kind of insight it would not have otherwise secured. That insight alone is often worth the investment.

I'm Not Comfortable with the Risk

This argument and the next represent a type of honesty and transparency not often found in companies that question the value of innovation investment. There are proven ways to reduce and mitigate such risks. Developing a more empathic approach to customers; emphasizing small, iterative investments; and hiring, developing, and retaining the most successful innovators will take the unnecessary risks of innovation off the table.

We Don't Know How to Innovate

Sit back, relax, and consider the rest of this book. We hope you will be pleasantly surprised by your options to renew.

THE WAY OF INNOVATION SUCCESS IN SMMES
In the End, It's About the People

Despite the arguments presented so far, moving beyond optimizing the enterprise to renewal through innovation often is justifiably called into question by senior leadership. For every success story, there are tales of wasted investment and dashed hopes.

What differentiates those companies that succeed from those that fail? What can you do to significantly improve your company's chances for a successful outcome?

The unmistakable pattern is that successful innovation capabilities are built upon an accurate premise about innovation's underlying nature. Innovation is the very human act of discovery—an act requiring a company to hire the right people and to acquire and establish the right attitudes, insights, culture, and business practices to achieve and sustain it.

Only with the right people who possess or grasp these attitudes, insights, culture, and business practices—along with a fair amount of hard work—does innovation successfully fulfill its significant financial promise. And it does so with a much more modest investment and lower risk than most expect.

Senior Leadership's Critical Role

Once senior leadership understands and accepts what is necessary for innovation success, what is required of them to fulfill their innovation responsibilities? Innovation requires the owner, board, CEO, and president or GM and their leadership team to make real, sustained commitments:

- A commitment to bring prudent courage to your innovation investment, recognizing that your and your employees' livelihoods depend on it
- A commitment to accept uncertainty while expecting serendipity
- A commitment to hiring the right people and a commitment to providing them with the financial and other resources, including time, necessary to discover innovation opportunities
- A commitment to foster a renewal-friendly culture, including the difficult responsibility to challenge a culture that has ossified in its inability to embrace innovation

- A commitment to resist the temptation to pull innovation investments inappropriately (material, financial, or human) onto the "problem of the day" to extend maturity—or at least do so in a measured, insightful, disciplined way
- A commitment to establishing the processes, tools, and strategic context necessary to support innovation
- A commitment to challenging each innovation proposal in a manner neither less nor more than how the market and competition would challenge them

Some desire no such commitment. Some try to get by on marginal commitment, investing less than what provides critical mass for innovation success. In such instances, the likelihood of success is so diminished that the potential return is not worth even the minimal funds and attention invested. At some point, it becomes more of a management distraction than an investment.

THE CASE FOR INNOVATION: SOME CLOSING THOUGHTS

Ignoring or insufficiently committing to innovation may look good on a company's bottom line for a time. Its near-term profit will not be affected by what appears to be a risky, speculative investment. Yet over time, the company will bear the risk of being blindsided by a competitor. It also runs the risk of missing a significant opportunity for renewed growth or margins. While we understand and appreciate the need to balance this priority against the tyranny of today's business, for the company's sake, we encourage each of our readers to commit sufficiently to innovation.

If you rise to these expectations and challenges, you will have served all. You will have played a key role in bringing valuable new products, processes, or services to customers—or in reframing your company's business model. You will have fulfilled the most challenging investment expectations, both near term and long term. You will have provided the environment in which all can succeed and experience fulfilling careers. You will be known and remembered as a wise and efficient steward of what has been entrusted to you.

We hope that all who read our book will succeed and that you will take up the challenge by leading and inspiring others, either formally or informally, in your organization in a manner not often witnessed.

KEY POINTS AND TAKEAWAYS

- SMMEs that succeed at investing in innovation survive and thrive.
- Investing in innovation must coexist with optimizing your existing business within the current paradigm.
- Innovation done right does not translate to risk, and to ignore it is to do so at your own risk.

CHAPTER 2

Design Thinking

"The future belongs to a very different kind of person with a very different kind of mind—creators and empathizers, pattern recognizers, and meaning makers. These people—artists, inventors, designers, storytellers, caregivers, consolers, big picture thinkers—will now reap society's richest rewards and share its greatest joys."

—Daniel H. Pink, *New York Times* bestselling author[1]

PRELIMINARY QUESTIONS AND INTRODUCTORY THOUGHTS

- What is innovation?
- Is there a methodology that captures the essence of innovating—regardless of whether we consider product, process, service, or business model innovation?
- How might I most quickly get started with innovation?
- Further, how might I start innovating while assuming the least risk and making the smallest investment?

As we committed to in this book's Introduction, our focus is on renewal that leads SMMEs to survive and thrive. We dedicate Chapter 2, our first "how to" chapter on innovation, to providing a concise yet rich discussion of a proven methodology used to accomplish just such renewal, design thinking. In doing so, we emphasize design thinking's critical importance to SMMEs as it enables a low-cost, low-risk means to explore innovative possibilities.

Through both descriptions and stories, we illustrate how SMMEs can successfully apply design thinking. Throughout, we reveal the critical role of courage as practiced by company leadership, illustrated by the often challenging decisions they must make, albeit made easier and with a greater reward for many by using design thinking methodology.

THE WHAT AND WHY OF DESIGN THINKING

As early as 1969, Nobel Laureate in Economics and computer scientist Herbert Simon referred to design as not only a science but also a way of thinking. Simon espoused prototyping and observational testing as a methodology; thus arose what we commonly call "design thinking." Simon noted that "to understand them, systems had to be constructed, and their behavior observed."[2] As obvious as that might seem too many, it did start an empirical, exploratory methodology that would be as critical to innovation and as significant a breakthrough as Total Quality Management is to manufacturing.[3]

Why Should We Care?

Design thinking is a methodology that should result in innovation. And since successful innovation is our desired goal, it appears wise first to address the often-abused word, "innovation." What is it? And after answering that, the next question is, What is design thinking? We will learn to "make sure you're solving the right problem," as Marne Levine, currently Facebook's chief business officer, very neatly put it.[4] We will learn what actions to take to find out the right problem and how you solve it.

Prelude: What Innovation Really Is

Let's start with "innovation" and why we see it and hear it so often in our everyday lives. Abuse of this word appears everywhere and often outside of industry. Walter recently saw a truck with the byline, "innovative plumbing." Really? Do you genuinely wish to have innovative plumbing, or do you simply want that leak repaired? Since the word "innovation" is so abused, could that be the real issue, that so much of what we call innovation . . . isn't? We want a simple, shared definition of innovation, understood by all, to discuss design thinking.

Innovation is not "creativity," nor "something new," nor "something different" as is too often the response. Innovation also is not "technology," although technology can play a role. Instead, for this book's purposes, innovation is the commercialization or actual productive use, based on creativity, of products, processes, services, or business models—commercial use with financial impact. It is the reduction to practice of creativity. If it's not in the market or public use, it is not innovation addressing a user's needs.

Ideas, and Lots of Them

Now, let's talk about design thinking. The words have become the new mantra for creative problem solving, irrespective of industry and issues. But what is or should be design thinking? And is there a methodology that one can use, as a standard, for the practice?

Let's begin by briefly clarifying what design thinking is not. It is not "group thinking" or "brainstorming." Those may contrast with design thinking.

Instead, it is about some things that appear counterintuitive to problem solving, such as the need to recognize and accept ambiguity. It's an amalgam of individual actions that include curiosity, empathy, and an open mindset. It's also a recognition of risk and embracing it. It's collaborative and constructive as well as holistic and nonjudgmental in views and approaches. And by views and approaches, we mean lots of them. It's about exploration, not a quick response of believing you know the answer but curiosity-driven exploration—and not just some exploration but lots of it. As Linus Pauling, Nobel Laureate in Chemistry, is so often quoted, "The best way to have a good idea is to have a lot of ideas."[5]

As it turns out, lots of great works resulted from lots and lots of more work. When we reference some of the known great works, the references, in general, have us believe that all of the creators' work was "great." That's not true, as it's really about playing the odds. Psychologist Dean Simonton recognized that the great works of those we consider genius result from the production of an enormous amount of work.[6] This vast output acknowledges the reality that, simply based on the odds, one should have at least some standout of a recognized individual piece.

Consider the famous Picasso painting *Guernica*; seventy-nine different drawings led to it. Mozart composed over six hundred pieces but is only known for a very few. Bach wrote more than a thousand. The same result; most know only a very few.

So one of the features of design thinking includes the exploration of multiple solutions. We need to recognize that the most ultimate success stories have been accomplished as a percentage of "tries." The more one explores, the more one learns and discovers, the greater the opportunity for success. From a personal perspective, Walter notes that he has never personally developed a design, nor has ever been involved with a design team, that did not explore multiple options and innumerable concepts until finding resonance with the intended audience. And the exploration of a hundred variances is not unusual.

Empathy: Understanding What Drives Your Customers

For those of us who do not see ourselves as a Picasso, searching for the ultimate impression of Guernica to satisfy ourselves, design thinking is a methodology that involves looking at a problem from the user's point of view, relative to needs for the many. And those needs are seen at the highest level. "At the highest level" means a deeper appreciation of what the problem is and how it should be interpreted, not what it appears to be. One tip for understanding the problem is a deeper dive into the user's actual experiential needs and emotions.

Here's a simple example. When Toyota recognized the need for a higher-value product they would brand as Lexus, the classic engineering requirements included specifications for all electrical and mechanical parts, based on a product requirement document. Thus one might express the force with which a door closes in newtons. But if you're a consumer, you don't care about whatever a newton is. If you're in marketing, you better translate that newton specification into a user's need and emotion as a follow-up to the product requirement document. For those end-users, you want a closure that translates into a user perception of a sound that is perfect, assuring, and stable. No one cares about units of force or acceleration, but they do care about the experience, even if it's "just a door closing." Toyota recognized that Lexus had to impart a feeling that would translate into a promise "that you will feel pampered, luxurious, and affluent."[7] Thus the understanding of an experiential focus became their overriding DNA.

This "reflective" viewpoint is all about the meaning we give to a product or service. It's a "reflection" from a user's point of view, and it's what makes us fall in love with a product or a service. The product or the brand can be so strong that a user and a fan could be willing to tattoo one's body with a corporate logo. That's not as crazy as it seems, as it is not unusual to see a "Harley" tattoo. This then takes us into a deeper side of emotion: the organization's culture itself.

Understanding Risk

We talked earlier about risk, and you might wonder, If we're talking about product or business development, using design thinking, why do I want to get involved with risk? The simple answer is that we're not talking about Las Vegas and gambling with a win-or-lose attitude but rather a culture that accepts and recognizes risk-taking in the creative phase that allows for innovation. Think of it this way. There are times in the new product development process that demand accuracy and adherence to rules, formulas, and regulations. Indeed, this would be the case in any engineering discipline if one is finalizing engineering release documentation. And that culture demanding accuracy, at that point of development, is critical. But if one is at the beginning of the creative process, albeit using the same team, a culture of stretching, which clearly will include risk, is critical. The requirement for a corporate risk-taking culture assures those who are dreaming up the next best thing that they will not be at risk for their creative thinking, recognizing that some pathways may not be correct. This cultural DNA allows for and encourages risk, and it allows for taking leaps that leave the competition behind. A corporate culture of risk-taking, not career safety, is critical for leadership, recognizing that moving ahead means never being behind.

Testing Ideas with End-Users and Constantly Iterating

Design thinking enables creative solution-based innovation, developed and iterated, focusing on human behavior in the context of a product's use. The basic methodology is understanding real people, trying and reviewing multiple and rapid mockups and prototypes, and continuously iterating.

The endpoint is innovation, which by definition, as noted earlier, is a reduction to practice in the marketplace with a real product or service. Design thinking is a solution-based methodology based on human behavior. It is important to note that design thinking is also reasonably rapid in getting to the ultimate solution and appropriately "framing" the problem. The "rapid" side of this is based on quickly building mockups and trying and retrying to find the answer that only end-users can provide.

The previous thought cannot be stressed strongly enough: "reviewing multiple and rapid mockups and prototypes, and continuously iterating." The iterating component is based on ongoing reviews with real users. This point has to be made, as those who are creating anything are too close to their own work to possess perspective. We all tend to think we're always right. While attempting to develop the "answer" to the opportunity space, it needs to be recognized that the so-called "obvious" solution is never the solution. However, too many of us do think that way. There's a name for that: it's called "confirmation bias," a bias that "occurs from the direct influence of desire on beliefs. When people would like a certain idea or concept to be true, they end up believing it to be true."[8]

A classic case of confirmation bias, which we see as the poster child for this subject, is the Segway, developed by Dean Kamen. "Kamen claimed the Segway, with its built-in gyroscopes, computer chips, and tilt sensors would make getting around cities so easy that automobiles would become unnecessary."[9] And Kamen himself believed the Segway "would be to the car what the car was to the horse and buggy."[10]

Kamen's confirmation bias is understandable, as this device was of his thinking and belief. Unlike most of his work, this one did not come from an outside request noting a specific problem but instead came from Kamen himself. He believed the technology he developed, based on gyroscopes, while expensive, would nevertheless be wholeheartedly endorsed by the general population, solely on the basis of remarkable technology. He was so sure of his invention that he forecast sales of ten thousand units per week. In actual counts, Segway only sold approximately thirty thousand units in six years. The reality is that it's challenging, if not impossible, to be objective when reviewing your own work.

In a research study by Dunning, Heath, and Suls based on interviewing engineers in different companies, between 32 percent and 42 percent believed they were among the top 5 percent of performers.[11] And you might not ever wish to listen to college professors, as 94 percent of them think they're doing above-average work. Someone's lying.

So, what do all of these thoughts mean? It means that if you genuinely want to get a sense of your work's viability, you better talk to someone besides yourself. And that someone had better be an end-user whom you ultimately will ask to pay for your product.

DESIGN THINKING: WHAT DOES IT LOOK LIKE?

While every story about the practice of design thinking is unique, Simon's simple takeaway, emphasizing the value of prototyping and observational research and the critical elements of ideas, empathy, risk, and iterating with customers, remains. A review of two organizations will give us a better sense of what this looks like, with one being a traditional third-generation family-owned SMME and the second being a dramatically smaller organization that could almost be viewed as a "one-man-show."

Breuer Electric Manufacturing Company:
The Company That Almost Didn't Have a Future

Our first example is a project performed some years ago before the words "design thinking" even emerged. This is a brief story that will quickly impart the concept.

A family-owned SMME with sales under $100 million and run by the founder's granddaughter was experiencing severe problems.

Breuer Electric Manufacturing Company was founded in 1927 and was devoted to electric cleaning equipment. Manufacturing included electric blowers, industrial vacuum cleaners, hot air blowers, sprayers, and dust collectors. In 1938, the company moved from their small operation in downtown Chicago and ultimately settled in Chicago's northwest side. Eventually, a third-generation family member, Linda, was running the company that her grandfather founded. She was proud that many third-generation employees worked for the manufacturing firm, just as she was doing.

The growth of the family company was based on the business of commercial floor cleaners. The company and its competitors in floor cleaners grew out of addressing customer needs. The industry comprised many SMME manufacturers, all producing in a job-shop mentality, meaning that all these competitive companies were appropriately responding to all of the individual requests from their customers. That translated into small volumes and a variety of finished products that closely met demand.

All manufacturers in the industry shared a common denominator of fabricating multiple-sized floor-cleaning machines based on customers' requests for specific volumes of water required. The cleaning activity allowed for scrubbing a floor and was coupled with the need to vacuum the dirty water from the floor.

The variety of different-size floor cleaners on the market reflected the floor area that users had to clean. As a result, machines were being manufactured with ranges from nine gallons to thirty-five gallons of fresh water, with an equal or greater volume container to allow for the vacuumed clean-up water.

With the large number of smaller manufacturers competing with each other, the inevitable took place, consolidation in the hope of manufacturing efficiencies. The mergers and ensuing efficiencies worked for those that formed new coalitions but clearly put the few remaining independents, including Linda, in a precarious position.

The mergers and takeovers of these companies would continue to disrupt the few remaining independents unless or until innovation could give any one of them enough competitive advantage to compete against the newer, larger firms, who were all producing with greater operating efficiencies.

Linda recognized the issue and called Walter's design development firm, Herbst LaZar Bell (HLB; his firm is now Herbst Produkt), with a not yet fully defined problem. Such a vaguely defined problem was not unusual, as Walter had had similar requests over the years from those who wanted to capture more market share but didn't really know how to do so. Linda believed the answer to her survival might lie in the functional design of the floor-cleaning equipment, believing she was reliant on her existing manufacturing operations. While all competitors used the same technology, their operations were more optimized, based solely on a larger volume of orders.

Rather than calling in a management consulting firm that could offer marketing or internal structural changes, she was willing to make a bet on design innovation. We're now talking "risk" and lots of it, but as noted earlier, in the very beginning, one is simply searching for strategic competitive advantage. Without recognizing that risk was at play, the future was going to be very dim.

Placing Bets

Early on, the risk assumed in design thinking should be a very low-level bet. Let's relate this to gambling. If you know nothing, you make little bets. The more knowledge you acquire, the less risk there is, thus allowing you to make larger bets. You see this kind of thinking in card games such as poker and blackjack. You make increasingly larger bets toward the end if you ultimately hold a good hand and fold them if you do not. The design thinking product development process is perfectly aligned with that mentality. In the beginning, the bets are small because the uncertainty and risk are so great. As one reduces risk, one can increase the bet. In this case, we are talking about overall costs relative to knowledge gained.

Linda's bet was reasonably small. The beginning of this entire endeavor did not require any significant capital expenditure. Relative to the total funding ultimately required, the thinking stage was a small percentage.

Linda hoped HLB could develop a design solution that would create a strategic competitive advantage for her company, which was now in danger of failing. None of the HLB team could delineate the problem other than, "The company is in trouble and will not survive on the path it is on." Her concern was not only for herself failing as the third-generation leader but also for all those who worked for the firm, especially so, again, as many employees were third generation. She had to make a bet.

She further recognized that a vital trade show was only six months away and whatever the solution, it had to be dealt with by show time if the company was to survive. Using design thinking and methodology to take HLB and Linda to the answer, the first question was, What could the differentiation be that would enable the company to survive and thrive? And then the question would become, How fast could we get, whatever it was, to market, in time for the upcoming trade show in six months? This rush to the show with strategic competitive advantage was a "do or die" situation for all involved. No misses could be allowed, or it would all be over. But the opening bet was small, as the initial activities were all human-centered, focusing on understanding the problem and ideating many solutions. So HLB budgeted no engineering development time, which could be substantial, and certainly no capital requirement, as there was nothing to capitalize at the moment—just research and thinking.

Methodology Is the Answer

HLB was new to the commercial floor-cleaning-machine business but did have a design methodology it believed in. HLB adhered to design thinking not because it was advocated for by experts in the business and popular press, which would come to be the case years later, but instead because the methodology made sense to them. An orderly phase-gate process (more on this in Chapter 4) had proven itself irrespective of industry. The initial "phase 0" (see Figure 2.1) was an investigative research phase, exploring issues and opportunities, wants and needs. The research phase for this project was similar to any other, consisting of a review of the competition and manufacturing options, both internal and external. While the process preceded what is now known as "design thinking," the methodology is identical.

Remember, design thinking is a solution-focused methodology based on observing human behavior. So if the solution was to be based on human behavior, the HLB team needed to become anthropologists in thinking about and studying users. Driving the design team was an insatiable curiosity and the need to appreciate the end-user fully. This need and understanding became a principal component of phase 0. Thus a broad net was cast for pure research exploration.

HLB's design process (see Figure 2.1; we discuss aspects of this process in additional detail as part of our review of the phase-gate process in Chapter 4 and in still greater detail as Appendix 1) was critically important for success. The process included conducting manufacturing assessments and

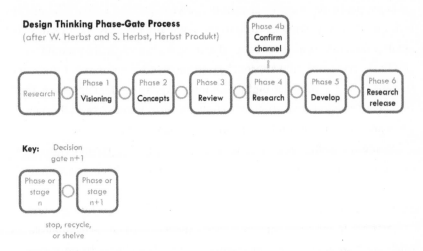

FIGURE 2.1. The design thinking methodology used by HLB in the Breuer Electric Manufacturing Company story.

understanding core competencies, deep research dives into understanding the ultimate users and their needs, and considerations of the efficiencies of operation. The core team consisted of designers, engineers, and researchers.

The plan was to quickly appreciate secondary and primary research based on the industry as a whole and the end-user in particular. The primary research component meant HLB team members had to meet with and understand who the users really were as well as the "gatekeepers" who purchased the floor-cleaning equipment to be utilized by the users. Secondary information would be obtained by understanding the competitors: their product lines, the evolution of their products, if there was any, and the gathering of any and all literature and collateral material on the subject.

The research phase had many critical moving parts, including a manufacturing review. The review confirmed the job-shop mentality that HLB believed it observed during early discussions with Linda in that different-size floor cleaners were produced in small volumes and "to order." The primary manufacturing methods of these commercial floor cleaners were based on sheet metal that underwent various operations. The break-formed steel housing line culminated with welding, grinding, and painting. The multiple processes were by themselves inefficient and costly. The operation's inefficiency dated to early in the company's history, as it dealt with small production runs that required extensive labor time. The mentality of this basic manufacturing approach continued unquestioned over the years, irrespective of somewhat higher volumes. Updating the current method into greater operational efficiency could require excessive capital expenditures and investment funds that were just not available.

While the design engineering team was reviewing factory competencies, the research team focused on discovery as part of the research phase. It was in the field, understanding gatekeepers and end-users while simultaneously using the devices themselves in a replicable setting. The use model of integrating design team members into a lived experience was indelible, as now they fully appreciated the nuances of use. They knew, by observation, that the machines were big, but now they experienced it. Trying to clean the aisles of a mocked-up supermarket with loaded shelving systems and cleaning close to the shelves became a real challenge. Both viewing and using the devices was an eye opener and critical to the design thinking exercise's research phase. The research exercise's immersion component provided much-needed depth that could not be secured in any other way.

Of no surprise was that many of the gatekeepers were not end-users. Instead, many of the gatekeepers were distributors or purchasing agents of large organizations. Since this was commercial cleaning equipment, it was not surprising that the gatekeepers did not use the equipment. So while gatekeepers were critical since they represented most sales, the end-user held the key to success. Fortunately, the end-user was at times also the purchaser since sales were made to individual independent contractors in the cleaning field through a distributor.

The actual reviews of independent contractors as well as cleaning personnel working for contractors were incredibly illuminating. The small independent contractor worked alone, which meant driving a van with the cleaning equipment from job to job. That operation demanded moving the machine from the van into the facility to be cleaned and then back again into the van for the next job. Furthermore, as we will develop further, it was no surprise that almost all of the independent contractors interviewed were male and of large physical stature.

Recognizing that the local research and interviews with North American gatekeepers and end-users would only secure data on a specific subset of the market and could skew the design direction, the research team also probed the users in the international market. This opportunity reflected a meaningful percentage of the existing market and thus had to be heard from. Traveling the world to perform the research was not only outside of the budget, it was not within the timeline as well. However, what was included within the budget and the timeline was talking to those representing the international user's needs.

Sales knew that the Asian and Latin American markets were important. To serve those markets with in-depth research on users, some representative research could be conducted with domestic, regional travel. To better understand any nuances with Asian users, trips were made to San Francisco and Chicago's Chinese neighborhoods. In addition, to study Latin American users, trips were made to San Antonio and Miami.

From its successful earlier interviews, HLB recognized the depth of insight that could be secured from those interviews. For this initial work, a "shadowing" methodology was chosen to observe real end-users operating this equipment in real work situations instead of limiting research to interviewing users. In the extended community research, actual end-users of either Asian or Hispanic descent were observed to be physically smaller than many of their Caucasian counterparts. Many were users, owners, or both of small cleaning services. So why should that matter? The answer was apparent in that the current machine was large by any standard, heavy by any standard, and difficult to maneuver by any standard. Thus the end-users' physical characteristics could have a dramatic impact on their purchase decision.

From a design thinking point of view, HLB stayed within the methodology's parameters, employing an amalgam of research actions, including curiosity, empathy, and an open mindset. This behavioral study gave the design team insights to fully appreciate the physical machine-human relationship and understand the basic use model. In other words, could one, neither trained nor able to read directions, be able to use the device as presented to them? The quest to better understand the entire range of end-users and needs had to go beyond large male physical stature to smaller-statured users, including female users. This duality of behavior included not just the usability but also an understanding of the user. The combined knowledge would ultimately guide HLB in the overall design direction.

While research (phase 0) was conducted with gatekeepers and end-users, the design engineering team was doing their factory and manufacturing exploration. It did not take much time to recognize that manufacturing techniques other than the current break-formed sheet metal methodology could dramatically improve operations. The HLB engineering team also realized that the company's existing equipment and operator skill base were not up to changing manufacturing methodology. The skills learned over many years were focused and well-honed, and likely resistant to change. And if a change was required, would the workforce be sufficiently skilled to meet the challenge? Time was not on Breuer's side.

Engineering and operations recognized that the company could outsource alternative manufacturing on a bid basis and that this approach could allow for increased efficiency and lower costs. Of equal importance was that since outsourcing was an option, capital investment for new manufacturing capabilities would be minimized as capital costs would be limited to tooling only and not equipment. This significant opportunity with massive change meant that Linda had to make a major decision that would affect both the business and her many workers.

The technology advanced by the HLB team to replace the very costly break-forming, welding, grinding, painting operations for metal housings was roto-molding to create large plastic housings. The factors leading to this preferred method included the potentially low cost of tooling, the opportunity for competitive quoting from various external molders, and a manufacturing method that demanded neither high production runs nor secondary finishing.

The manufacturing methodology decision involved shutting down a significant portion of the Breuer Electric Manufacturing Company factory. To survive, the company had to change to manufacturing methods not currently known to Linda's team. That decision, unfortunately, would require having to say goodbye to a substantial number of employees. Yet doing so would save the company and many other jobs and allow the business to grow with new technology.

The units' total redesign to allow for roto-molding had an added benefit in that the design team could start with a "clean sheet" of paper. The clean sheet of paper and design thinking mentalities allowed for a range of design and human factor possibilities. The most obvious would be the form itself, as it no longer had to be the classic "boxy" shape based on break-formed metal parts, which generally yielded hard angles and square or rectilinear shapes. For the first time in this industry, the fabrication technology would allow for more subtle forms, as there was no longer any welding and grinding and finishing to take place. In other words, the overall aesthetic would be "nice" looking, would have some "emotional" content, and would be user-centric in that sightlines could be dramatically improved, especially for smaller-statured users.

Keep in mind that the time expended for the research methods and the review of potential manufacturing methodologies was still minimal. Linda's bet was still a small one compared to the entire potential investment that might ultimately include significant capital investment for new production equipment. However, she received enough information that would encourage her to recognize that a larger bet should be made to advance the new product development project, recognizing that some of the risk was already mitigated.

Now that the design team had a clean sheet of paper for the manufacturing component, design thinking could continue on the basis of the early explorations and the team's understanding of the use model. Recognizing the end-users of the devices and their nuances and their issues, resulting from "shadowing" and becoming one with the end-user, the HLB team could allow empathic exploration to begin. The HLB team had a good sense from its research that the end-users experienced multiple frustrations that did not come out in questioning but did emerge during observation.

None of the independents complained about or thought anything unusual in unloading these large devices from their vans, providing the cleaning required, and reloading them into the van. All appreciated and accepted that the floor-cleaning machines were large. And from the user's vantage point, they had to be, as they were required to carry clean water, which would get deposited on the floor, with a liquid cleaner, plus the machine had to be large enough to then pick up the water that had been dispersed on the floor. And the dirty water volume had to match the clean water deposited equally; thus the housings were large and cumbersome.

It also needs to be noted that the large size became a significant problem when used in an environment that required some degree of careful operation. Again, if one was cleaning a supermarket or big-box type of store environment, the chances of doing damage to the store's products by the equipment's sheer bulkiness while ensuring proper cleaning close to shelving became a problem. Shadowing observation confirmed the user issues, as the devices' bulkiness resulted in a visual barrier at the large machine's front.

Research Completion

With the research in hand and a potential manufacturing methodology, the design team now had a starting point. As is critical to design thinking, no preconceived mindsets had gotten in the way.

The design team next questioned more deeply what the users did not comment on, the overall size. All users appreciated that the volume was rather large but accepted that as reality. When purchasing the equipment, there was no significant variance of choice; the assumption was that the equipment had to be of the size it was for the job to be done. The competitive developers were all in the same boat. All the equipment currently on the market was almost indistinguishable. All were big and boxy, and all were overly large. All machines were the size they were because of the two volumes of water—one clean, one dirty—they were dealing with.

The questions the design team asked of themselves were, "What if the machines were smaller? Could they still do the same job?" This sounds a lot like the ambiguity and curiosity that started this chapter to define design thinking. The big question was, "What if they did not have the mass of the current devices? And if not, how could we reduce the physical size but not the volumes required to do the job?"

There was one other but very theoretical opportunity advanced by engineering, and that was the potential that within this new molded form, one might be able to insert a bladder. This bladder would be separate from where the clean water had been held, allowing for the retrieval of dirty water to displace the space where the former clean water had been, yet not contaminate the volume used to store clean water. If this were really possible, the total device would be half the size of conventional models.

This represented the kind of innovative breakthrough insight that could renew the basis of competition within this industry.

A high volume of creative exploration was next going to be expended to ensure comprehensive exploration and eliminate any internal biases of what a floor-cleaning machine could or would look like. The design team knew from their many investigations on various prior projects that there was no "obvious" answer.

Increasing the Bet

The bet was now being increased as the risk was systematically decreased. The design team had a potential direction that appeared to have enough success elements to allow the bigger bet.

The design work started as design-thinking-based projects always do. The designers, some of whom were part of the user research team or the engineering research team, began design concept exploration (phase 2 in Figure 2.1; see also Appendix 1). This exploration was in the form of simple sketches. The basic exploration continued with a dedicated team of three designers for one week. At the conclusion of the week, an extended team reviewed the hundred-plus ideations posted on the studio's walls.

The sketches were in the form of "thumbnails," which by design definition are one per page, sketched using either pencils or fine-liner pens, and minimally colored with pencils or markers or both. The key was broad exploration, and the numbers reviewed supported that.

Explorations included new forms that would allow for better sightlines based on "soft" molded forms rather than break-formed steel housings, variations in wheels or tracks to enable ease in going up and down stairs for entry into facilities, and early sketch explorations of smaller sizes based on the theoretical opportunity of reducing the overall size by as much as half. The one constraint placed on the project was one of "ease of use." The unit had to be easily handled by an end-user with a broad range of body types.

Following the thumbnail exercises, internal reviews were held with the engineering team and studio designers who did not participate in the activity (phase 3 in Figure 2.1; see also Appendix 1). The fresh eyes of others were vital to ensure minimal bias based on comments from the designers working on it and potentially falling in love with their creation. The idea of other designers reviewing colleagues' work is more accurate in finding the appropriate direction than allowing external test audiences when it comes to creative work.[12]

Feasibility, Viability, Desirability

Starting with a feasibility review, the innovation funnel, as Robert Sutton describes, is "where a lot of ideas are whittled down to a precious few."[13]

The overriding decision was based on what all had to consider. From an engineering point of view, the question that had to be answered was, Were any of the concepts feasible? For any new product development project, feasibility is an obvious requirement. Could contract manufacturers produce the chosen design with the new technology, and could they perform within a required timeline? Would the selected ultimate approach be able to deliver the promised experience?

If the chosen direction was "feasible" from an engineering and production point of view, would it be viable? Viability would be judged by the resulting solution supporting a sustainable, profitable business model.

While Linda did not have many requirements, she was aware, as HLB was, of having a minimal budget for tooling. And the ultimate price of the device paid by end-users would continue to be critical in their decision to purchase one of her products. Thus the housing technology took on a more significant role relative to costs.

Following those variables, the next and only variable left that had to be met positively were the questions, Was it desirable? Would anyone care? And the "anyone" had to include purchasing agents for extensive facilities as well as independent operators. Would they buy it at a price sufficient not only to return Breuer Electric Manufacturing Company to profitability but also enable it to thrive?

Best Research Practices

To continue along the path of design thinking, and with an understanding of primary user-needs research as a starting point coupled with a broad exploration of potential engineering solutions, the team moved on to funneling the concepts (still phase 3 in Figure 2.1).

The methodology used for funneling, searching for the most promising ideas among many, was supported by the best practice of having work reviewed by peers, evaluating ideas by one another rather than any other reviewers. Justin Berg, an assistant professor of organizational behavior at Stanford, performed research on funneling, identifying best practices.[14] Berg's studies included a range of new circus-act reviews by performers versus circus managers. The research suggested that the initial evaluation of ideations should be left to the creatives that ideate new products. It is incredibly valuable when peers have backgrounds and interests in the area under review.

To support the concept of having peer reviewers as opposed to "outsiders," we offer as a contrast a review of two supporters of Dean Kamen's personal transporter discussed earlier in this chapter, the Segway. Steve Jobs and John Doerr, two of the original investors in Google, were early enthusiasts and significant supporters of the concept. Between the two of them, they offered $143 million to be "in" on this investment. But what did they know about the field? Or about users willing to spend more than $10,000 for a device that offered a different transportation mode, but not a better one than either the car or the bike? And the answer is . . . nothing. Thus, moving ahead with the early stages of funneling, the internal team needed a proper and intense review by peers.

The internal HLB team reviewed each of the hundred-plus ideas, recognizing that the device had to be introduced at a trade show in six months. In addition, it had to be based on a technology that would ensure the costs could be at least comparable to the existing product and hopefully more competitive. Thus feasibility and viability became vital drivers.

What was left as a variable to the creative team was the unknown of acceptability. For acceptability, it had to be desirable. The desirability metric was simply judged on the basis of appropriate demand from both distributors and end customers.

The three variables were critical, but of equal importance was the question that even if Breuer Electric could perform, could it protect this creative solution? Intellectual property protection—in this case, patents—had to take place, as any design without appropriate protection would be easy for competitors to copy. If the team could not cover both process and method with patents, Breuer Electric would have very short-lived success. While all should be concerned with intellectual property protection, the clock was ticking, as the team still had to find the winning idea with which to move ahead. Recall that the hundred-plus ideas were in the format of thumbnails, or very rough preliminary thinking. In that form, they could be quickly analyzed and reduced in number in the following manner.

Standard features were the first point of reduction to a manageable number for review. The team found that it could reduce the hundred-plus ideas to approximately six by reducing them to a set of shared features. The variations included common manufacturing methods, different drive systems, and various cleaning methodologies to reduce the size.

The team recognized from prior experience that, while they could begin the funneling and develop the concepts into more clearly delineated renderings, they also should show the renderings and talk to real end-users at this point. Further, the results would have greater accuracy if full-size volume studies supported the renderings. If complete volume studies were not used, the design and research team's concern was that the viewing audience would not fully appreciate the unit's ultimate size in terms of volume. The team employed a quick methodology to create full-size mockups of the final product.

Renderings were generated using a solid model database. By using the database, full-size foam-core mockups could be developed with accuracy. These full-size mockups were accurate in terms of overall form and volume. The team created five mockups, as the most critical responses required for the team to continue to move forward were based on size, sightlines, and wheels versus tracks. And for the potential of reducing size, two different volumes were developed, one based on the current methodology of dual tanks and the second based on the prospect of a dramatically smaller size using a theorized bladder solution.

The same individuals were reinterviewed, but now, rather than shadowing users at work and interacting with them, these sessions were devoted to showing concepts as renderings and full-size mockups. This time the format was dramatically different in another way than the one-on-ones held previously. HLB called in approximately five to seven individuals in groups, creating the groups on the basis of commonality. Two groups were devoted to only large male users, another two groups to Asian users and Hispanic users to better understand stature and culture. A fifth and much smaller group was dedicated to other gatekeepers who, in this case, were distributors. While most researchers might call these sessions "focus groups," we carefully avoid the phrase and the methodology.

The Danger of Using Focus Groups

Let us start with the methodology for those who have never worked with a focus group. Focus groups have moderators using a script based on the information required. The required information usually deals with preferences, pricing, and several nuanced needs of the client. The moderator addresses the needed information by opening up a discussion. Usually, the moderator plays the role of someone not only neutral but also possessing no knowledge of the product. This is designed to ensure that the participants are not asking any technical questions that might get in the way of the initial and emotional responses. The moderator's role is to ensure, in the time allotted, that all questions that are critical for the client team are responded to. In reality, this becomes a big "chat room" with all those participating under the moderator's control.

Problems arise with this "chat room" format. As one might expect, there is usually one self-described "expert" in the group, and that expert tends to dominate. It becomes easy to visualize a so-called expert taking control and making a negative statement that all could interpret as a genuine expert review. In the Breuer Electric case, the concern was that the reality of a dramatically reduced machine size—based on new technology—might elicit a response such as, "A real professional cleaning person would never use a smaller device like that, as we know it would not work!" Those of you who have experienced a focus group can readily identify with such a comment.

Customer Feedback

Standard focus groups are similar to the groups HLB employed—but in the following manner only. There were mockups and renderings of the new designs, a machine currently on the market for comparison, a moderator, and participants seated around a table. All guests were end-users, either as employees or those running their businesses, or, in the distinct fifth group, gatekeepers.

The significant variation was in the way the questions were asked. Rather than an impulsive response to the moderator, all participants received the questions beforehand. Participants then had to write their answers to the questions, which were queries regarding personal likes, dislikes, and expected costs. As this early round of research in response to design options had only renderings and foam-core mockups to relate to, the emotional reactions were noted. Thus users could not move or use the devices. They could, however, stand and pretend to be operators.

This controlled group method ensured the elimination of bias, which generally occurs with focus groups that yield to the room's strongest voice. With each respondent having put forth their initial point of view, they were comfortable in their position and able to further articulate nuances.

For the design and engineering team, the research's central illumination was relative to the device's overall volume. The potentially reduced overall size struck a chord with all users, irrespective of their physical size. This level of enthusiasm came from both end-users and gatekeepers. The distributors loved the idea of smaller size with the same liquid volume, as it reduced their floor space requirement for inventory. Every research session had a plurality of all participants who immediately recognized the smaller device's overall value. While admittedly they did not understand how the volumes of liquid could be the same as in the units currently being used, they all agreed that they were very interested in the direction.

The overriding enthusiasm put pressure on the design development team. While they had postulated that they could reduce the overall size by almost half, they were not yet sure about the specifics. Knowing this smaller volume was the winning direction and recognizing that if the method of a flexible bladder within the volume of the basic unit was possible, all felt comfortable they would be granted patentable protection, which they ultimately were.

Breuer Electric Manufacturing Company: The Outcome

The ultimate product solution, created using design thinking, reduced the machine's size by as much as 40 percent, as illustrated in Figure 2.2. The

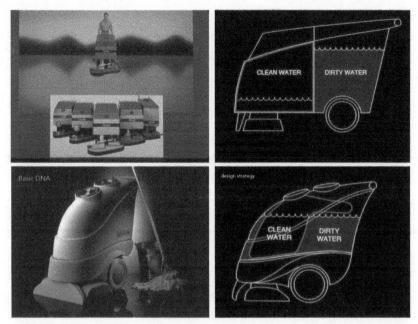

FIGURE 2.2. Breuer Electric Manufacturing Company's commercial floor-cleaning machine before (upper left and right) and after (lower left and right) renewal. An integral bladder and roto-molding manufacturing technology enabled significant design improvements valued by their customers.

research indicated a substantial number of end-users were not of large stature, and the new and reduced-size product not only would be easier to use but would dramatically reduce any damage to surrounding fixtures.

Differentiation based on thorough research and design thinking did allow the company to survive and thrive. Ultimately, Linda sold the renewed company and the patented technology. On the basis of the actions described here, the company grew to be a leader in the floor-cleaning equipment industry.

Slice: The Kind of Company That Could Eat Your Lunch

Our second illustration of design thinking follows a company that, while small, is not yet mature. It did, however, take on a very mature industry, the manufacture of box cutters. As you read their story, ask yourself, What if, as the owner or an employee of a company making box cutters prior to Slice, I had tried what they did? What if I made a relatively small, reasonably low-risk investment in the type of renewal that gave rise to what Slice is today? What if I hadn't and now must compete with Slice?

What if?

A Different Approach Based on Design Thinking

Another methodology for design thinking follows the path of Slice.[15] The owner, TJ Scimone, used a variance to the more classic method pursued by Breuer Electric but still followed the basic philosophy of design thinking. As noted earlier, design thinking includes curiosity, empathy, an open mindset, and recognizing and embracing risk, and at the top of the list, it is human-centered. It also demands a deeper appreciation of what the problem really is, not what it appears to be. For understanding what the problem really is, one needs to take a deeper dive into the user's actual experiential needs or emotions. TJ may not have been formally schooled in the process, but he certainly understood the means for success.

TJ partnered with the design firm Herbst Produkt in a highly collaborative, constructive, holistic, and nonjudgmental approach with their out-of-the-box design thinking consultancy. He was entirely open for any and all directions.

TJ is the classic entrepreneur who explores opportunity and white space. Being the sole proprietor in a company of one at that point in time, he could act incredibly swiftly and with remarkable efficiency. His company, Slice, started with recognizing a potential need relative to using the classic stainless-steel-blade box cutter. His starting curiosity component of design thinking triggered the questions, Why were these blades potentially so dangerous and Why had no one ever explored a better solution in this category?

Staying true to the methodology, TJ began by confirming that he was not alone in recognizing how dangerous box cutters were. His personal encounters included his prior entrepreneurial experiences as an importer and total sole responsibility for opening incoming and shipping outgoing packages. Keep in mind, TJ was the classic "one-person show" company when he started Slice.

Since TJ found box cutters dangerous, could he confirm that others recognized that as well, and could he prove that he might have found a "white space" opportunity? A quick search online confirmed his answer. According to one blog, "30% of workplace injuries involve lacerations, and 70% occur on the hands or fingers."[16] Apparently, box cutters are dangerous enough that one can actually purchase safety posters for the workplace addressing "utility knife safety instructions." And while the literature supported his exploration into the opportunity space, conversations with other users confirmed his thinking.

Unlike Dean Kamen with his Segway, with TJ's design-thinking mentality, his hypotheses of recognizing the dangers of box cutters and the need for instruments that could perform the same function, but with safety, was now confirmed by end-users. In an interview for this book, TJ quickly confirmed that when he considered entering this marketplace twelve years ago, there was no data on the safety cutter market size.[17] Nevertheless, he confirmed that since multiple major players were in the market and all sellers were producing almost identical products, the risk of exploration appeared to be well worth it. Using design thinking and partnering with Herbst Produkt, he began the search for a strategic competitive advantage.

While TJ could only present those products already on the market to the team, the team recognized their similarity. Next, the design team, following design thinking tenets, began the project with their own research.

The research results had a commonality that helped set ideation direction. Initial research revealed that many users of box cutters also observed that, when opening boxes, they often had to contend with heavy-duty staples that helped secure the closures.

In addition, there were constant complaints that one could accidentally put the box cutter in one's pocket, which led to numerous accidental jabbing and cutting incidents. Industrial end-users, as well as do-it-yourself end-users, shared other concerns, which became insights.

True to design thinking methodology, approximately a hundred ideations were developed as thumbnail sketches for the first pass. It also needs to be noted that the entire design team had backgrounds in using box cutters. With the review of their own research, they could more fully appreciate those drivers that might take this new generation of products to another level.

TJ and the Herbst Produkt team were equally concerned, as they had to "hit this out of the ballpark" since they were a new player in a mature industry and market, competing against major, recognized brand names. On the basis of the team's personal experience and referencing research with a wide background of end-users, the team delineated the early sketch ideations into three major categories. These categories included an exploration of the cutting blades themselves, exploration of the physical format of the knife to ensure a more user-centered approach, and exploration to minimize any accidental stabbing and cutting.

Supporting the idea of a breakthrough product, the material exploration for the cutting blades themselves led to a precision ceramic blade. TJ was quick to recognize ceramic was dramatically more expensive than a stainless-steel blade; however, the strategic competitive advantage was that the blade would last ten times longer. In addition, ceramic would allow a slightly rounded point to ensure one could never get "stabbed" as the point was blunt.

The second category of opportunity recognized the potential, while using a standard box cutter, of literally ripping one's knuckles if the box had industrial staples for additional closure protection. A new design format would be able to protect the knuckles of one's hands.

The third category of opportunity was during "non use." Some of the early explorations considered the hands-free transfer of the knife itself.

Examples of the kinds of ideas generated as part of this phase of the design process appear in Figure 2.3.

Research Confirmation

Holding to the design-thinking mentality of ensuring confirmation of the overall design and recognizing the minimal budget for total development, the full team was forced to make a critical decision. The Chicago International Housewares show was forthcoming at McCormick Place. While TJ was ready to be an exhibitor with his current houseware products, the decision was made to have a working prototype of the new-to-the-world box cutter and introduce it there. This housewares show presentation and

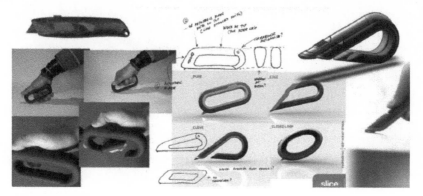

FIGURE 2.3. Initial "thumbnail" sketches, early mockups, and a solid model rendering for Slice by Herbst Produkt.

initiation of this new out-of-the-box concept would serve as confirmation research in a public forum rather than the more classic research forum. As we noted earlier in this chapter regarding placing bets, the risk had decreased on the basis of the prior research performed. Simultaneously, the financial bet increased as the working prototype alpha model had to be a perfect "alpha." Alpha, by definition, is a looks-like, works-like prototype. In this case, it was critical to reaching the professional retail buyer and merchandise manager levels. A comparison of a conventional stainless-steel box cutter and the Slice box cutter appears in Figure 2.4.

Of some surprise, the unit was remarkably well-received. Still, the major retailers were understandably concerned not only with the change in technology of a standard box cutter but with the risk of getting involved with a brand-new vendor in an old, secured, mature category and at a higher price point. The greatest surprise came from the business-to-business category, in contrast to the more traditional business-to-consumer category. Interest was extremely high from the business-to-business category, and, given that, TJ immediately pivoted. The excitement from that category was centered around the blunt tip of the ceramic blade, which presented a remarkable shift to safety and reduced insurance costs. The required open mindset of design thinking for TJ was immediate. TJ and the team would shift and focus on the industrial safety cutter market. Thus began the development of multiple products, which was quickly and easily accomplished.

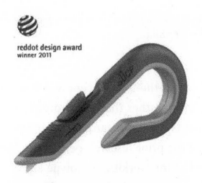

reddot design award
winner 2011

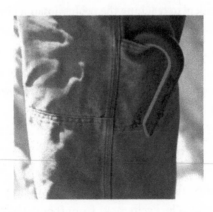

FIGURE 2.4. Comparison of a standard stainless-steel box cutter (top) and a new Slice ceramic-tip box cutter (middle). How the simple design enables the easy, safe, comfortable, accessible carrying of a Slice box cutter in a user's pant pocket is illustrated at bottom.

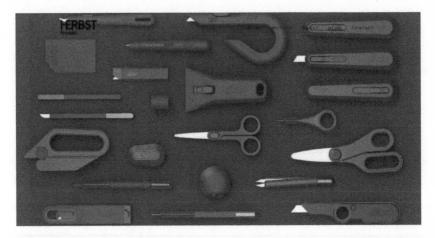

FIGURE 2.5. Twenty-four of Slice's currently forty-two stock-keeping units (image courtesy of Herbst Produkt).

TJ now recognized what design thinking could do for Slice and especially so as they were small and agile. They readily admitted they did not know the market. Still, design thinking, starting with research and customer needs, would quickly give them the appropriate answers. TJ's attitude, which holds well for SMMEs, was that "the big guys cannot get out of their own way." End-user research took them into a diverse product line to include ice scrapers, leather tools, deburring blades for manufacturers of injection molded plastics, seam rippers, scissors, precision knives, and a multitude of others, now counting forty-two stock-keeping units, many of which appear in Figure 2.5.

DESIGN THINKING: SOME CLOSING THOUGHTS

Most SMMEs fall into the range of the two companies reviewed in this chapter. The intentional reference of Linda's $100 million enterprise and TJ's one-person startup confirms the reality that irrespective of SMME size, design thinking is a methodology that works.

By its very definition, design thinking includes exploring multiple solutions once end-user needs are recognized and understood. Unlike attorneys or MBAs who often seem to know the answer before asking the question, designers—those for whom Daniel Pink argues the future belongs—have no idea what the answers are before they begin. Thus a complete exploration is a requirement. The greater the exploration, the greater the opportunity is for success as long as the end-user plays a significant role in the opportunity's research.

In this chapter, we have made many references to deeply understanding the customers and their needs. Understanding customers falls under the concept of the "voice of the customer."[18] While perhaps you have implemented something that you have referred to as voice of the customer, we suspect that the approach presented here and in the references provided in note 18 may be more rigorous than what your practice has been. If so, you need to get used to this deeper level of effort and resulting insight. It should be part of your vocabulary and toolkit going forward, as it drives everything that leads to successful innovation.

This chapter described situations in which those practicing design thinking probed potential customers and end-users with the simplest form of a product, possessing the most essential features. If you already are acquainted with the lean startup concept (discussed in detail in Chapter 4), and this looked familiar to you, you would be right. Like lean startup, design thinking involves creating a minimum viable product to quickly engage potential customers, enabling the designer to learn and, as necessary, pivot to best address customer needs.

In this chapter, we also spoke broadly about showing working models to end-users to enable efficient engagement to understand their needs and innovation as responding to change rather than being wedded to a plan. This too may appear familiar to you if you have experience with agile development.[19]

Not surprisingly, some of the best ideas used elsewhere to reduce risk and minimize up-front investment—such as "voice of the customer," lean startup, and agile—will appear again and again as we discuss innovation.

Research requires a deep dive into the users' needs and emotions. Those needs are often unarticulated, under-met or unmet, and unrecognized. For all SMMEs working to develop opportunities for such undefined or vaguely defined needs, the value of ambiguity needs to be recognized. Too early a definition of the problem, a solution, and the potential method for solving it often kills the best ultimate solution.

Design thinking may appear counterintuitive to problem solving, such as the need and recognition of ambiguity and accepting it as a starting point, allowing for broad exploration. For SMMEs, it's an amalgam of individual actions that include curiosity, empathy, and an open mindset. It's also a recognition of risk and embracing it. It is collaborative and constructive and holistic and nonjudgmental in ideas and approaches. And ideas and approaches mean lots of them. It is about exploration, not just a quick response of believing you know the "answer," and not just *some* exploration but *lots of* exploration.

KEY POINTS AND TAKEAWAYS

- Design thinking is nothing new.
- Design thinking is a methodology, not magic.
- Design thinking requires exploration, empathy, and depth.
- To succeed, design thinking requires practitioners to be focused, without bias, on end-users, deeply engaging with and understanding them.
- Design thinking demands incremental, small bets—assuming little risk and moving quickly—when properly employed.

CHAPTER 3

Emotional Design

"I like the red one."

—an anonymous shopper overheard
having just decided which car to buy

PRELIMINARY QUESTIONS AND INTRODUCTORY THOUGHTS

- Having grasped the basics of design thinking in Chapter 2, what must I consider to implement it most successfully?
- In Chapter 2, you stated that "to succeed, design thinking requires practitioners to be focused, without bias, on end-users, deeply engaging with and understanding them." What must I most clearly understand about my customers to succeed?
- What gives design thinking its greatest financial boost?

The proposition is straightforward. When looking in any competitive product category, one is generally drawn to the product or service that evokes an emotional response. It may be as simple as color evoking the response. An early research exploration conducted by Walter took him to a used-car lot of remarkably inexpensive cars. A husband and wife were there, along with their three kids, looking at equally priced vehicles that appeared to share the same attributes. No dents, no rust, reasonably equal in speedometer mileage, the same age, and all other visual aspects, supported by their window stickers claiming other nearly identical attributes. Again, all the cars they looked at appeared to be equal. The close of the deal came when the wife simply said, "I like the red one." That was it, a purely emotional response that elicited the sale—their purchase decision's visceral component was based solely on an emotional response to the car's color.

This chapter will deal with the reality of emotional design, whether it be a service or physical product, whether it be the product itself or the package it comes in. Given a choice, most users rely on a simple gut reaction dealing with the very basics of which one of "these" will do the job better, and, absent any third-party review, the choice is almost always emotional.

Keep in mind that we are not limiting this conversation to "style" when we say "emotional design." Design here is the "big D," the totality of a product or service, not just the aesthetic of style. Think, instead, How easy will this be to use or even to understand how to use? Will I need a ten-page use-and-care manual just to turn on my device? Design is the totality of our products and their ease of use as well as any "back room" support.

Think Uber and its use model. Download an app, activate it, wait for an instantaneous response loaded with the simple basics: what type of car, what color, who is driving, where they are now, and when they will arrive. What, why, when, where, who, and how are the unknowns that need an answer. And when most are present, you've taken your first step of great emotional design. If it's obvious and easy to use and understandable and evokes a positive emotion, that all falls under the heading of "emotional design."

EMOTIONAL PRODUCTS HAVE ADDED VALUE

Irrespective of any specification and the ultimate promised delivery, the purchase of any product or service has emotional content. To support that thought, we offer the following two, very different, introductory cases, Pattern and OXO.

Pattern: A Journey from Function Alone to Function+Emotion

A mechanical engineer, an electrical engineer, and a dermatologist wanted to start a microbiology company.

No . . . this is not the beginning of a bad joke.

They had a vision and needed funding. They were not academics, nor were they scientists. However, they all shared a common concern, and none had a built-in bias to a specific solution, as is common with academics and scientists. That thought is important, as academics often develop technology based on personal interest and develop answers in search of a problem. What the engineers did know, and what was at the basis of seeking funding, was the reality that pneumonia was the number one infectious killer around the world, especially so in children.

Nick, one of the co-founders, kept asking himself, Why does it still take almost a week to diagnose something as common and fast-moving as a life-threatening bacterial infection? The answer, he realized, resided in the surprising complexity of bacterial resistance and the fact that bacterial infections, like cancer, required targeted treatment of a few "bad cells" living in a sea of "good cells." An electrical engineer by training, Nick suspected that single-cell isolation using a type of biochemical "digitization" could quickly and accurately reveal the key bacterial resistance and population characteristics of an infection. He wanted to start a company, which became Pattern, with the goal of drastically improving antibiotic treatment decisions.

Bryan, the dermatologist, decided he would provide the "pre-seed" funding that allowed all three of them to prove whether they could isolate and identify live cells and then measure their response to antibiotics.

The pre-seed funding was used for research that could prove a potential solution and then move on for outside seed funding that would allow them to expand the team. Nick's new hires had the job of acquiring lots of automated data and building a small but operational biosafety lab for continued development, which was critical, as they were working with some hazardous microbes.

The efforts were successful enough; they now had automated the cell analysis, evidence that analyses could be done in a three- to four-hour time frame, and had a proof-of-concept box that could take them into Series A funding (see Figure 3.1, top image). They believed they had a revolutionary technology with the potential to drastically change outcomes for millions of patients. They also believed that their customers, medical directors of

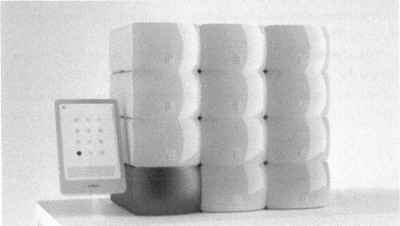

FIGURE 3.1. The preliminary proof-of-concept design (top) of a micro-fluidics device that analyzes potential treatment within three to four hours and the final design (bottom) using a modular methodology for multiple testing in labs.

hospital microbiology labs, would agree and be excited once they understood the platform's capabilities.

So, while they had a "box" that worked, they recognized that they needed customers to viscerally "want" the product, even before they could verify the clinical impact. They knew that a hospital microbiology lab's medical director is still a consumer, who can be moved by a beautiful product he or she would want to have in a lab. The partners recognized the need for great design and beautifying the product, even in an industry in which design and beauty aren't part of the value proposition.

The "want it" part of this gets to the emotions and is essential for all SMMEs that desire to take anything to a more final road to success. When medical directors have an emotional "I want it" response, developers (in this case, Nick) are given the time to explain further how things really work as opposed to presenting pure analytics.

The design firm Herbst Produkt was called in for a complete assessment of laboratory usage, manufacturing methodology, and overall industrial design and to investigate the potential user's habits and practices. The Herbst Produkt design team recognized that what Nick and the team were developing used optical patterns for differentiating bacteria inside microscopic droplets and allowed them to create a design language for the company, "Pattern."

Nick, the CEO, noted, "The main reason we invested in the design is because the instrument is the 'face' of the company and will be our ambassador to the market. It's more about what we think it will do rather than what it has done, as we're not yet on market." The final design (see Figure 3.1, bottom image), being clearly emotional, could now get to their customers' hearts, not just their brains, and is allowing Nick and the team to make the mission statement of "improving the world's most important health decisions" about to come true.

Most Consumption Has Emotional Content

In thinking about emotional design, it certainly is not limited to large capital investment projects. What needs to be brought forth is the reality that a basic product has to function and has to do so with reliability; it must have human factors support in that a product must be obvious, intuitive, and usable. If we put that into a Maslow-like pyramid, the very tip-top should undoubtedly include the word "pleasurable."[1]

In that regard, we can think of the basic functional carrot peeler (introduced in Chapter 1), which typically retails for under two dollars, and review what Sam Farber and his OXO Good Grip concept did in converting that purely utilitarian product into a highly emotional and higher-perceived-value product (Figure 3.2).

FIGURE 3.2. Comparison of a utilitarian, functional carrot peeler (left) versus OXO Good Grips emotional peelers (right).

Take a serious look at the blades on both the functional and the emotional design peelers. Surprisingly, the blades are almost identical. It's the dramatically different handles—again, coupled with nearly identical blades—that yield dramatically different price points and margins. This solidifies the argument relative to the value of emotional design.

At the time of writing, one can purchase the "Royal Roy 1062 Peeler" (the functional design in Figure 3.2) for $0.67.[2] The "OXO Good Grips Swivel Peeler" (the first of the three emotional designs in Figure 3.2) can be purchased directly from OXO for $9.99[3] and as low as $8.99 elsewhere.[4] Based on an emotional response to the OXO peeler, this significant price difference is derived from a well-designed plastic handle that includes sensitive "crush" ribs built into the handle to ensure a universal, highly comfortable grip.

So let's dig into this a bit more to see just how important OXO's emotional design is to the bottom line. We estimate that the steel frame used for both peelers is produced for approximately $0.13 (one-fifth of the Royal Roy peeler's retail price, a standard heuristic for commodity products to cover margins for all in the supply chain). We also estimate, on the basis of experience, that the OXO peeler's plastic handle, which encases a steel frame virtually identical to the Royal Roy peeler, is produced for approximately $0.45. Thus we estimate that the Royal Roy peeler costs $0.13 to make, while the OXO peeler costs $0.58 to produce. This means that the OXO peeler could be priced as low as $2.90 (again, the five-time multiplier to cover margins in the supply chain).

But wait; there's more . . . and the more is that the retail value of good design, in this case, provides a multiplier of approximately *seventeen times the manufactured cost*, not five times. Recognizing there is a dramatic difference between the methodology and the supply chain of the two devices, and even if we were off by 100 percent for the OXO unit, one would still achieve an eight-time manufactured cost based on sound, emotional design.

PRELUDE: THE INFLUENCE OF BRAUN AND DIETER RAMS ON EMOTIONAL DESIGN

As we explore next, emotional design is anything but new. And while many think of Apple when they hear the words "emotional design," many of the foundational insights upon which Apple has built its success predate it by decades and come not from Silicon Valley but Europe.

Design Values Are International

Braun GmbH, the German appliance company, headquartered in Frankfurt, Germany, and currently wholly owned by P&G, was founded in the early 1920s by Max Braun.[5] Braun, a brilliant German engineer, began his company with a device dedicated to fixing or modifying drive belts for machinery. Shortly after founding his business, Braun quickly shifted to the then new commercial radio product technology. Braun figured out a methodology for this new technology that made it easier for listeners to tune their radios with the crystal cylinder he invented. That venture into radio allowed the company to not only manufacture these tuning devices but also expand their manufacturing to include amplifiers. This move allowed for a reasonably easy pivot to developing the entire radio as a product for the new and very successful company. From there, it was an easy jump to include turntables and then the integration of both radio and turntable into a single unit.

World War II resulted in significant damage to the Braun facilities. Yet the company rebuilt and was revitalized with Braun entering the kitchen appliance and electric shaver markets. With Max Braun's sons, Arthur and Erwin, leading the company in the 1950s, they established a strategy emphasizing design to improve their relationship with customers.[6] Supported by the results of a public opinion study titled "The Perception of Living Styles," suggesting that Germans in the 1950s desired modern home design, the brothers recognized the need for change from a more traditional design. While this would be a challenge, Arthur and Erwin recognized the potential for long-term gains.

In the early 1950s, the design profession barely existed and certainly not within Braun. At the time, there was no such thing as a design department or even a "designer" within their organization. Fortunately for the Braun brothers, there was a newly established school of design nearby. The Brauns immediately contacted the school's faculty and developed a new design direction based on Bauhaus teachings, which stressed minimal design using clean contemporary forms.

Braun introduced an entirely new line of radios with these new, more modern forms at the International Radio Exhibition in Düsseldorf in 1955. The brothers were "hip" enough to decorate their booth with Knoll International furniture, designed by Ray and Charles Eames. They did that to support new radio designs, which reflected the look of popular furniture and was now being carried over into housewares, specifically radios.

Fortunately for Braun and their recognition of design as a differentiation strategy, they hired a young architect named Dieter Rams, who joined them to help design their offices, showrooms, and guest rooms. However, it did not take long for Rams to also become involved in product design. Rams had a basic philosophy of "less but better" and joined the company in 1955. Design became such a critical competitive advantage for Braun that they established a permanent design team. Rams became their chief design officer, retaining that position until 1995.

Dieter Rams's genius is best exemplified by a design methodology of moving household appliance design away from what physically looked like traditional furniture (think of the vintage wood or early phenolic plastic radios). His early record player (shown in Figure 3.3, center left) was so pure looking and unusual for the times that it was known as "Snow White's coffin." Adding to the purity of the lines was the clear acrylic cover, which never before had been used in consumer products.

Dieter Rams understood emotional design starting in the mid-1950s with a simple set of principles. Good design had to be innovative, useful, aesthetic, understandable, unobtrusive, honest, long-lasting, environmentally friendly, and attentive to the last detail. And good design had to be as little design as possible. In effect, it had to be less but better.[7]

By the end of the 1950s, Braun had become a household name on the basis of the pure, clean, simple, and iconic forms found in all their products, the breadth of which is illustrated by the examples shown in Figure 3.3. The company won numerous national and international prizes and became known as a "design brand." The design brand label was easily supported, as their products became part of museum collections and exhibits worldwide. By concentrating on and creating their own DNA of design, Braun grew from a postwar SMME to become a critical strategic component of the Gillette company in 1967 when Arthur and Erwin sold a majority stake in the organization founded by their father fifty years prior.

The Design Impact of Dieter Rams on Apple

Jony Ive, director of design for Apple, readily admitted Dieter Rams was his inspiration and that Rams's philosophy became the design credo of both him and Steve Jobs. And Rams returned the compliment by noting that Apple is one of the few companies designing products according to his (Dieter Rams's) principles.[8]

The pure simplicity that Rams brought to Braun was summarized by Steve Jobs in referencing Apple's design intent: "Simplicity is the ultimate sophistication . . . it takes a lot of hard work to make something simple, to truly understand the underlying challenges and come up with elegant solutions."[9] Jobs also has said, "Design is the fundamental soul of a human-made creation that ends up expressing itself in successive outer layers of the product or service."[10] And, "Most people make the mistake of thinking design is what it looks like. People think it's this veneer—that the designers

FIGURE 3.3. Several of Dieter Rams's designs for Braun Manufacturing.

are handed this box and told, 'Make it look good!' That's not what we think design is. It's not just what it looks like and feels like. Design is how it works."[11]

Jony Ive, beyond just being a great designer and champion of design—which is why he now holds the title of "Sir" Jony Ive—has always been an outspoken commentator on the subject. We love his comments, such as, "It's sad and frustrating that we are surrounded by products that seem to testify to a complete lack of care"[12] and "I think we are surrounded by hundreds and thousands of products that show companies don't care enough about what they design. . . ."[13]

The clean, simple lines of Apple products convey a design philosophy that is highly emotional, but beyond the emotion is the obviousness of their products and ease of use "standard," which is the basis of user delight. This visceral response informs user joy, which then becomes the basis not only of consumption but also advocacy.

Here's another way to think of that. Assume you're delivering a product or a service that entices consumption. People buy it. People use it. But then what? Do they tell their friends? Do they extol your products' virtues? Do they become your advocate? If the answer isn't positive, you need to review what you previously thought was a successful product.

SOME EXAMPLES OF EMOTIONAL DESIGN

Having laid the necessary groundwork, next we consider a range of examples for how emotional design leads to innovation success for various types of companies and applications.

Everyday Emotional Value Issues

Let's begin with an almost ubiquitous, everyday-use product example. How about your need to toast a few slices of bread. Maybe throw a bagel in as well. Chances are good you have a toaster oven for the job. Chances are good it can toast four slices of bread at a time. Chances are good you can even cook a nine-inch pizza. Chances are good that it can bake up to 450 degrees, and broil, toast, and keep food warm. Chances are good there is a reasonably precise timer. Chances are good it has an easily cleaned, removable crumb tray. Chances are good it has some sort of a brushed chrome face with a large window so that you can see inside, and three easy-to-use knobs. Let's all recognize it's "'kind of'" ubiquitous in that toaster ovens share many common attributes.

Would someone like to tell us why—when we have the option of paying $29.99 for a Black+Decker Model TO1373SSD[14] (Figure 3.4 top) or paying $99.99 for the nearly identical size and features relative to usage for the Cuisinart Model TOB-40N[15]—we should purchase the more expensive Cusinart (Figure 3.4 bottom)? Might we suggest, from a personal point of view, that the Cuisinart is a nicer-looking unit? Further, might we suggest that both of us would rather have a nicer-looking unit on our countertop given a choice and given the money to make that choice? And yes, at one heck of a premium price. And yes, without any additional discernable features relative to what our needs are for toasting, baking, broiling, warming, and timing the process.

We're hoping by now that you are appreciating the case we are attempting to make with emotional design.

We can continue this conversation to include many everyday items produced for comparable costs and that perform comparably the same job. Yet one has some emotional content that we value, resulting in a more positive user experience, with our response being purely psychological. That response would be purely reflective, as it is solely based on our feelings for the product or service we are involved with.

One can purchase an adult toothbrush with a very simple plastic handle, with literally no unique shape, for $0.06. We know that sounds crazy, but look it up, and you'll see it's true, at least at the time of writing.[16] Or one can purchase a lovely handle shape, including a softer finger grip, for about $4.00. Granted, the bristles may have a flair shape between rows or some other nuance, but it turns out they are all produced in pretty much the same manner. They all have nylon filament bristles. They all have plastic handles in various forms. And the new, more expensive ones are all manufactured with a process that allows for a softer grip for your fingers.

We recognize that the $0.79 toothbrush we used as kids had bristles that were probably not as well designed as today's bristles. Today, most seem to come from DuPont with a "fancy" branded bristle called the Tynex filament. And we recognize there are nuances in the angles of how the bristles

FIGURE 3.4. Comparison of Black+Decker (top) and Cuisinart (bottom) toaster ovens.

are seated in the handle. But the reality is that the molding machine and the machine that inserts the bristles into the handle do it in the same amount of time as the minimally priced brush. With the direct manufacturing cost of production for the two brushes being roughly at parity, and distribution costs not incredibly different, the retail cost indicates remarkable margins based on the user's perceived value. We admit to the reality that the new ergonomic brushes probably feel better in your hands, but then again, this is a use model that rarely takes more than two minutes.

The bottom line is simply that the variation of today's better plastics and better bristles don't necessarily justify the dramatically more expensive product. We are talking pennies of difference in product cost versus the dramatic difference in retail price. So at the end of the day, you all, we all, feel better and might actually believe we're doing a better job with the $4.00 toothbrush than with the $0.79 toothbrush. But we're not.

And do we really need a tea kettle with a bird whistle, designed by Michael Graves, that can retail for $190[17] with the exact same number of parts as a Mr. Coffee Carterton stainless steel whistling tea kettle for about $14?[18] At the end of the day, all we want to do is boil some water. Or do we?

Packaging Can Also—Should Also—Be Emotional

We noted earlier that emotional design, which by now perhaps we should start calling good design, was clearly not limited to the product itself but would undoubtedly include the packaging and any supporting service aligned with it. And for all SMMEs, the lesson should be clear. Whatever it is you're doing, whether it be a physical product or a service, your counterpart on the purchasing and using side should have some delight in the relationship of its use.

Walter happens to like the DeWalt brand of drill bits. Not long ago, he needed a new set of spade bits. The carded, rack-mounted set of six sold for $10.98, reduced from $22.27, on Amazon. At the higher $22.27 price, each bit sells for $3.71. Walter searched a bit further and saw an eight-piece set that sold for considerably more money, $49.95, or $6.24 per bit. These were the identical drill bits, from the same manufacturer, with the exact specifications, but there were two more bits included in the second set. Each bit was approximately two times the price of the card-mounted ones. The primary difference was that the eight-bit set came in a simple, injection-molded plastic case that, when opened, exposed all eight drill bits, each within its own holder. Walter estimated the plastic case, which included a simple little locking mechanism, to cost less than $0.50 to manufacture. Assuming a five-time multiple of cost, the value of the case at retail should be less than $2.50. But rather than paying the $3.71 each for eight or just under $30 for the complete set, plus a $2.50 case for a total of $32.50, it is more than evident that a dramatically higher margin was attainable simply because of a better use model by virtue of including the plastic case. Walter recognized that his purchase was on the emotional side of consumption. The "two-and-a-half-dollar case" made it all the more worthwhile for him, and he had no reservation in purchasing it at the much higher price.

So while the case above references an unexceptional drill bit, think of your purchase of most any laptop computer or any other high-end electronic product. Walter recently purchased a MacBook Pro, some earbuds, and a remarkable magnet-based dashboard holder from Logitech for his cell phone. All of the products supported a wondrous out-of-the-box experience. In one case, when he opened the lid of the outer package, the product itself rose up from the base of the packaging to present itself in an anointment-like affair. It became regal. It was as though a third hand was presenting him with a gift of extraordinary value. It allowed for an initial presentation that convinced Walter that the product itself was worth every dollar he paid for it. As opposed to expressing these merely as "opening a box," all presentations suggested the manufacturer truly cared for him on a personal basis. It was at its best a highly emotional design that can only be expressed as being visceral. Walter knew the products would be everything he had hoped they would be. The benefit of that expression did indeed start a bit of a love affair. And as with any love affair, he was going to tell all.

Now we ask you, what is that worth? How many people that purchase your product or service want to tell everyone about it?

Emotional Design Is Always Good Design, Including Nonconsumer Items

While the drill bit vignette dealt with a consumer-based product, albeit a do-it-yourself hardware product, good design is good design, irrespective of it being a consumer product or an industrial part.

Manufacturing Hub, a manufacturing industry online newsletter, reviewed design decisions and how design translates to dollars.[19] They took a business-to-business part for analysis, a battery tray for the Ford Taurus, first introduced in 1985. The battery tray seemed simple enough. There were three main components: a base with all four edges turned up to contain the battery, and two L-brackets mounted to the two side flanges for final assembly into the vehicle. All three separate parts were break-formed in steel and assembled with several fasteners. The fasteners required to hold the battery in place included bolts, nuts, and J-nuts. The basic form was appropriate for its task of holding a battery in containment and allowing it to be easily bolted to another structural member.

If one counted up all of the individual parts, they numbered sixteen, and the assembly of all the parts required three-and-a-half minutes. Those three-and-a-half minutes of labor, including overhead, yielded a total labor cost of $2.36. The pieces themselves cost $11.08. A cost-of-quality burden of $0.59 was applied, giving the total cost of $14.03 for the battery tray. It turned out that all of the tooling costs were also significant and ran $476,316.

Here's where "good design" comes in. And if you're in the accounting department at Ford, this could quickly become "emotional." When they looked at the piece parts and assembly time, their question was, Could the part be optimized to save not only material costs but also labor as well? While steel by itself is relatively inexpensive, all the parts and the assembly justified a review. They also thought a design review could lead to a decreased number of parts.

The answer was a new plastic design. A single molded container and an innovative redesign achieved all the benefits hoped for. The sixteen parts of the original design were now replaced by six. The three-and-a-half minutes for assembly was now replaced by less than two minutes. The number of fasteners dropped from eleven to four, but best of all, the piece cost went from $11.08 to $3.22. The new plastic part's tooling bill was $85,000, resulting in a cost savings of over $2.25 million. That translates to "emotional design" for anyone motivated by financial return.

As described in Chapter 2, another industrial example was a commercial floor-cleaning machine. When we think of the category, our brain's image is usually something big and ugly, a boxy hunk of steel with brushes on the base. In that case, the big, ugly steel box was thrown out and replaced by a roto-molded plastic product with a high aesthetic value. Upon initial review, it was emotionally received in a very positive light. And on further examination, the strategic competitive advantage of reduced volume with other attributes identical proved to be an instantaneous hit.

THE VALUE OF EMOTIONAL DESIGN LEADERSHIP

Not only do companies that successfully embrace emotional design perform better financially than those that don't, but those enterprises that assume a *leadership* role in emotional design have the opportunity to succeed in ways that many others do not even consider.

Emotional, Great Design Is Good for Business

According to a McKinsey study, "Companies that excel at design grow revenues and shareholder returns at nearly twice the rate of their industry peers."[20] According to interviews of a hundred executives and two hundred senior design leaders, 90 percent of all companies were not reaching what McKinsey suggests is their full design potential. That top executives do not understand or believe in a user-centric strategy—which is easily defined as understanding your end-user—is astounding, for lack of a better word. In addition, for those that do employ senior designers, those folks are not invited into the "C-suite."

Having lived in the design consulting world for his entire professional life, Walter was not surprised to read in the report that only one-third of the CEOs and their direct reports surveyed understand what the head of design is responsible for, and only one in ten acknowledge that their directors of design play a meaningful role in defining corporate strategy. So who cares, and why does that matter?

It matters because design is good for business.

Design Leadership

Bracken Darrell, the CEO of Logitech—and for full disclosure, a client of Herbst Produkt—is a strong supporter of design and describes his company's use of design in three stages. There is a narrow focus on pure aesthetics in the first stage, often toward the end of the development process. That focus can include the form, color, materials, and finish of discrete products. It's like "dressing" the product at the end of the process. When companies mature and understand design a bit more, Darrell puts them into the second phase. In this phase, they recognize that design is a way to build an experience around the user. Companies exist at many levels within this stage, he says, from highly mature, like Apple, to much less mature. Companies never stop improving in this stage of building experience around the user rather than building products with user input. There is a third stage of design, but Darrell doesn't believe any, or at most *very* few, have made much progress toward it. In this stage, a company would include design in everything they do and infuse it within the entire organization. Logitech is starting down this path, but he views it as a very long-term goal. Darrell supports his hypothesis by recognizing his role in the company, which began in 2013. Through 2019, he saw the market value of Logitech increase seven times (at the time of writing in 2021, it is fifteen times).

The Logitech story is important, but the bigger story is the correlation between organizations that highly value design compared to the rest. In another study, McKinsey took a look at the top quartile of design-centric organizations versus what they consider to be their industry benchmarks.[21] Revenues in general increased substantially faster over five years for the design-centric organizations, which exhibited 32 percent larger revenue growth and 56 percent higher return to shareholders. This result was blended between medical technology, consumer goods, and retail banking to ensure appropriate reporting. Those industries obviously relate to discrete goods, digital products, and services. Among the companies not in the top quartile of design industry performance, over 40 percent admitted that they do not talk to their end-users while developing new products. Over 50 percent admit to not having a way to assess or target their design teams' outputs. Clearly, there is a leadership issue, and one that can be easily overcome, according to McKinsey.

These observations remind us of some great leadership comments used as a basis for moving companies out of the doldrums, with two immediately coming to mind. The CEO of T-Mobile, for example, has a personal motto of "shut up and listen."[22] And IKEA's vision is "to create a better everyday life for the many people."[23] If you're not paying attention to the people who consume your goods, there is no way to create a better everyday life.

EMOTIONAL DESIGN: SOME CLOSING THOUGHTS

We are sadly fascinated to know the stories shared here and read of the survey results referenced earlier, only to realize that design often has little or no voice in many companies. The summation for SMMEs—irrespective of whether you sell a physical product or service and whether your customer is a consumer or another business—is that your bottom line can be dramatically improved by paying attention to the user's emotions and by relying on design to play an important role. Importantly, all this is available by taking on a manageable level of risk and making reasonable cost investments.

It is to be expected when rolling out your new product or service that you have resolved issues of feasibility and have done enough to understand its viability.

But do you fully appreciate its desirability?

KEY POINTS AND TAKEAWAYS

- Consider your customers' emotions broadly.
- Good emotional design leads to competitive advantage and financial success.
- Those who ignore the value of emotional design are destined to compete on the basis of cost in a race to the financial bottom.

CHAPTER 4

Innovation Processes and Tools

"Every activity, every job is part of a process."

—W. Edwards Deming, noted twentieth-century
American quality consultant[1]

PRELIMINARY QUESTIONS AND INTRODUCTORY THOUGHTS

- What processes and tools are available to help me and others in my company learn the basics of innovation?
- What common and valuable processes and tools are available—and relatively easy to implement—to help me manage innovation just like other business investments?
- How might I most effectively implement innovation process tools in an SMME, especially when many seem to be developed for use by larger, mature companies or executed on a more ad hoc basis by startups?

With W. Edwards Deming, we affirm that "every activity, every job is part of a process." And innovation is no exception. Processes and tools serve an essential yet intriguing role within the innovation endeavors of any company. Important because some form of a process or tool is necessary for innovation success; they ensure that you will pursue innovation correctly. Intriguing because none is sufficient to ensure innovation success.

Innovation processes and tools are necessary because they help us manage to success measures, much like other metrics used in any ongoing operation. Innovation metrics include but are not limited to commercial success, efficient use of resources, return on investment, speed to market, and, ultimately, the long-term viability of your company. We optimize such metrics by employing innovation processes and tools that ensure high-quality information and insight, provide rapid and inexpensive learning methods, reduce risk, optimize resource allocation, and establish a clear strategic role and context for innovation.

This chapter focuses on the necessity of the innovation processes and associated tools most useful for SMMEs, identifying and briefly fleshing out five of the most critical (with overlap among them): phase-gate process, lean innovation, open innovation, 2x2 matrices, and product and technology roadmaps. We return to and address the insufficiency of innovation processes and tools in Chapter 5. There we discuss those who innovate. We review the people who grasp and work out the details of operating effectively within an atmosphere characterized internally by strict operational standards and protocols and externally by significant volatility, uncertainty, complexity, and ambiguity. Such innovators bring to life the necessary but insufficient processes and tools discussed in this chapter.

THE PHASE-GATE PROCESS

The most ubiquitous of all innovation processes, the "phase-gate process,"[2] represents something of a "master tool" of innovation, providing discipline where it might otherwise be lacking. This section introduces it and then discusses its value to the company, how to implement it with particular attention to its use in SMMEs, and some notable limitations.

Prelude: The Front and Back Ends of Innovation

The most commonly held view of innovation accepts that two very different, complementary activities exist in series. First, there is a creative, opportunity-recognizing "front end of innovation." Second, an implementation, idea-developing, and commercializing "back end of innovation" follows the front end.

The front end of innovation is most fully characterized by its component described as the "fuzzy front end" of innovation. The fuzzy front end deals explicitly with only three variables: the business opportunity plan, which includes a market and financial analysis, a pretechnical evaluation, and competitive research.[3]

The fuzzy front end carries the unarticulated assumption that, while we can successfully apply the "design thinking" techniques discussed in Chapter 2, we cannot explicitly fully grasp the details of how the innovative insight emerges in the innovator's mind. Such a "fuzzy" view acknowledges the intuitive, creative aspects of innovation and seeks to not overcontrol it. It is also "fuzzy" due to the initial lack of absolute product definition, which emerges over time.

Because of its seemingly "black box" and "messy" natures, the fuzzy front end appropriately opens up possibilities to embrace the volatility, uncertainty, complexity, and ambiguity that characterize breakthrough innovation and the associated renewal it drives. Thus, while necessarily tethered to customer needs and wants, the front end emphasizes the apparently random nature of innovation. The front end of innovation also involves an initial round of idea screening to ensure that only those ideas with the potential to be innovations—commercially successful and not merely curiosities or inventions—are allowed to receive further investment and consideration. As we will discuss shortly, such opportunity recognition and screening represent the phase-gate process's first phases and gates.

Some may see our description of the fuzzy front end as being a bit fuzzy itself. Yet we seek to emphasize the simultaneous reality that, while a lack of the methods and processes we shared in Chapter 2 and here in Chapter 4 all but guarantees failure, no technique or process ensures innovation success. Why is this? It is because you just may find, after extensive exploration, no viable opportunity for commercially successful, competition-changing innovation at the time you look for it. You also may miss something along the way that results in your not seeing that which is necessary to renew your company. Does this mean that you should not pursue innovation? Absolutely not. But it does mean you must accept that this is the nature of such endeavors if you hope to succeed in their pursuit.

Finally, in the back end of innovation, we dedicate ourselves to converting screened ideas into commercialized products, yet doing so in a fiscally responsible, step-wise way, incrementally investing in development only when progress toward commercialization is deemed favorable. The back end of innovation carries with it the unarticulated assumption that we can systematically develop and evaluate promising innovative concepts: that is, that we can reasonably grasp and proceed toward innovation.

The Phase-Gate Process

Any attempt to renew an SMME that lacks either a formal or informal process inevitably results in unnecessary waste. Whether due to a lack of strategic alignment, detachment from customer needs, individuals or groups working at cross purposes, scope creep, failing to learn from past mistakes, insufficient commitment, or investing time and money without assessing the likelihood of success, something regularly gets in the way of progress.

In response to the disarray arising when no process is employed, innovation best practice involves structuring the front and back ends of innovation, tying innovation to strategic initiatives, and only allowing authorized, identified individuals or teams to take action or make informed investment decisions. Further, when appropriately implemented, such structuring provides the discipline to not assume unnecessary risk by investing too much effort or too many resources before systematically vetting an idea to ensure that it and your company are ready to proceed to the next level. A phase-gate process is a simple yet powerful way to structure innovation. In its most basic form, a phase-gate process is a series of increasing investments and activities (phases) separated by decisions on whether or not to continue (gates).

This phase-gate process view of innovation appropriately systematizes innovation activities in ways that characterize how most other, non-innovation processes in the firm work. It ensures that critical information and thinking are not missing or ignored; it formally brings the customer's voice to innovation; it trains less experienced people in the innovation process; it helps those who have mastered innovation to recall and concentrate on the details. Such an approach is disciplined, not chaotic. It makes innovation more uniform and more predictable, minimizing variation in the innovation process. Finally, it reduces the risk of failure and loss of investment due to innovation process mistakes. Thus the phase-gate process emphasizes the apparently recipe-like nature to ensure opportunity converts to innovation.

Not surprisingly, numerous phase-gate process variations exist. Three examples, each illustrating a somewhat different perspective, appear in Figure 2.1 (Walter and Scot Herbst's Generic Design Thinking Phase-Gate Process) and Figure 4.1 (Robert Cooper's generic Stage-Gate Process and Karl Ulrich, Steven Eppinger, and Maria Yang's generic New Product Development Process). Cooper's generic process, typical of those possessing a conventional business-process perspective, provides little explicit detail regarding how the preprocess, "Discovery: Idea Generation," occurs. Yet it provides a relatively balanced view in terms of activity from start to finish. In contrast, Ulrich, Eppinger, and Yang's process emphasizes design activities, dedicating two phases to them. And in contrast to both Cooper and Ulrich, Eppinger, and Yang, Herbst and Herbst emphasize front-end activity with development and reduction-to-practice left to the final phase and interspaced with ongoing research and confirmation.

Upon additional consideration, these differences should not be surprising. Cooper, possessing both a terminal academic degree and a faculty appointment in business administration, presents the most uniformly weighted generic process from a business perspective. Ulrich, Eppinger, and Yang, each possessing a terminal academic degree in engineering and either affiliate or primary faculty appointments in engineering, present the most engineering-design-centric generic perspective. Finally, Herbst and Herbst, both of whom possess design-based degrees and extensive practical client experience, emphasize the process's design thinking and nonlinear aspects.

Implementing a Phase-Gate Process

The first step in implementing a phase-gate process is to understand your company's strategic objectives and key success factors. This activity will enable you to select a process most closely aligned with your needs. With

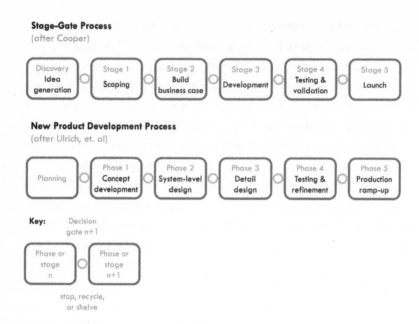

FIGURE 4.1. Generic phase-gate processes suggested by Cooper and Ulrich, Eppinger, and Yang. Source: (top) *Winning at New Products: Accelerating the Process from Idea to Launch* by Robert S. Cooper, copyright © 2017. Reprinted by permission of Basic Books, an imprint of Hachette Book Group, Inc. (bottom) *Product Design and Development, Seventh Edition* by Karl T. Ulrich, Steven D. Eppinger, and Maria C. Yang. Reprinted by permission of McGraw Hill, copyright © 2020.

our discussion of Cooper's; Ulrich, Eppinger, and Yang's; and Herbst and Herbst's processes, we hope you have begun to see which of these processes represents the best fit for your organization. Indeed, while it is best to start with one approach, your phase-gate process may evolve into a hybrid process over time. For example, an organization lacking both strong customer engagement and good overall process discipline might eventually synthesize aspects of Herbst and Herbst's and Cooper's process insights. The principle difference is the additional user research phases of Herbst and Herbst.

Having selected an approach, implementing such a process requires addressing a series of questions about each phase and gate. Examples include the following. For each phase,

- What output is required?
- What activities should we expect to perform?
- How are the activities funded? Who makes the funding decision?
- What roles are involved? What are the responsibilities of each role?[4]
- Who are the participants? Who allocates their time to this activity?
- Who has overall responsibility for the output and activities performed?
- What information or strategic context from outside the phase-gate process must be available to the participants? Who is responsible for providing it?

For each gate,

- What are the decision criteria for each possible outcome: proceed, stop, recycle, or shelve?
- What roles are involved? What are the responsibilities of each role?[5]
- Who or what group has the ultimate decision authority?
- Who are the participants? Who allocates their time to this activity?
- What information or context must be available to the participants beyond that coming from the output of the phase immediately preceding this gate?

To illustrate a typical phase-gate process implementation, consider the example of the adjacent Stage 1 and Gate 2 in Cooper's Stage-Gate Process. An idea enters Stage 1 after being screened at Gate 1 to ensure alignment with company strategy (we address the strategic context of innovation in Chapter 6) and its commercial viability potential. That is, with little investment of time or money, it appears feasible to reduce to practice, the market seems attractive, and we have identified no fatal flaws. In Stage 1, the executive responsible for new product development assigns the idea to a "product development manager." This individual could be the idea creator or someone else appointed to lead the concept through development. They serve as the point person responsible for preparing a "Scoping" analysis, a more detailed summary and consideration of the idea than that performed during "Discovery: Idea Generation," and carrying the idea into subsequent phases should additional investment be deemed appropriate. This analysis requires a deeper level of investigation and, as a result, yields more learning than that pursued for moving past the initial screen conducted in Gate 1. Here the product development manager (with a team, if assigned) probes multiple sources of information, possibly including but not limited to literature and database searches, internal and external experts, conversations with potential customers, initial market research, and competitor analyses. In the Stage-Gate Process, the product development manager then assimilates and compiles this information into a coherent, increasingly refined narrative that includes some preliminary financial analysis.

At this stage, the product development manager (again, with a team, if assigned) carefully explores risk factors, as missing them here can result in costly mistakes. One story worth sharing here involved an electronic component envisioned for a mass-market application, requiring a relatively rare mineral as part of its fabrication. Only later did the idea generator (who pursued the idea to development without the benefit of a phase-gate process) realize there was not enough annual production of that mineral globally to meet market demand. At that point, interest in the project waned. Another relevant story is that of an idea generator who invested six months in developing a product based on demand insight gleaned from a fellow engineer at a customer company. Only at the end of that time did the idea generator learn that, while his engineering counterpart genuinely was interested in his work, those in the customer's purchasing organization saw no value in it. These failures could easily have been avoided, much earlier and at less cost, by following a simple risk analysis of the type appropriately pursued in Stage 1.

Having completed this Scoping assessment, the product development manager should convene a team review gate meeting (Gate 2) to decide whether or not to proceed with additional investment. The review team typically comprises representatives of primary functional groups, often including functional management. Participants bring their expertise, insight, and a firm grasp of the company's strategic investment requirements to bear on the decision, either made or deferred, pending further assessment, by the end of the meeting.

Both Cooper's and Ulrich, Eppinger, and Yang's processes appear in some detail in readily available references. Therefore, we continue our commitment to design thinking as discussed in Chapters 2 and 3 by expanding on Herbst and Herbst's Design Thinking Phase-Gate Process (described in detail in Appendix 1).

As noted earlier, the phase-gate process is a series of increasingly larger investments and activities. Recalling our discussion of design thinking in Chapter 2, we can relate the phase-gate process to gambling. In the beginning, we know very little, and therefore, we are going to risk a very small bet. As the phases continue and as we continue to learn more, the bet can be allowed to increase as we decrease the chance of failure.

As part of the fuzzy front end, the design thinking process ensures a minimal bet, as the initial work is pure exploration. There are not many individuals involved nor long periods of time for involvement. Strategic plans are reviewed, as is the competitive environment, while a market analysis segmentation is beginning, as the end-user opportunity is explored. Concurrently, a manufacturing and technical assessment is also performed. None of this should result in heavily detailed and voluminous reports. The entirety of this design thinking is research-based, resulting in customer definition and the general direction the project will take. This work culminates in the form of a product requirement document. Product requirement documents can be thought of as the basis of a contract. The requirements allow all to understand what that product or service should do.

There are two ways one can create a product requirement document. One is a reasonably short document delineated line by line and referencing the descriptive verbs "shall," "should," "may," and "could" when describing the preliminary requirement. The reasoning for those verbs is the elimination of absolutes, as it is early in the game and absolutes become specifications, which occur further down the line.

An example is as follows and references the development of a line of transportable containers for keeping contents cold (think lunchbox):

- They should be easy to carry by users ranging from five years of age and up.
- The user group may include students, professionals, children, and anyone with party needs.
- The materials used could be easily cleaned with soap and water.

When the project does not include a complex development, the short lineal layout as above should be used. However, for anything more complex, the product requirement document becomes a major document supported by a table of contents that includes the following:

1. Purpose
2. Document scope
3. Program scope
4. Design documentation
5. Hardware documentation
6. Validation
7. Physical requirements
8. Electrical requirements
9. Functionality

Recognizing that a product requirement document can be reasonably complex, the ongoing use of the verbs "shall," "should," "may," and "could" throughout—just as in the short version of the phase-gate process, to avoid early specifications—supports the words "fuzzy front end."

Once a product requirement document is established, as the beginning deliverable for a design-thinking-based phase-gate methodology, the design team leads a Visioning component. Visioning supports the ultimate direction based on the product requirement document, as the team should now have a direction for the product to continue. What needs to be appreciated is that no one product can satisfy everyone, and therefore, the visioning allows the entire team to appreciate the end-user. That appreciation began with the previous step that included end-user research. That segmentation will lead to greater targeting of the end-user, including insights, trends, and inspiration. Since there are multiple user groups, and now that we recognize that one product does not fit all, directing the design to the ultimate user for a greater emotional response is critical.

That greater emotional response is recognized as aspirational. And aspiration does drive consumption. In other words, we purchase on the basis of an identity we wish to be affiliated with. Multiple examples abound, but vehicle purchases provide a good example. For the purchaser, a Hummer vehicle reflects an identity of brute strength, toughness, and indestructibility. Having noted that, personal reference suggests most Hummer owners live in suburban towns where roads and general transportation needs do not require any of the above. A similar comment might be made for one who wears a Harley t-shirt. Once again, it is an identity projection and need not reference Harley ownership.

Many who use Joseph and Joseph plastic food storage containers recognize these do the equivalent job of a very low-end generic food container. Yet Joseph and Joseph product customers use them to reflect their identity of someone with greater taste.

The design thinking methodology of end-user-driven emotional response will allow the design team to move ahead into a Concept phase. To ensure the direction is appropriate, and recognizing that early research will have taken them to this point in time, the complete team must review the concept work for ultimate production capability and success. Still, a vital review must be undertaken to ensure potential end-user success.

Design thinking methodology in a phase-gate structure minimizes the potential of failure in all areas. While we have focused on the comparatively unique first phases of the Herbst and Herbst process, we include additional detail in Table 4.1.

Implementing a Phase-Gate Process in an SMME

While the phase-gate process is ubiquitous in large, mature enterprises, this is not the case in SMMEs, especially as company size decreases. If your SMME has no process in place or even one you are not satisfied with, we recommend starting with a simple implementation that you can improve upon over time and tailor to fit your company's needs, what one might consider a "phase-gate light" implementation.

TABLE 4.1. First-level details of Herbst and Herbst's Design Thinking Phase-Gate Process.

	Phase	Summary	Output (if decision to proceed)
0	Research	Synthesize end-user and competitor insights	Product requirement document
1	Visioning	Generate insights by looking to external trends and inspiration, as well as technical architecture	Framed problem
2	Concepts	Brainstorm, breadboard, and develop concepts	Product concept 1.0
3	Review	Refine product concept 1.0 iteratively, develop product image or story	Product concept 2.0
4	Research	Test and Validate product concept 2.0	Product concept 3.0
4b	Confirm Channel	Test and Validate product concept 3.0 proposed distribution channel	Confirmed distribution channel
5	Develop	Complete engineering release "Alpha" to commercialize product concept 3.0	Alpha product release
6	Final Research Release	Confirmation with targeted market	Commercialized product

The first step in a successful SMME phase-gate process implementation is to ensure that you have a firm grasp of the overall decision criteria and strategic context for commercialization. We regularly observe SMMEs that are unable to articulate what constitutes innovation success. Appropriately, this activity starts at the top, with owners, board members, and CEOs openly considering what they hope to accomplish with such investment. This discussion concludes with a clear, concise, and written description of what is acceptable strategically and what constitutes an adequate financial return for each innovation investment. If the owners, board members, and CEOs, often in collaboration with the president or GM and their leadership team, cannot reduce their expectations on these matters to a concise written form, it will be impossible for those engaging directly with current and potential customers to succeed. If anything, it becomes a futile effort of "go slay a dragon, and we'll tell you later if it's the right one."

The second step in SMME phase-gate process implementation is for the management team (which includes formal functional leadership), often jointly with informal functional leaders' guidance, to establish decision criteria for each gate. These include the specific market, technical, manufacturing, and operational hurdles used to decide whether to stop, recycle, or approve next-stage investment. This step also should include identifying assessments and assessment tools that may be used or considered at each phase, such as the following:

- *Market*: Market attractiveness, customer buying behavior, distribution, pricing, promotion
- *Technical*: Technical feasibility, design robustness, patentability
- *Manufacturing and operations*: Cost, capacity, supply chain
- *Financial*: Profitability, cash flow, return on investment, time to breakeven
- *Strategic*: Strategic alignment, strategic position, competitive advantage

Our advice is to start by keeping these simple and concise—just enough rather than too much—as a means of maintaining momentum.

Having identified these decision criteria and assessments, those implementing the phase-gate process can assign individuals to specified roles. This step should also involve establishing position descriptions (including statements regarding the required skills and expertise) for the product development manager and the review team participating in decision making at each gate. Note that the review team's composition will likely change as you move further along within the phase-gate process, with higher-level approval often required as investment increases. Also note that the product development manager role, not unlike a more general project management role, represents an excellent opportunity for a functional expert to develop cross-functional and interpersonal skills. In addition to deep product and customer insight, successful product development managers develop expertise in accounting and finance, marketing, negotiation, and influencing others.

Once launched, follow-up assessment and adaptation of an SMME's phase-gate process is critical. A final phase, requiring documenting results (both successes and failures, including return on investment, time to market, and specific reasons for failure), enables innovation leaders in the SMME to identify patterns of strengths (or weaknesses) that the company can build (or improve) upon in subsequent commercialization efforts. A not uncommon example of improving on a pattern of weakness is to insist on early and regular consumer engagement by idea generators and product development managers, something often resisted by general management and those in other functions, such as sales. Further, some companies establish different phase-gate processes for incremental and potentially breakthrough ideas, with breakthrough ideas requiring more careful consideration to ensure that unarticulated assumptions become neither inappropriate barriers nor free passes to proceed. Similarly, some companies implement different phase-gate processes for different business units, especially those with different strategic expectations.

Phase-Gate Process Limitations

Having argued on behalf of the value of the phase-gate process, we note that it does carry with it limitations. First and foremost, a phase-gate process does not make up for lack of commitment to and investment in innovation efforts. Too often, executives fail to provide appropriate support for innovation initiatives once a process is in place. For example, the most common phase-gate failure occurs when projects languish, waiting for a gate review meeting or funding. Such failure typically is observed in companies that are good at generating ideas and starting projects, but not sufficiently disciplined to see them through to completion or at least an explicit decision to stop. Second, commercial risks exist, as even potential innovations developed in a phase-gate process regularly fail in the marketplace. Failure in the "Phase 0" fuzzy front end that feeds the phase-gate process often is characterized by a heroically technical success or insight that finds no place in the market. This is particularly the case when design thinking methodology is ineffectively or not pursued. Failure within the phase-gate process itself often is characterized by incremental rather than breakthrough success. Perhaps most important, the combination has the appearance of an inefficient production line, generating large amounts of product (generating potentially breakthrough ideas in the front end of innovation) followed by filtering out the defects (filtering of ideas in the phase-gate process). In the ridiculous extreme with this perspective, we close our eyes, grit our teeth, and throw ourselves in a direction (in the fuzzy front end), after which we learn whether or not it is the right direction (in the phase-gate process). Such an endeavor often is exhausting, expensive, and not entirely satisfying. The only way to overcome this limitation is to improve the quality, alignment with strategy, and commercial viability of incoming ideas and opportunities.

LEAN INNOVATION

Emerging from a single origin yet developing by way of two independent paths, "lean innovation" represents an attempt to reduce waste in the pursuit of innovation. This section introduces lean innovation from the perspectives of both the quality community and the entrepreneurial community. We then discuss the "minimum viable product" concept, including how to implement it with particular attention to its use in SMMEs. Finally, in our discussion of lean innovation in SMMEs, we note some potential pitfalls in its application.

Prelude: Perspectives of the Quality and Entrepreneurial Communities

A concept dating to the 1990s, "lean," in the context of production and quality, can be framed as the pursuit to eliminate three categories of wasteful practices:

1. Activities that neither add value for the customer nor necessarily support those that add value for the customer (known as *muda* in Japanese)
2. An unevenness of production flow (*mura*)
3. Unreasonable work expectations (*muri*)[6]

Eliminating *muda* begins with a deep understanding of customer needs. Those responsible for lean production propagate this understanding throughout the production system, removing wasteful steps such as the unnecessary, non-value-adding movement of work in process through the production line. Eliminating *mura* involves such activities as leveling production so that work in process neither unnecessarily accumulates nor dries up through the production line. Such smoothing of flow results in the efficient use of both equipment and labor. Finally, eliminating *muri* involves establishing standardized work, which also can have an impact on *muda* in that wasteful steps become less likely to find their way back into the production process.

After developing "lean production," quality experts found success in applying these concepts across various enterprise functions in the form of what they refer to more broadly as "lean thinking."[7] What occurred next is critical to understanding lean innovation as it exists today, as two relatively different perspectives and approaches to innovation grew out of lean thinking. Both the quality and entrepreneurial communities look to this expansion to lean thinking as the foundation for their lean innovation views. Therefore, and unsurprisingly, their independent literatures bear some similarities, most notably that each focuses on the critical importance of customer value. In addition, both appeal in places to a kind of simple, iterative pursuit of insight to innovation, such as that described by W. Edwards Deming's Plan-Do-Check-Act Cycle.[8]

Yet these two literatures diverge in critical other ways in how they define, present, and pursue lean innovation. You tend to find a discussion of what is known as "lean product and process development"[9] emerging from the quality community and, separately, a study of what is known as the "lean startup"[10] arising from the entrepreneurial community. Incremental innovation is more consistent with the language and concepts used to describe the context of "lean product development" (cost reduction, predictability, stability, reliability, simplicity, moving toward the known). In contrast, breakthrough innovation is more consistent with the language and concepts used to describe the context of the "lean startup" (revenue growth, uncertainty, volatility, agility, complexity, moving away from the unknown). These differences mean that both perspectives have value—yet, a different type of value—to the SMME.

By way of the quality community's perspective, lean product development concepts are appropriately applied to improve, for example, an

SMME's phase-gate process. The process improvement benefits provided by the quality community's approach tend to result in incremental innovation success. In some respects, this is not surprising, as lean concepts typically are familiar to those in—and implemented widely across—successful mature enterprises, especially manufacturing companies, and increasingly so as company size increases.

In contrast, SMMEs apply lean startup concepts to move into new markets and realms of competition. The customer development benefits provided by the entrepreneurial community's perspective are more likely to open the door to the kind of breakthrough innovation that leads to renewal. This view also is not surprising, as the lean startup concept, which emerged from the new business development aspects of entrepreneurial practice, emphasizes customer development over speculative product development.

This distinction rarely is made, with those in SMMEs at best choosing to pursue only one or the other approach and then most often selecting the more familiar, lean product development perspective of lean innovation. The unfortunate consequence of such a choice is that renewal opportunities often are missed. For this reason, we emphasize the entrepreneurial community's lean startup perspective here, introducing our SMME audience to concepts frequently not encountered or embraced.

Lean Innovation: The Minimum Viable Product

Perhaps the most crucial idea arising from the lean startup is that of the minimum viable product and its use to help entrepreneurs quickly engage potential customers, enabling them to learn and, as necessary, pivot to best address customer needs.

A minimum viable product is the simplest form of a product, possessing the essential features that the entrepreneur seeks to test with potential "lead" customers or early adopters. Such lead customers are those most likely to work with the startup to refine the product concept to the point that it is valued later and ultimately by a larger segment of the marketplace. With this concept, you avoid the time and money spent developing additional "bells and whistles" features that, while perhaps interesting, do not directly address and probe lead customer needs and wants. In this way, the entrepreneur streamlines innovation, and as the name "lean innovation" implies, eliminates waste. In addition, it allows one to have a product in the market—importantly generating early revenue—in a timelier manner and accepts potential improvements along the development path as next-generation developments.

The value of the approach is that it addresses two common commercialization errors experienced by entrepreneurs. First, some entrepreneurs develop and launch products searching for a market without the benefit of deep customer insight of the type discussed in Chapter 2. In such cases, they often exhaust their resources, focusing on their personal preconceptions of customer preference without ever learning directly from customers what they prefer. We illustrated such failure with our discussion of the Segway. Instead, the minimum viable product approach consists of a series of quick development cycles of relatively simple product concepts, getting them in front of customers to iteratively secure feedback. Each minimum viable product development cycle represents a low-risk, high-return investment, with successive cycles permitting design modifications or pivots in new directions.

The second commercialization error addressed by the minimum viable product is more subtle than, yet can be as important as, the first. Some entrepreneurs pursue a "release early, release often" strategy to implement a series of quick development cycles of relatively simple products. In doing so, they launch products broadly across their entire potential market landscape. This shotgun approach can lead to conflicting feedback, with different customers representing different market segments preferring other product characteristics. Companies that take such feedback to heart without understanding the underlying nature of the market segments addressed can find themselves bullwhipped, pulled in different directions almost randomly over time, as they first pursue one customer's needs and then those of another. In contrast, the minimum viable product approach focuses on customer engagement by limiting it to so-called "lead" customers and then generalizing such learning to the larger market.

Slice's story, presented in Chapter 2, is a perfect example of successful lean innovation. Slice started with a basic manual box cutter, addressing the needs of a specific market segment. It then went to the auto-retractable box cutter, then to the manual carton cutter, then to the smaller "pen" cutter, then to the auto-retractable pen cutter, and finally to the manual mini-cutter. All of these have achieved success. All found a niche market.

Notably, lean innovation advocates for getting a minimum viable product out quickly, refining it over time, rather than waiting to make a "perfect" product as a first launch.

Implementing Lean Innovation in SMMEs

As noted earlier, perhaps the most significant barrier to successfully implementing lean innovation in SMMEs is that context and perceptions tend to favor the lean product development approach over the lean startup perspective. As this is not an either-or proposition, the SMME is best served when those responsible for innovation leadership clearly and effectively understand and communicate these differences and their implications. Too often, we have observed a willingness to proceed in these directions in a tentative, step-like manner, first by (at most) embracing lean product development and only later followed by (at most) considering but not necessarily implementing lean startup concepts. As with all of our cautionary notes, this timing could very well put the SMME in a precarious, life-or-death situation as current or potential competitors move first into new modes of competition.

A second barrier to implementing lean innovation of the type described by the lean startup approach is that many SMMEs limit contact with current and potential customers to those in sales functions. Even when other functional experts are included directly in the discussion, they are often managers, not necessarily those with deep insight into current technical capabilities. As we discuss in Chapter 5, such siloing of activity limits the opportunity for holistic thinking and thus the kind of breakthrough innovation that leads to renewal.

A third and final barrier to SMMEs implementing lean innovation of the type described by the lean startup approach is that its iterative, non-linear path often appears to contradict the linear view embraced as part of a phase-gate process implementation. Those in the most successful SMMEs understand that these two approaches must be reconciled and coordinated to succeed. Doing so requires that all who are implementing and managing innovation understand and accept the role and importance of each. Unfortunately, this often is not the case, with individuals or entire portions of an SMME either actively or passive-aggressively seeking to undermine the organizationally-foreign, fluid, iterative, and nonlinear approach used when employing a minimum viable product to gain customer insight. To some, a minimum viable product may seem like a waste of time, as innovation efforts start, stop, return to the starting point, and resume again, usually multiple times. Only the kind of patience that comes from grasping and accepting the minimum viable product approach will enable SMMEs to succeed in ways otherwise impossible.

The Pitfalls of Implementing Lean Innovation in an SMME

Having identified and briefly discussed the wasteful practices (*muda, mura, muri*) addressed by lean production at the beginning of this section, it seems fitting to close this section with a discussion of their innovation equivalent, the wasteful practices of innovation. In doing so, we expose the challenges of implementing lean innovation in an SMME.

Eliminating *muda* in innovation begins with securing a deep understanding of customer needs, just as it does with lean production. Here, the minimum viable product enables innovators to test ideas simply and quickly while generating revenue, rather than investing more than necessary to decide how to proceed. Unfortunately, a misguided interpretation of eliminating *muda* is possible by not considering the minimum viable product's fluid, iterative, and nonlinear characteristics. Gaining the insight necessary for commercial success requires sufficient time and focus. It can appear to be, yet not be, non-value-adding. Executives, who seek to know enough to make decisions, often are at odds with innovators who must know enough to create. Therefore, executives must open themselves to seeing this apparently messy process as the innovator's value-added work. This level of awareness can be incredibly challenging in more operationally focused SMMEs.

Eliminating *mura* by smoothing flow in innovation also requires a nuanced perspective. Innovators need time to ruminate; innovative insight does not merely emerge on demand. Yet, as we explore in more detail in Chapter 5, proven innovators are often called on as the company's best solvers of current problems. By combining these two roles—strategic renewal and tactical triage—in one exceptional individual, SMMEs get the best of both worlds. It is just such smoothing that leads to both current and future financial success. However, we lose the opportunity to smooth if these individuals are pulled from innovation so much or so often that they become ineffective at driving it.

Finally, eliminating *muri* requires addressing unreasonableness. In lean production, this involves establishing standardized work. Lean innovation also requires managing executive expectations, just as we detail here in our *muda* and *mura* discussions. Without senior leadership—whether owners, board members, CEOs, or presidents or GMs and their leadership teams—grasping breakthrough innovation's unique character and value, they place unreasonable demands on their innovators, destining their SMME for failure.

OPEN INNOVATION

Emerging as an explicitly defined, standalone concept in 2003, "open innovation," in its simplest form, encourages innovators and forward-thinking companies to shed a "not invented here" attitude when it comes to new ideas and insights.[11] This section begins with open innovation's most commonly depicted context, the "innovation funnel." Next, we make a case for open innovation, suggest some options for implementing it, and conclude with a brief discussion of the opportunities and pitfalls of pursuing it within an SMME.

Prelude: The Innovation Funnel

Immediately behind the most common front and back ends of innovation and phase-gate process depictions of innovation, the innovation funnel conveys the sense that a relatively large number of untested ideas are winnowed down over time to a manageable and proven set, ready for commercialization. As depicted in Figure 4.2, the funnel is just that, a horn-shaped drawing that accepts a large number of untested ideas on the left end and launches a small number of validated ideas on the right end. While the phase-gate process schematics of Figures 2.1 and 4.1 clearly illustrate the process nature of innovation, the innovation funnel schematic depicts the structured selection process's focusing result.

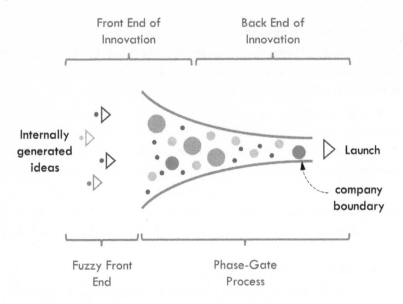

FIGURE 4.2. Schematic of the innovation funnel depicting the relative positions of the front and back ends of innovation, as well as the fuzzy front end and phase-gate process.

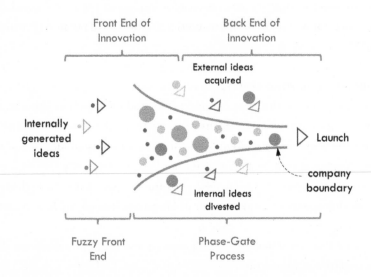

FIGURE 4.3. Schematic of the innovation funnel depicting how open innovation allows external ideas to be acquired and internal ideas to be divested.

The Case for Open Innovation

Worth noting in the innovation funnel of Figure 4.2 is the unarticulated assumption that ideas only enter the company at the far left end and leave at the far right end. It is just this perspective that open innovation challenges. In contrast to the innovation funnel shown in Figure 4.2, Figure 4.3 illustrates the reality that ideas can flow into and out of the company at any point from conception to commercialization, a simple yet powerful insight. In this way, open innovation represents the application of supply chain considerations to innovation, as we reconsider the flow of ideas and insights across company boundaries historically understood as impenetrable.

Such openness can take several forms. It can most simply represent a passive acceptance of ideas suggested by those outside the organization. It can manifest itself as an active solicitation of ideas by putting forth a need and allowing external individuals or organizations to respond. It can mean licensing someone else's technology or engaging a consultant or advisor. The external source of innovation insight may, at one extreme, be a relatively small but likely essential contribution from an outsider. It also may take the form of full innovation outsourcing at the other end of the spectrum. In this case, an external individual or organization independently develops a new product concept to the point of commercialization.

The critical insight is that a company can leverage its existing internal innovation capabilities by looking outside for complementary ideas and insight.

The case for open innovation, then, is simple. By employing open innovation, a company can reduce expenses associated with internally generating innovative ideas and also expand the pool of innovative ideas to which it has access. Further, the company can generate income by divesting ideas that, after some development, are found to have financial promise elsewhere yet be poorly aligned with the company's strategic goals.

Implementing Open Innovation

Building on the underlying assumption that companies benefit from being open to and importing ideas from outside traditional company boundaries, open innovation requires a different posture and investment profile than traditional innovation. The most significant difference lies in the types of people employed to pursue innovation as well as their skill sets.

In a more conventional innovation environment, full-time employees who succeed at innovation are highly skilled at learning and developing ideas. If they acquire insight from outside the organization, it typically is very granular and requires significant development in combination with internal insights to bring to commercial fruition.

These same companies primarily manage their intellectual property defensively as assets to protect their ability to function profitably.

In an open innovation environment, full-time employees who succeed in implementing innovation are highly skilled at identifying ideas outside of their company that can be brought to significant commercial fruition when combined with some internal competence. This internal competence can vary widely and include but not be limited to manufacturing expertise, access to specific markets or customers, and products that might benefit from external technology. The distinction observed in those companies most successful at open innovation is that they are experts at leveraging but not solely relying on internal expertise, connecting external ideas with ideas or skills already possessed internally.

In companies employing open innovation, intellectual property groups become revenue generators in addition to their role as asset protectors, licensing or selling patent rights to noncompetitors.

To illustrate these differences, consider a company that sells chemical products. A more traditional approach to innovation typically would involve employing a chemist or chemical engineer who possesses outstanding technical depth in a relevant field and demonstrates a firm grasp of customer needs. This potential innovator would seek to develop new features on their own, building on existing expertise or that which they might easily add.

Further, this company's intellectual property activity would actively employ defensive strategies such as establishing a "picket fence," a barrier of multiple patents covering the innovator's inventions (perhaps covering both products and processes). Such an approach would enable the company to use the innovator's insights commercially without the threat of direct competition.

In contrast, an open innovation approach typically might involve employing a chemist or chemical engineer who possessed broad familiarity across a wide range of technical fields and who, again, also demonstrated a firm grasp of customer needs. This potential innovator—having the expertise to evaluate external independent individuals and organizations and their ideas—would explore external sources of ideas that the company could leverage to its advantage.

This open innovation company would actively employ an intellectual property strategy that includes disposing of unused assets or assets that would generate *more* income by teaming with an external partner than by commercializing them internally. In this example, the company might license patented chemical products or processes employed by the company in its industry to noncompetitors in other sectors.

Note that such approaches need not, perhaps even must not, be considered exclusive. Chemists and chemical engineers exist who are both deep—at times multiply deep—and broad. As we will discuss in Chapter 5, such individuals exhibit the flexibility to implement either a more traditional approach or open innovation, whichever benefits the company most. Similarly, intellectual property groups exist that implement both defensive and revenue-generating strategies.

Not wanting to suggest that these examples are exhaustive, here are some common ways companies can employ open innovation to their advantage.

External Ideas Acquired

- Sources can include other companies (small, medium, or large enterprises; startups and mature; domestic or foreign), government laboratories, universities, consultants, part-time employees (often retired with relevant industry experience), anyone participating in crowd-sourcing activities.
- Actions can include teaming with noncompetitors, crowd-sourcing ideas, contracting with or part-time hiring individuals or groups, and licensing-in or acquiring intellectual property.

- Opportunities with universities include engaging university faculty as consultants, contracting with university faculty to conduct research, engaging university student teams (typically undergraduate students working on capstone projects), accessing specialized university facilities and equipment.
- During crowd-funding activities, since those participating demonstrate a willingness to purchase your product, you could make them a form of "lead customer."

Internal Ideas Divested

- Targets include other companies (small, medium, or large enterprises; startups and mature; domestic or foreign).
- Actions can include teaming with noncompetitors, licensing-out or selling intellectual property.

The Opportunities and Pitfalls of Pursuing Open Innovation Within an SMME

When implemented effectively in SMMEs, open innovation overcomes financial, human, and capability limitations found in such companies.[12] The most significant opportunities that open innovation provides for most SMMEs is that it leverages the typically limited resources available to the SMME and generates income not otherwise possible due to limited sales, marketing, or manufacturing capabilities. Such opportunities can generate significant windfalls for the SMME. Yet SMME leadership must be aware of potential pitfalls experienced when implementing open innovation. These pitfalls typically emerge due to insufficient internal expertise, a substantial mismatch of needs between the SMME and its open innovation partner, or an imbalance of power between the SMME and its open innovation partner.

As an example of insufficient internal expertise, consider an SMME that places responsibility for inbound open innovation in the hands of an individual lacking sufficient ability to see or implement connections between external technologies and internal needs. In an attempt to minimize internal investment, such SMMEs go too far. The lesson to be learned here is that open innovation success requires a minimum investment and expertise. Anything less represents a waste of time and money.

As an example of potentially mismatched needs, consider technology transfer opportunities from universities to SMMEs. Research-intensive universities generate intellectual property in the form of insights and patents as well as graduates. To remain competitive in receiving federal government research funding and to establish a prestigious reputation—the coins of the realm in research-intensive universities—faculty members in the United States must focus on current and emerging trends. In contrast, SMMEs typically base their competitive position on relatively mature technologies. As a result, hiring faculty consultants or funding graduate-level research from these universities is challenging, as the fit often does not exist. Add to this the reality that federal law enables universities and faculty inventors to receive financial windfalls from technology licensing, and preference is given to those companies that provide the greatest likelihood for financial success. The result is that most university technology transfer offices license their intellectual property almost exclusively either to large corporations or to faculty and student startups. They work with those large corporations that possess market access or manufacturing infrastructure to speed and help ensure successful commercialization. Similarly, they work with faculty and student startups having intimate familiarity with the technology, again, to speed and help ensure successful commercialization and reward the faculty and student inventors.

Does this mean that SMMEs have no opportunity to benefit from open innovation opportunities from universities? Not at all. Typically, the best match between research-intensive universities and SMMEs occurs by working with student teams participating in competitions or implementing sponsored capstone course projects under a senior faculty member's tutelage. However, when doing so, the SMME must pay attention to the terms of its agreement with the university if it hopes to secure intellectual property rights, as these are not always guaranteed.

As an example of an imbalance of power, consider SMMEs working with large, mature enterprises' open innovation efforts. For SMMEs, collaborating with large, mature enterprises can represent an apparently attractive opportunity. With their considerable volume potential and, often, profit potential, large, mature enterprises can take on the appearance of a proverbial "pot of gold at the end of the rainbow." Yet for every SMME entering into such collaboration, countless others lose out on the opportunity. As a result, large, mature enterprises typically are in a position to negotiate an SMME partner's share down to razor-thin margins. Therefore, SMME leadership is wise to set expectations appropriately when pursuing open innovation relationships in which they divest ideas to large, mature companies.

2X2 MATRICES

Business strategists have employed simple matrices for decades as planning and communication tools. As innovation is inherently strategic, a handful of such matrices may appropriately find their way into conversations around renewal in any company. This section introduces business matrices and then illustrates two applications that are particularly useful for SMMEs: exploring white spaces for product opportunities and project portfolio mapping. It concludes with a brief discussion of the opportunities and pitfalls associated with such tools within an SMME.

Prelude: Strategic Business Planning Matrices

While many people can process a great deal of information verbally, a simple schematic often helps cut through potential confusion. Two possibly familiar examples are the Ansoff Growth Options Matrix and the BCG Growth-Share Matrix. We illustrate both in Figure 4.4.

Dating to the 1950s, Ansoff's Matrix depicts four primary growth options (displayed as quadrants) available to any company when limiting focus to new markets and new products. The company can further penetrate existing markets with existing products (lower left), develop new markets with current products (upper left), create new products to address existing markets (lower right), and, finally, diversify by developing new products to address new markets (upper right). In addition, by noting that new market development often is less expensive and risky than new product development, and that pursuing both is riskier than either in isolation, this matrix helps the company quickly and easily visualize more than just the existence of four options.

Ansoff Growth Options Matrix

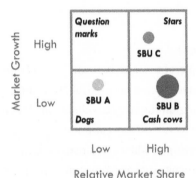

BCG Growth-Share Matrix

FIGURE 4.4. Two simple 2x2 matrices commonly used in strategic business planning, the Ansoff Growth Options Matrix (top) and the BCG Growth-Share Matrix (bottom).

First deployed by the Boston Consulting Group in the 1970s, the BCG Growth-Share Matrix is used to depict the state of a portfolio of strategic business units on the S-curve (see Introduction and Chapter 1). A great deal of uncertainty exists during a high-growth phase, as leaders (Stars) run the risk of being overtaken, and followers (Question Marks), while still in the running, run the risk of being left behind. At maturity, when growth flattens, leaders (Cash Cows) become entrenched at least for a time, and it becomes increasingly difficult for low-share competitors (Dogs) to displace them. The names assigned to each quadrant depict how BCG suggested managing business units therein. As with the Ansoff Matrix, the BCG Matrix helps one quickly and easily visualize multiple portfolio characteristics. Such enhanced visualization is especially possible when the user depicts, for example, business unit size by the size of the circle used to identify it, as shown in Figure 4.4.

We can generalize these two charts by noting that the essential act in their development is selecting two axes that, when used together, depict the most valuable information for the practitioner. It is just this selection criterion that we will use next to illustrate several potential uses for such 2x2 matrices in innovation.

White Space Mapping

A simple first example of using a 2x2 matrix to advance innovation is to map white spaces, unaddressed yet desirable product price-performance characteristics. Building on the story developed in Chapter 2, we use Figure 4.5 to depict how Slice identified and communicated just such a white space.

By locating competing products on a map of feature desirability versus price, the Slice team recognized an opportunity for a new product that enabled cleaner, safer cuts relative to conventional box cutters. Slice's ceramic blade renewed the industry. In contrast to the inconsistent cuts of varying depth realized by using traditional, metal-knife box cutters, Slice's ceramic blade resulted in more controlled cuts. Further, Slice's unique design protected users from box fragments, such as staples and sharp edges.

Project Portfolio Mapping

Similar to a BCG Growth-Share Matrix used to map strategic business units and a white space planning matrix to map products, innovation practitioners benefit from mapping projects as a means of both visualizing and communicating investment allocations. Two such examples appear in Figure 4.6: pursuing economies of scale by applying Michael Porter's generic strategies[13] and pursuing economies of scope by diversifying.

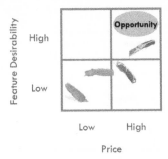

White Space Planning Matrix

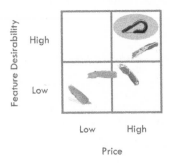

White Space Implementation Matrix

FIGURE 4.5. White space planning (top) and implementation (bottom) matrices employed by Slice in their pursuit of industry renewal.

Figure 4.7 illustrates the use of the economies of scope (diversification) strategy map by depicting two possible innovation investment portfolio scenarios. Portfolio 1 comprises four projects, three of which are at the extreme limit of projected time to market for this company. Further, each of the four addresses new-to-company markets with new-to-company technologies, significantly increasing the risk relative to Portfolio 1. Portfolio 2 also comprises four projects, each of which has a roughly one-year or less

**Economies of Scale Strategy Map
(Porter's generic strategies)**

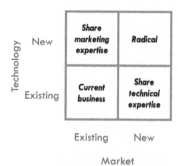

**Economies of Scope Strategy Map
(diversification)**

FIGURE 4.6. 2x2 matrices used to depict pursuing economies of scale (top) and scope (bottom).

projected time to market. Each also leverages existing market competence as a means to commercialize new-to-company technology.

Companies most effectively develop such maps iteratively and collectively. Whoever leads the innovation effort may appropriately construct the first-pass map. Formal and informal functional leaders—and then other relevant individuals and teams—can provide a subsequent review, suggesting possible changes, including project location on the map and time-to-commercialization estimates. Additional map variations can prove

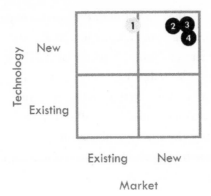

Portfolio 1

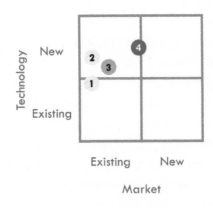

Portfolio 2

FIGURE 4.7. Two possible innovation investment portfolio scenarios, depicted in an economies of scope (diversification) strategy map.

useful if, for example, they depict both the current state and either a real past investment state or a desired future investment state—or if the marker size represents the size of a project's potential market opportunity.

Not surprisingly, other valuable project portfolio mapping options exist. Perhaps the most important is that depicting investment by project. Many firms overcommit and do not adequately allocate resources.[14] By visualizing, in a simple 2x2 matrix, the strategic allocation of resources among projects competing for scarce resources, leaders must confront the reality of their decision-making processes. Like production systems, innovation cycle time skyrockets when innovation work in process grows beyond capacity. As a result, a simple visualization tool, such as a 2x2 matrix, can facilitate a discussion that leads simultaneously to reduced investment and shorter time to commercialization.

The Opportunities and Pitfalls of 2x2 Matrices as Innovation Maps Within an SMME

As noted at the beginning of this section, 2x2 matrices serve as effective planning and communication tools. Introducing them for use in SMMEs is particularly valuable, as such organizations often lack the kind of broad palette of tools employed by large, mature enterprises.

Such tools' successful use requires an increasingly sophisticated understanding of customer needs, core competencies, competitive challenges, and company strategy. To the extent that those in an SMME either possess or seek insight regarding the most important two factors that serve as the maps' axes, these 2x2 matrices represent potent tools. However, for those who use them casually, these matrices can mislead with less-rigorously chosen, less-useful axes, encouraging SMMEs to focus on less-than-critical opportunities and issues.

PRODUCT AND TECHNOLOGY ROADMAPS

"Product and technology roadmaps" provide a clear, concise visual summary of and the link between customer requirements and company product and technology development plans over time. This section introduces product and technology roadmaps, addressing their value to the company as both a planning and a communication tool, external and internal. We conclude by discussing the challenges of implementing them.

Prelude: Project Timelines

Timelines, such as Gantt charts, are among the most familiar and commonly used project management tools. They illustrate schedules and the dependency between various tasks. The project timeline, constructed during the project planning process, is a valuable resource during project implementation. At a moment's glance, one can visualize project status and consider how to best adapt to delays.

Product and Technology Roadmaps

Product and technology roadmaps often take the form of a series of parallel timelines, each depicting a different yet interrelated set of information about your customers' needs and your company's capability to fulfill those needs. By constructing product and technology roadmaps, your company can anticipate customer needs and act sufficiently in advance to be ready to address those needs on time, enabling your company to secure that business.

A useful hierarchy of roadmap options begins with identifying your customers' product plans—not their plans for your products, but their product plans—and then successively digs into and then deeper into your organization's capabilities. A relatively complete set of roadmap options includes the following:

- *Your customers' products.* This roadmap depicts your understanding of a high-level view of your customers' product development and commercialization plans. Ideally, insight regarding your customers' strategy supports this roadmap. This supplemental information might include a description of their target customers and markets, their products' intended position in these markets, and the trajectory that they anticipate for these markets and their product positioning.
- *Your customers' requirements for your products.* This roadmap depicts a complete set of critical specifications to be addressed

by your products. It represents your customers' anticipated time-varying demand for what you produce. Your customer should articulate the connection between these specifications and their product roadmap, enabling you to understand not only what they want but also why they seek the progression of performance characteristics they desire.

- *Your products.* This roadmap depicts your planned response to customer expectations. It serves a useful role in discussions with current and potential customers and during internal planning processes. In dialog with current and potential customers, this roadmap puts forward what you believe your customers might want over time and how you plan to address their needs. In dialog internally, this roadmap provides a clear set of performance characteristics necessary to sustain customer engagement. Ideally, these two conversations produce a future "making of the market" negotiation and understanding between your customers and internal-to-company capabilities.

- *Your technologies.* This roadmap depicts those capabilities necessary to address customer needs over time. It ties inextricably to your product roadmap, with technology availability driven by product characteristic timing, which in turn is driven in a cascading manner by customer requirements.

Both "Your products" and "Your technologies" roadmaps depict something directly controllable by your company. As a result, considerable information is appropriately communicated internally through their use. Product and technology roadmaps commonly feature color-coded entries to depict a state of availability, investment, or activity. This state is most easily accomplished with a three-color, green-yellow-red stoplight style scheme. Color-coding can involve using

- Green for available (sufficient investment or complete),
- Yellow for nearly available (some investment or some effort),
- Red for unavailable (no investment or inactive).

As should be clear, a "red" entry for a relatively near-term need enables practitioners and executives to communicate critical challenges without exchanging a word. Such blunt transparency often is vital for high-functioning teamwork.

Implementing Product and Technology Roadmaps

In direct collaboration with your customers, you construct the first two sets of roadmaps ("Your customers' products" and "Your customers' requirements for your products"). Roadmap conversations ideally occur quarterly, or at least semiannually, and involve sales and marketing representation and engineering for highly technical products. In these same meetings, your company representatives present your existing product plans ("Your products"), if any, and perhaps even your technology plans ("Your technologies") to the extent that sharing them helps your customer anticipate both opportunities and challenges. As nondisclosure agreements constrain this information's use by you and your customers, these roadmaps illustrate what your company sees but does not share with your customers' competition and what your customer sees but does not share with your competitors.

After securing this long-range customer input and insight, your next step is to update—or construct if they do not yet exist—the bottom two sets of roadmaps ("Your products" and "Your technologies") internally. This process challenges all to either buy into or question the proposed plans. It also requires those involved to assign color-coding for each entry.

The Challenges of Implementing Product and Technology Roadmaps Within an SMME

No obvious downside exists in implementing product and technology roadmaps specifically within an SMME. The greatest challenge within any organization in using a tool referenced quarterly at most is that those applying it often forget how to interpret the various entries. The most common error involves forgetting which color-coding scheme is used for each roadmap. To ensure clarity of interpretation, documentation should include comments noting the color-coding method applied, and multiple roadmaps depicting the same content, but different color-coding options, may be constructed.

INNOVATION PROCESSES AND TOOLS: SOME CLOSING THOUGHTS

The processes and tools discussed in this chapter, with the design thinking methodology of Chapters 2 and 3, form a strong and robust toolkit for any SMME seeking to invest in innovation. A phase-gate process instructs the novice and reminds the expert of all they must consider and do as they seek to move potentially innovative insights into the marketplace. In doing so, it reduces risk and moderates up-front investment unless or until the innovative insight proves itself worthy. Lean innovation reinforces the importance of deeply understanding customer needs, reduces risk and initial investment, and encourages innovators to pivot, when appropriate, to pursue real needs. Open innovation reduces risk and investment by relying on those outside your organization rather than forcing you to build all expertise internally. The 2x2 matrices provide a means to both visualize and communicate innovation portfolio investment options. In doing so, they help an organization develop a concise, shared language as to the most critical innovation parameters. Product and technology roadmaps also provide a means to both visualize and communicate innovation portfolio investment options. But they go further, as they give you and your customers a valid reason and means to share and negotiate plans for the future.

As with any toolkit, innovation practitioners must choose which tools most appropriately address their needs. Just as a carpenter would never dream of using a screwdriver to hammer a nail, those investing in innovation—at all levels—must possess position-relevant insight as to which tool to use when. And just as there are different types of hammers and screwdrivers, the processes and tools we discussed in this chapter take various forms for different situations. Recall that we discussed three very different phase-gate processes. This was intentional, serving as an introduction to the multiple appropriate ways to deploy a phase-gate process, again, based on need.

With Chapters 2 and 3, Chapter 4 addresses the "how to" aspects of innovation. As we move into Chapter 5, we make a slight transition. While

Chapter 5 considers the "how to" related to who often leads innovation in an SMME, we also emphasize the *who* of innovation in SMMEs. Returning to this chapter's opening paragraphs, we next move from the necessary methodologies, processes, and tools to those who bring them to life, the innovators themselves.

KEY POINTS AND TAKEAWAYS

- Innovation processes and tools guide those less experienced in innovation and remind those who have mastered innovation of what they might have forgotten.
- Innovation processes and tools help us manage to success measures.
- Innovation processes and tools are insufficient in themselves to guarantee success. As we will discuss in Chapter 5, they require a skilled innovator to bring them to life.

CHAPTER 5

The Innovators and Those Who Manage Them

"We have a guy like that; his name is Kevin."

—Stephen McShane, founder and CEO
of Midtronics, Inc.

PRELIMINARY QUESTIONS AND INTRODUCTORY THOUGHTS

- If, as you have mentioned in Chapter 4, innovation processes and tools are insufficient to succeed at innovation, and skilled innovation practitioners are required, who are these innovators?
- How do I identify true innovators, if one even exists in my company?
- How do I most effectively manage or collaborate with an innovator?
- What about the rest of the employees in my company? Can they effectively contribute to innovation? If so, how do my colleagues and I harness their potential?

When owners, boards, CEOs, and presidents or GMs and their leadership teams begin to think about investing in innovation, they inevitably talk about processes, tools, culture, and organizational models. This behavior is understandable, as such a perspective is consistent with the current view of management. Processes, tools, culture, and organizational models are the levers of control most familiar to executive leadership.

Yet we are emphatic in our position that while processes, tools, culture, and organizational models serve a critical role in enabling you to succeed, they are insufficient on their own. In the end, the right people make innovation investments work. Not having such people yields innovation failure.

Hiring people who "get it" when it comes to innovation will cost you more in salaries and wages than if you had not. Yet doing so will significantly reduce the risk of innovation failure and greatly increase the potential for financial return on your innovation investments. Hiring the right people addresses all six of our book's major themes and insights, either directly or indirectly.

This chapter focuses on those rare individuals who make innovation happen in SMMEs. We begin by considering a people view, rather than a process view, of breakthrough innovation in mature companies. We do so by introducing Griffin, Price, and Vojak's concept of "Serial Innovators."[1] Next, we systematically expand our discussion from the role of individuals to pairs and teams. At this point, we gather and apply these insights to SMME renewal. We follow this by considering how best to manage Serial Innovators in SMMEs, in contrast to innovation as a process. In addition to discussing our primary concern, renewal driven by breakthrough innovation, we close by providing our perspective on the challenge of broadly engaging an SMME's workforce to address incremental innovation opportunities.

A PEOPLE VIEW OF INNOVATION IN MATURE COMPANIES

For decades, practitioners and scholars alike have embraced the perspective that innovation in a mature company can be managed like any other complex process. In contrast, in this section, we introduce a people view of innovation in mature companies.

After first providing context on entrepreneurs in startups and how the process view of innovation emerged, we briefly summarize the work of Griffin, Price, and Vojak on Serial Innovators: the cutting-edge thinkers who repeatedly create and deliver breakthrough innovations in large, mature organizations. We then extend the understanding beyond the rare, relatively unknown individuals in large, mature companies to pairs and teams, and then how this insight applies to SMMEs.

Prelude: Entrepreneurs in Startups

Entrepreneurs capture the imagination of contemporary society. The most successful among them change our lives and define a vision for the future. Their originality, their unconventional insights and approaches, and, at times, their quirky personalities attract the public's attention.[2] Aspiring entrepreneurs emulate their nonconformist personalities. Even those who fail, whether honestly or perhaps by deceit, cause us to reflect on what might be.[3]

Entrepreneurs are intuitive in their approach, regularly lacking formal business education such as an MBA. The most successful learn what they need when they need it, a type of "just in time" approach to personal development. They tend to eschew processes (at least in startup mode) and instead pivot as necessary, doing whatever it takes to succeed.

Those with characteristics and personalities seen as "entrepreneurial" often find no place in mature companies. Their feral nature does not fit with the kind of process systemization necessary to optimize a business within a paradigm, the existing basis of competition.

Given these features and characteristics, we have no difficulty thinking of entrepreneurs embracing and engaging in a people view of innovation.

Prelude: How Did We Get to a Process View of Innovation?

To move beyond a process view of innovation in mature companies, we benefit from understanding how we got there in the first place. That a process view of innovation is so prevalent suggests that it represents a perceived improvement over what previously existed. It is safe to say that no one would argue that innovation did not exist before the process view. So how did this process view emerge?

In broad strokes, the history of the process view of innovation grew from a scientific approach to management of the type advanced by the likes of Frederick Taylor[4] and Frank Gilbreth at the onset of the twentieth century. As forerunners of today's quality initiatives, their work addressed the pursuit of efficiency. By analyzing and optimizing business activities in a manner not unlike how an engineer analyzes and optimizes physical systems and processes, managers appropriately mined newfound opportunities for profit.

Best practices in mature businesses often reflect just such a process perspective. Further, this view represents the norm in the content taught in contemporary MBA programs. Despite protests to the contrary, management regularly takes precedence over leadership.

Note that we embrace the value and importance of processes and process optimization in all companies. Further, we acknowledge that some process-based perspectives, such as lean initiatives, demonstrate respect for the individual when properly implemented. Yet, while unarguably admirable, process efficiency initiatives not only hit natural limits, they also are deadly for a company to pursue on a standalone basis. By doing so, you become myopic and miss opportunities to grow and renew.

Serial Innovators

The decade-long research of Griffin, Price, and Vojak zeroed in on people, the cutting-edge thinkers who repeatedly create and deliver breakthrough innovations in large, mature organizations—Serial Innovators.[5] Serial Innovators are rare, real people with special, powerful skills and perspectives. As key contributors to a company's financial success, they have demonstrated significant, repeated breakthrough impact on their companies and industries. Based on interviews with dozens of Serial Innovators and an even larger pool of their co-workers and managers, this work revealed critical insights about identifying, developing, understanding, emulating, enabling, supporting, and managing these unique and essential individuals for long-term corporate success.

Nancy Dawes is a Serial Innovator.[6] Across her several-decades career at Procter & Gamble, leading to her appointment as a research fellow in P&G's prestigious Vic Mills Society, Nancy repeatedly had an impact on P&G's top and bottom lines. Through her efforts, she led breakthrough changes in both the food and beauty industries.

Early in her career, Nancy applied her deep and broad technical and consumer insight holistically to reinvent and triple the once-stagnant Pringles brand by innovating and defining a new "crisps" product category.

She pursued industry renewal rather than a more traditional approach that would yield incremental innovation, such as merely improving Pringles to taste more like a conventional potato chip. In doing so, she established Pringles as the only US top-ten snack business not owned by Frito-Lay.

Later, Nancy grew Olay® to one of P&G's Billion-Dollar Brands by reframing the beauty aisle in mass-market retail stores, creating a new "masstige" (mass market plus prestige) anti-aging skin care category. Again, she pursued industry renewal rather than a more traditional approach that would yield incremental innovation, such as merely creating a better conventionally priced facial moisturizer. In doing so, she filled this new skincare category with multiple new-to-the-world products such as Olay Total Effects®, Olay Regenerist®, and Olay Definity®.

Serial Innovators Versus Entrepreneurs

Many ask, "Aren't Serial Innovators just entrepreneurs?" This question is best answered by comparing the most successful entrepreneurs, the glamorized "guy in the garage"—think Jeff Bezos or the late Steve Jobs—with Serial Innovators, the unknown "guy in a large, mature company"—think Nancy Dawes or her late P&G colleague, Tom Osborn.[7] In some respects, the similarities are strong. Each of these individuals possessed deep and broad insight and the creative power to envision new possibilities. Each also had the drive, discipline, and initiative to make things happen.

Yet the distinctions between entrepreneurs and Serial Innovators are both several and salient.

First, entrepreneurs must start from scratch, while Serial Innovators work within an existing structure. They do not need to "waste" time establishing operations and, instead—despite all the organizational challenges facing Serial Innovators—can leverage the company's resources. Second, some entrepreneurs initially risk "everything," going even so far as mortgaging their homes to pursue success. In contrast, Serial Innovators assume at most the risk of losing a job, something that many of those who ultimately proved themselves were dangerously close to experiencing. Third, while entrepreneurs can shop their ideas to multiple funding sources, Serial Innovators are challenged by being held captive by one "banker," the company for which they work. Fourth and finally, while the public often glamorizes entrepreneurs and many entrepreneurs encourage the mystique, Serial Innovators are the most important people you never heard of as they deliver results in relative obscurity. Along with other characteristics discussed next, these distinctions will begin to help you identify who might most appropriately drive innovation in an SMME.

Serial Innovator Distinctive Characteristics:
How They Stand Out from the Rest

Serial Innovators possess a profound mastery of their trade. They see things before others. They see things that others do not. They make things happen that others cannot.

So, other than a repeated, significant financial impact on their company, what differentiates them from the rest? Serial Innovators display the following characteristics:[8]

- *How they engage with problems.* Serial Innovators actively engage problems. They are exceptionally curious as they seek to understand a challenge they are confronted with, seeking deep and broad insight and asking tough yet appropriate questions. As they gather clues, Serial Innovators begin to seek patterns in the data. In this way, they are holistic, systems thinkers. In the process, they display above-average creativity in their thinking, not willing to rest in the first or most convenient interpretation of the problem.
- *How they engage with projects.* Once engaged on a project, Serial Innovators are tenacious. Unlike those who are easily discouraged, Serial Innovators see projects through to completion. This tenacity may merely involve testing hypotheses that ultimately are not worth pursuing. Yet these individuals stand out in their willingness to try the idea, rather than speculating an outcome and resigning themselves to it. A prime example of such behavior is their deeply probing both articulated and unarticulated customer needs. Serial Innovators do not rely on guesswork when customer engagement or a simple experiment provides unrefutable insight.
- *How they engage with business.* In contrast with those who are merely creators or inventors, Serial Innovators understand the

need to bring ideas to market successfully. This is more a distinctive characteristic in large, mature companies where many become isolated from the market, rather than in SMMEs where limited resources rarely allow this possibility.

- *How they engage with people.* Unlike the commonly held stereotype of the lone, socially awkward inventor, Serial Innovators value people. They see the strengths in others and value and enlist them to help accomplish the company's strategic goals. By establishing a reputation based on trust and respect, Serial Innovators use informal leadership skills to bring others along with them in ways rarely seen. Because they are self-motivated to solve customer problems, Serial Innovators accept responsibility to make things happen. They do so by possessing a willingness and developing the necessary skill to influence and convince others as they seek to create value.

Note that it is the complete set of these distinctive characteristics that make Serial Innovators so powerful. The absence of one or more reduces the aspiring Serial Innovator's effectiveness as they will be unable to affect the type of change necessary for the company to succeed at renewal.

Serial Innovator Distinctive Characteristics: The Path They Travel While Innovating

While we could include numerous other topics to characterize Serial Innovators, perhaps the best is to compare the path they follow with the phase-gate process (covered in Chapter 4). As Griffin, Price, and Vojak discuss in detail, Serial Innovators traverse a path illustrated by the Hourglass Model of Figure 5.1.[9] The Hourglass Model comprises five primary "states."

To orient the reader, we note that Serial Innovators begin at the upper left of the Hourglass Model, self-motivated to innovate, as we discussed earlier. Having first identified a problem worthy of their effort ("Find the Right Problem"), the Serial Innovator follows their curiosity to understand it deeply and broadly. They intimately grasp customer needs, competitive positions, technical possibilities, and manufacturing options, to name a few ("Understand the Problem"). Only then do Serial Innovators begin to prototype options and iteratively test them ("Invent and Validate"). These

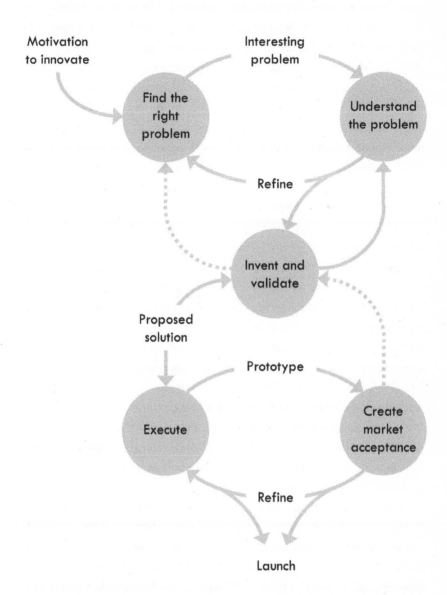

FIGURE 5.1. The Hourglass Model of innovation. Source: Abbie Griffin, Raymond L. Price, and Bruce A. Vojak, *Serial Innovators* (Stanford University Press, 2012). Reproduced with permission from Oxford University Press, *The Oxford Handbook of Interdisciplinarity*, edited by Robert Frodeman, associate editors Julie Thompson Klein and Carl Mitcham (2010), (Figs 37.2, pp 546-559) from Ch 37. Bruce A. Vojak, Raymond L. Price.

upper three activities constitute the front end of innovation, as discussed in Chapter 4. Solutions deemed to have market potential drop down to the back end of innovation, where Serial Innovators continue engagement as commercialization proceeds through a gated process ("Execute"). While not commonly witnessed in others, such post-invention attention ensures that their innovative insights are not lost after initial conception. Further, Serial Innovators often appropriately continue their customer and market involvement, begun in the front end, in the back end of innovation, aiding market acceptance ("Create Market Acceptance").

The Hourglass Model differs from the phase-gate process in several fundamental ways—the most essential three for this book we discuss here.

First, the Hourglass Model depicts a nonlinear path, contrasting with the phase-gate process's linear flow. Not surprisingly, innovation—especially breakthrough innovation—traverses a nonlinear way forward. While the general direction is ahead, innovators often follow a recursive path, backtracking and reconsidering earlier steps. We observe some of the most significant innovations arising from a reframing of the problem, that is, a return to the very first step ("Find the Right Problem"). Nancy Dawes's experiences, shared earlier, illustrate this approach. With both Pringles and Olay®, Nancy's reframing of the industry (to "crisps" and "masstige," respectively) ultimately led to her significant commercial contributions to P&G. Earlier, we discussed similar examples in SMMEs, with Wes-Tech Automation Solutions, Breuer Electric Manufacturing Company, and Slice returning to redefine the basis of industry competition only after deeply understanding the problem.

Second, the Hourglass Model is descriptive of the path that innovators follow, contrasting the phase-gate process's prescriptive use. We intentionally use the word "states" rather than the word "phases" (as in a phase-gate process) to distinguish these two diagrams' nature in this regard. Moving between each of the five primary "states" of the Hourglass Model is contingent upon that which is known and, to a certain extent, sensed. As Serial Innovators possess the insight to see patterns not observed by others, it often is just such an intuitive sense—only later validated in the marketplace—that they follow.

Finally, since a phase-gate process is a management tool, while the Hourglass Model describes a commonly followed path of an individual, it is critical to understand that they are not intended to conflict with each other. When it comes to a phase-gate process and the Hourglass Model, it is a both-and, not an either-or situation. Serial Innovators work within each of the phases and gates defined by their company's phase-gate process. Simultaneously, they discover and innovate along the path they travel within the Hourglass Model.

Innovative Pairs

While Griffin, Price, and Vojak explored individual exemplars representing a people view of innovation, people sometimes work together closely to innovate. At its simplest, complementary pairs form a natural combination. Joshua Wolf Shenk effectively employed narratives to illustrate the innovative power of such pairs.[10] In contrast, yet drawing similar conclusions, David Goldberg's simple quantitative approach suggested that pairs could easily be twenty or more times more productive than individuals working alone.[11]

Opportunities for pairwise innovation success in industry abound, including pairs representing various combinations of technical experts, design experts, marketing experts, and managers teamed with any of these experts. Which combination is most impactful will depend on both the nature of the challenge addressed and who is available and sufficiently skilled to partner in this way. For example, we commonly observe managers effectively running interference for technologists and playing the role of a sounding board. And in one case, Bruce enjoyed watching two highly skilled technologists repeatedly and together bring products and processes to market. Their complementary expertise and personalities provided fertile soil for fresh perspectives with commercial potential. Their combined insight always exceeded what either could bring to the table alone, and trust that each was powerful on their own. Seeing them in action together, one might mistake their at times almost heated discussions as a negative. Yet in reality, what played out was the engaged passion of two very insightful individuals—each of whom trusted and respected the other—working closely together to address challenging problems. So inextricably intertwined were their contributions that a contraction of their two names became the working name of several successful projects.

Innovation Teams

Moving from pairs to teams of three or more, we find some conflicting trends. Most apparent is that, while adding to the depth, breadth, and diversity of insight brought to bear on a customer need, communication becomes increasingly complex. Not only does the communication network grow exponentially with each additional team member, requiring more and more complex combinations of individuals in dialog, but establishing a shared understanding among this larger number of people represents a significant challenge.

So what have we observed as best practices when forming teams that seek to renew their companies? Two generic approaches exist, with the first being most common:

1. A top-down approach in which management brings together a diverse—in terms of innovative insight, expertise, and skill—group to form a small team at the start of the effort
2. A bottom-up approach in which a Serial Innovator forms the team by inviting individuals onto and off the project as needs demand

The top-down approach can work well when the company is in exploration mode and assigns just a few, very high-quality participants to the team. Unfortunately, the best potential participants in terms of expertise and team skills often are not selected. Instead, management errs by seeking functional representation—the business equivalent of democracy—or, worse, the loudest voices as the forming theme. Bruce has observed such a team-forming approach hindering progress, as participants chosen for these reasons become more of a burden than an asset, defending functional turf, not grasping the need for innovation, or not possessing the kind of expertise necessary for renewal success.

The bottom-up approach works very well when a proven Serial Innovator exists in the company. They, too, can operate effectively in an exploration mode, calling on others to contribute as necessary.

Some of the most successful companies implement a combination of the two approaches. The top-down approach serves to guide the overall innovation investment. Individual team members then apply the bottom-up approach as they take the lead to explore specific customer needs in more detail.

Most important is that team leadership cannot be diffuse for such an investment to succeed. In the end, committees do not succeed at renewal efforts. Someone must have both the responsibility and the authority to make decisions to ensure success. Even if peers constitute the team, a first among equals must emerge for the kind of innovation investment that can lead to renewal not to languish.

A People View of Innovation in SMMEs

So, what does a successful "people view of innovation" that leads to renewal look like in an SMME? Over and over, we have observed the same pattern. An individual, perhaps with a peer partner or two—working closely with those in the existing business—emerges to make renewal happen.

At first, what surprised Bruce was how often this differed from that observed by Griffin, Price, and Vojak in large, mature companies. He expected to find a Nancy Dawes–like individual in every successful SMME. And at times, he did. Kevin Bertness (mentioned by Steve McShane in the quote found at the head of this chapter and whose work we discuss in Midtronics' story, presented in Chapter 7) is just such an innovative exemplar. Kevin is a natural, textbook example of how one fits the Serial Innovator criteria in an SMME. He successfully and repeatedly engages with problems, projects, business, and people. Yet, while people like Kevin exist in other successful SMMEs, Bruce did not find an exact "Kevin" replica in every successful SMME. What he did find, however, confirmed his hunch that an exemplary individual, pair, or very small team must exist for an SMME to survive over the long term.

Besides an individual who precisely fits the Serial Innovator mold, a skilled pair, or a very small team, the two most common roles filled by those who serve as Serial Innovators for SMMEs are company president and external consultant.

The most common situation in which a company president fills this role is when an entrepreneurial founder continues to renew their company after its initial commercial success. This should not be surprising at some level, as this person possesses the requisite inclination and expertise. Less commonly observed is a second- or later-generation family member serving in this role. Unless the second- or later-generation family member has the natural temperament to innovate and self-develops over time to assume this role, they more commonly serve as optimizers—working within the paradigm, the existing basis of competition—seeking to protect the heritage rather than grow it. We often observe the same tendency when a nonfamily member serves as company president. Family board members are typically conservative with their investment and now have the added challenge of lacking an intimate, day-to-day grasp of the business and industry. Further, with each generation, if they prioritize optimization over renewal, operations naturally ossify. Only when a founder maintains a culture characterized by renewal and passes this culture, and associated values and processes, to subsequent generations, does a family business prove itself able to survive and thrive over time.

Engaging an external consultant to serve as Serial Innovator can be challenging to manage, as it requires a company president who can rally their team to support renewal. The Breuer Electric Manufacturing Company story we shared in Chapter 2 illustrates how one third-generation family member, company president Linda, successfully navigated these challenges. While some decisions were difficult personally, such as letting go of some long-time employees, Linda realized that a change in direction was necessary for the sake of those who remained. She took on new investment risk in working with the HLB external consultants led by Walter. Yet had Linda not accepted such risk, she knew the company would not survive.

In each of these scenarios, overcoming internal resistance to change is critical. It requires both deft and decisive interpersonal skills and strong business acumen, as the potential for failure at first seems far away and then suddenly looms large. The most commonly observed internal resistance, manifesting itself after an innovation investment commitment is made, takes the form of passive-aggressive behavior. This is especially true among those tasked with optimizing performance within the current paradigm, the existing basis of competition. These individuals still may not grasp or accept the value of company renewal. Instead, many see it as diverting resources away from their function or, even worse, adding more work to their already full plate. Not surprisingly, such attitudes lead to inefficiency and, eventually, failed investments and job loss for some, if not all.

MANAGING SERIAL INNOVATORS IN SMMES

In this section, we briefly review the basic tenets of managing Serial Innovators. Then we discuss some of the particular ways to apply these insights within the context of an SMME.

Prelude: Managing Serial Innovators in Large, Mature Enterprises

While Hebda, Griffin, Price, and Vojak discussed how to manage Serial Innovators in large, mature companies in detail,[12] for context, we believe it is essential to share some high-level perspective here. In a nutshell, managing Serial Innovators involves three activities: identifying, developing, and working with them (which includes retaining them).

Managers most easily identify Serial Innovators by their proven track record of repeatedly bringing significant new concepts successfully to market, renewing the company strategically and financially. Identifying aspiring Serial Innovators—those with potential but not demonstrated success—is complicated. Still, it is aided by comparing their daily behavior with the four characteristics discussed earlier in this chapter (how they engage with problems, projects, business, and people). Evaluating potential on the basis of these characteristics is possible for those in close, regular contact with the potential innovator. Ideally, those identifying potential Serial Innovators either are experienced Serial Innovators or have worked closely with one over time.

Developing Serial Innovators is a gradual, progressive process that occurs over several years, with most fully emerging by the time they have fifteen years of industry experience. Their development occurs in two broadly defined phases: an early development phase that lasts up to five years and a subsequent maturation phase that typically takes up to an additional decade.

Serial Innovators establish their fundamental expertise during the first phase. This is when they develop skills and work patterns while simultaneously gaining credibility with their colleagues and management. Challenging work assignments play a crucial role in this stage of development. As problems stretch aspiring innovators to their limits, the best learn how to reframe problems in a way that makes them manageable. Similarly, as interpersonal interactions can challenge aspiring innovators, the best acquire the rich and often nuanced interpersonal skills necessary to succeed. During this time, these employees should also begin to gain exposure to customers, suppliers, and competitors as well as external sources of potential new ideas.

During this first phase, it is essential to cast the net broadly, as you do not yet know who will emerge as a Serial Innovator. Only as some begin to demonstrate both the Serial Innovator characteristics and a pattern of commercial success should you begin to separate the best and provide personal, customized development, tailoring your focus on the emerging Serial Innovators. While this may seem obvious, it is not, as many large, mature companies do not actively develop those with such significant potential, at best allowing it just to happen, if it even does.

Serial Innovators reach maturity during the second phase of their development. They continue to add breadth to their expertise during this time while typically establishing depth in a second or third discipline. In this phase, managers should challenge them to identify commercially significant problems on their own as they continue deep customer engagement. Managers should resist the temptation to facilitate all of their growth, especially during this phase, as aspiring Serial Innovators must grow as self-directed learners to succeed later. Aspiring Serial Innovators benefit from an informal apprenticeship relationship with a proven Serial Innovator. By working alongside the established innovator, they witness how to reframe problems and generate impactful solutions. Even more important, they also gain exposure to how to navigate organizational politics effectively at all levels.

Once Serial Innovators have proven themselves, their managers are most effective when they unleash, not drive them. The best managers of Serial Innovators grasp how to engage and guide, not ignore or micromanage them. Such an interaction involves a highly individualized, relational form of management. It requires patience on the manager's part as they provide

Serial Innovators the time and resources needed to innovate. Managers also often need to run interference on the Serial Innovator's behalf in large, mature companies, intervening as necessary with higher-level executives to protect their investment. And all this occurs in an environment characterized early on by extreme uncertainty. The manager's responsibility is to accept such uncertainty while simultaneously expecting serendipity in the form of significant commercial success.

Yet all this is not sufficient. Just as the company must continuously renew itself with a pipeline of innovative products, processes, and services, the most successful companies build an innovator pipeline. They systematically track and develop high-potential, high-performing individuals who aspire to become Serial Innovators. These companies understand that their long-term success depends on not resting with who they have but instead always looking to develop the next generation.

Managing Serial Innovators in SMMEs

Much of what is necessary when managing Serial Innovators in large, mature enterprises also holds for SMMEs. One requires skill at identifying and developing Serial Innovators as well as building a pipeline. Serial Innovators in SMMEs respond best when teamed with and guided, just as they are in large, mature enterprises.

Some aspects of managing Serial Innovators in SMMEs require additional emphasis, such as ensuring that they are not only permitted but encouraged to engage directly with current and potential customers regularly. In addition, they deliver results best when not isolated geographically or organizationally from the core business they seek to renew. Such distance makes it all the more difficult to develop and ready the organization for inevitable change.

Perhaps the most significant difference between managing Serial Innovators in large, mature enterprises and those in SMMEs is that, below a certain size, SMMEs may not require an individual, pair, or team dedicated full time to innovation—or at least not dedicated full time to the kind of breakthrough innovation that renews an industry's basis of competition. As a result, Serial Innovators in SMMEs typically carry responsibility not only for renewal but also for solving current customer problems. There are real benefits to such an arrangement. First, by doing so, you are applying the expertise and insight of your company's best innovator to immediate issues that have an impact on current financial performance—a win. Second, you expose your company's best innovator to real customer problems—also a win. And finally, your company's best innovator lives with any issues that may have crept into the product, process, service, or business model of their creation—a big win.

Yet this also is where the real problems can begin for the SMME. While it is a very attractive option to assign your Serial Innovators to solve current problems, too much of it can be deadly. With no time to focus on renewal, it never happens, as the Serial Innovator is valued most for their firefighting skill. In the end, it's a matter of appropriately balancing short- and long-term needs. It's sadly fascinating to hear company leadership speak of their investment in those who can innovate yet have nothing to show for it in the end. This is a situation in which a little wisdom and a great deal of discipline can go a long way.

BROADLY ENGAGING YOUR WORKFORCE FOR INCREMENTAL INNOVATION

While we have focused on renewal by way of breakthrough innovation practiced by a few exemplars, pairs, or small teams, we would be remiss not to address incremental innovation as practiced by the rest of an SMME's employees. As many in SMMEs understand this practice as "innovation," we believe it essential to discuss how many misperceive it and help them improve on how to approach it.

This section identifies the two most common incremental innovation perspectives held in SMMEs and addresses how they fall short. Next, we discuss what incremental innovation looks like from a people perspective. In closing, we suggest how management might appropriately implement such a revised view broadly within an SMME.

Prelude: The Most Common Perspectives and Their Shortcomings

Two often unarticulated perspectives dominate how SMMEs approach incremental innovation for their "typical" employee, that "everyone can successfully innovate" and that "innovation can be successfully reduced to a simple, few-steps process."

That "everyone can successfully innovate" often is exemplified by companies setting aside, as policy, regular times—in some cases as much as 10 percent per week—for employees to explore potentially innovative ideas. It also appears in the form of "suggestion boxes" and internal, open-participation funding competitions, with the best ideas advancing for further consideration. The idea that "innovation can be successfully reduced to a simple, few-steps process" is illustrated by training that encourages the use of W. Edwards Deming's Plan-Do-Check-Act Cycle[13] or some variation of it.[14]

So why do we push back on these views as they currently are implemented?

First, while everyone might have some capability to innovate, there are limits to any one individual's expertise. As a friend's piano-teacher wife once said, "I can teach any student how to play the piano, but not all will perform at Carnegie Hall." Having acknowledged this, is it still appropriate to treat all equally? We believe not.

Second, SMMEs often ask employees to innovate only after successfully driving lean and quality optimization initiatives. They have squeezed the possibility of any but the most minor opportunity for change out of their systems. Working within such a narrow perspective, often without seeing the big picture, employees are hard-pressed to identify and develop ideas that represent meaningful contributions.

Third, even with those who possess the potential to innovate successfully, there are limits to how most companies prepare employees to do so. How many times have you observed the practice of creative activity in any field accurately characterized by a simple, recipe-like, few-steps process? Never. Which grand chef, who among the old masters of art, and what famous jazz musician—when describing their experience—revealed that they followed a few-steps process to create that for which they are known? None. So why do we expect this from our employees? It makes no sense.

Fourth, as we dig into the Plan-Do-Check-Act Cycle, from where exactly does the "plan" come? Management encourages employees to generate ideas, to "plan," and then move forward. Yet management rarely helps employees understand how to develop ideas and rarely helps employees know what constitutes a good problem to solve, let alone what a good "plan" entails.

Then, almost to add insult to injury, many SMMEs celebrate their unfortunately false innovation prowess, hoping to make employees feel part of an innovative team. It can be a fatally empty act.

Incremental Innovation for the Rest

So what should it look like when an SMME attempts to have its employees embrace innovation broadly? We return to this chapter's recurring theme: innovation requires a people perspective; it is a craft, with the best exhibiting inarticulable skill while still following a process.

Consider the example of a child learning how to ride a bicycle. Decades ago, children first learned how to pedal a tricycle or a bike equipped with training wheels (see the top image in Figure 5.2). These options enabled the child to ignore the need to balance, instead allowing them to focus on pedaling. Such approaches gave children a sense of success that they really were learning how to ride a bike, just like a parent or older sibling. Or were they?

Interestingly, while tricycles and training wheels remove the need to balance by keeping the rider from leaning too far and tipping over, they also prevent the rider from learning the kind of counter-steering necessary to turn a two-wheeler. Contrary to previous popular belief, as bicyclists turn in one direction (left or right), they first lean and steer slightly in the opposite direction (right or left). This quick, intuitive move is learned by experience, not by reading an instruction manual. In fact, for many years, most people did not realize that they were making this move. Further, children who learn to ride using a tricycle or a bicycle with training wheels learn to turn the handlebars the wrong way, an act which must be unlearned later! Instead, today many children learn how to ride a bike quickly by first learning how to maintain their balance on a two-wheeler without pedals (see the bottom image in Figure 5.2). As they glide, with relatively little risk of falling (just like the tricycle or bicycle with training wheels, yet now only with two wheels), children gain an unarticulated understanding of how to balance. Only later do they add pedaling to this now-intuitive balancing skill.

FIGURE 5.2. The traditional way of learning how to ride a bicycle by first using training wheels to facilitate balance (top) versus the contemporary practice of riding a bike by first learning how to balance (bottom). Source: iStock.

Implementing Incremental Innovation for the Rest

In light of this discussion of how to ride a bicycle, what does it look like to ask everyone within an SMME to consider innovating? What does it look like when we turn from a process view of innovation to a people view in this context?

First, begin by appealing to how employees already exhibit skill and expertise in nonwork environments, places where they are not as highly constrained as they are at work. Do they pursue a hobby or pastime in which they have exhibited growth in their skill and expertise? Are some participants on recreational sports teams? Do others express their creativity as amateur musicians, actors, or artists? Are there those in your midst who enjoy baking, grilling, or brewing beer? Perhaps some pursue crafts, and others are hobbyists who design and build remote control drones. You get the idea. Most employees have outside interests that they have freely pursued, activities that bring enjoyment. Start with these interests and get them thinking about what they have done to explore and learn and grow their skill and expertise in these situations. Challenge them to consider how they went about discovering new, improved ways to practice their hobby or pastime. How did they get their ideas of what to try? How did they test these ideas? How did they know which approaches were better or worse? In other words, help them realize, make the connection that what you expect from them in terms of innovation at work is essentially no different than how they approach these other activities.

Next, move, over time, to eliminate any "suggestion box" you have in place. By suggestion box, we mean an approach that only solicits suggestions without analysis performed by those who submit them. Such methods rob employees of the opportunity to learn what constitutes a real innovation. It prohibits employees from intimately engaging in the process in this regard, allowing them merely to toss potentially unqualified ideas into play. Management can still retain ultimate decision-making authority to implement. It is just that requiring employee participation in evaluating ideas is another step to develop them as innovators.

Finally, train and develop your employees to build a deep and broad understanding of their work and how it fits in the company's larger environment. Help them understand what constitutes an innovation. Get them in front of customers, either internal or external, to understand real needs. Challenge them to grasp the basics of financial analysis as it applies to their work. Expose them to company strategy, even if it requires articulating it simply and concisely. Encourage them to identify unarticulated assumptions that guide their work, beliefs that just might be unnecessary.

Work with them, side-by-side as appropriate, engaging them where they are. Such personal interaction could be on the production floor if we are talking about production operators. It could be accomplished by having less-experienced employees join those with more depth and breadth of insight on customer calls, allowing them to listen and observe.

Such apprentice-like engagement can enable innovation novices to develop mastery, but only if they work at it. As an example of a creative apprenticeship, renowned jazz musician Clark Terry summarized the art of learning jazz improvisation—a creative act that bears a resemblance to the kind of innovation we discuss here—as comprising three phases: imitation, assimilation, innovation.[15] This is similar to the process in which your employees must practice the act of innovation to establish and improve innovation skill. It's a good start if you—as the proven innovator with whom they apprentice—observe them noticing and then imitating your behaviors, perhaps asking questions and challenging assumptions as you may have done. Then, if you see that they have grasped them, recalling specific skills during subsequent conversations or while addressing the next problem, you and they are almost there, as they now have assimilated and possess individual skills as their own. Finally, when they follow a path not previously mapped out by you, they and you have established a new capability for your company.

Having done all this, here are some questions to ask yourself about those whom you seek to raise up as innovators in your organization.

Can they articulate a simple, clear economic case on behalf of their idea? Can they tell you who their customer is, again, whether internal or external? Can they qualify and quantify the commercial viability of their innovative ideas? Do they understand the difference between an innovation that leads to a strategically differentiated product or process versus one that lowers cost (more on this in Chapter 6)? And do they know not only why this distinction matters but also which is most desirable in their work? Can they explain how their work fits in the company's overall process of serving a customer? Do they see and understand what happens both upstream and downstream from their work? Do they understand how a change in their area has impacts on other areas, both adjacent and remote? And if not, can their colleagues and peers help them know how their work fits into the whole? Do they know who to turn to to help them understand what is necessary to advocate for their ideas? Do they understand that, in the end, successful innovators are those who take the initiative, grasp customer needs, engage and involve others, persevere, and at least try things, not giving up too quickly?

Can they prepare a simple innovation proposal that looks like what we described in our discussion of the ideation phase phase-gate process in Chapter 4? Just as before, we challenge employees to assume increasing responsibility to develop their ideas.

In the end, do they know whether someone in your company truly cares if they take the initiative to learn how to innovate in this way?

For that matter, do you and does your management team genuinely care and, if so, how do you and they convincingly communicate it?

Suppose you succeed at developing such capacity in even a fraction of your company's employees—at all levels of your organization—to master their work, innovate, and contribute. Can you imagine what this would look like and what commercial success you might achieve for the benefit of all?

THE INNOVATORS AND THOSE WHO MANAGE THEM: SOME CLOSING THOUGHTS

With this chapter, we made the transition from the "how to" aspects of innovation addressed in Chapters 2, 3, and 4 to the "who" of innovation, those who bring innovation to life, the innovators themselves. The Serial Innovators we spoke of, as well as the pairs and small teams, possess a mastery not often observed. Like any experts skillfully practicing their craft, they wisely and insightfully select and apply the tools introduced in the preceding three chapters.

For many, this chapter's contents may present a challenge, if not a stumbling block, as methodologies, processes, and tools are easier to manage than people, especially those gifted with innovation skills. Some may wonder, "How do I assess whether I have the right people, possessing the right skills, those who 'get it'?" Our answer is simple: "What have you observed?" Are those assuming leadership roles in innovation, either as innovators or managers, behaving as we described the exemplars here? If so, that's good. If not, you have a place to start. And, if they are behaving as we described and you have yet to see results, you must ask, "Why?" Is it too soon? Must you have patience? Or, perhaps, what might be wrong or missing? Or is it that no significant opportunity for renewal exists at this time? And, if so, what does that mean for you and your SMME?

We leave you with a lot to think about, a lot to explore, and a lot to try. If that is where you are, you're on the right track because, with innovation, that is a very good place to be.

KEY POINTS AND TAKEAWAYS

- A process-only view of innovation is insufficient. A people view of innovation is necessary to succeed.
- Successful Serial Innovators exhibit distinctive characteristics as they engage with problems, projects, business, and people. Also, they follow an often circuitous, nonlinear path as they move their company forward.
- Innovative individuals, pairs, and teams often emerge to drive breakthrough innovation in SMMEs successfully.
- Serial Innovators are most effectively managed relationally, neither micromanaged nor ignored.
- While innovative individuals, pairs, and teams often emerge to drive breakthrough innovation in SMMEs successfully, your other employees can also contribute. However, for them to have the most significant impact, you must learn how to engage with them as inherently curious and insightful people, behaviors they regularly exhibit when engaging in their passions outside of work.

CHAPTER 6

Strategic Innovation Management

"In one survey of 10,000 senior leaders, 97% of them said that being strategic was the leadership behavior most important to their
organization's success. And yet in another study, a full 96% of the
leaders surveyed said they lacked the time for strategic thinking."

—Dorie Clark, strategy consultant and executive coach[1]

PRELIMINARY QUESTIONS AND INTRODUCTORY THOUGHTS

- What are the most basic, easy-to-understand, and simple-to-
  communicate options available for defining and implementing
  strategy?
- What is objective-based planning, and what are a few variations
  that we might choose from to implement in an SMME?
- What roles do culture and organization play as we strategically
  manage innovation?

Innovation is inherently strategic. It's not a matter of "luck." And for those
SMMEs that believe that because they were able to roll out their very first
product successfully, ongoing rollouts would continue in the same manner, get ready for a grand awakening. Those that are successful, repeatedly
successful, have a formula. The formula involves a combination of the
right methodology and people. We dedicate this chapter to the methods of

strategic innovation management, methods that—as Dorie Clark notes—are valued, but regularly overlooked.

In this chapter, we first systematically introduce the concept of strategy and then turn our attention to the types of innovation available to any company. Next, from this foundation, we discuss the critical task of objective-based planning to align the work of everyone in the organization strategically. Finally, we conclude by considering the levers of strategic innovation management that executive leadership has at its disposal: culture and organization.

PRELUDE: STRATEGIES FOR COMPETITIVE SUCCESS

Before focusing on the strategic aspects of innovation management, let's begin with a brief discussion about what we mean by strategy and how it can lead to competitive success. While this topic is likely familiar ground for many, our intention is that a preliminary discussion will bring all to a shared understanding and language.

Strategy

A strategy ties a company's vision, objectives, and goals to its day-to-day activities. It's a broad philosophy followed while attempting to accomplish those objectives and goals.

As just an example, Honda's CEO was once said to have a vision, and a stretch vision at that, of placing "six Hondas in every garage." Now, these six could represent a portfolio of Honda products, such as one or two cars to get you around, a mower and a trimmer to care for your lawn, a snowblower to clear your drive, and perhaps a motorcycle or ATV. It's easy to arrive at this list quickly. Yet it was Honda's strategy at the time that made this vision possible. Honda's strategy was to favorably differentiate its products from the competition by its relentless pursuit of dominating internal combustion engine technology for its product applications.

Two Options

Following Pitts and Snow and as illustrated in Figure 6.1, two broad options are available for any company seeking financial success: seek market share or exploit synergies, or both.[2]

Market Share Enables Economies of Scale

Synergies Enable Economies of Scope

FIGURE 6.1. The logical connection between day-to-day activities, through strategy, to financial success.

Companies possessing dominant market share achieve competitive advantage from economies of scale (Figure 6.1, top).[3] These economies arise from spreading higher volume production over fixed costs, more significant learning over time by experiencing a greater number of design cycles, and increased market power over customers, suppliers, and competitors.

Companies exploiting synergies achieve competitive advantage from economies of scope (Figure 6.1, bottom).[4] These economies arise from sharing expertise and funds between related but not identical products or businesses.

Everything Comes Down to a Handful of Strategies

This quick reflection leads us to consider the strategies appropriate for each of these two broad options.

Market share strategies range from pioneering a business as an entrepreneur, to rationalizing a business by creating the infrastructure necessary to enable growth after the startup phase, to applying incremental innovation as a means of market segmentation, to exploring opportunities for breakthrough innovation as a means of revolutionizing an industry at maturity. Further, in each case, companies pursue these economies by applying Michael Porter's generic strategies: differentiating—ideally with a core competency that makes competitors "quake in their boots"—their offering from that of the competition, providing the lowest-cost offering, or focusing on an otherwise unaddressed niche.[5]

Synergy strategies take the form of sharing expertise between two or more products or business units, such as pursuing similar markets with differing products, pursuing new markets with existing products, relying on similar inputs, designing and selling products enabled by the same core technologies, or sharing funds.

Why Understanding Strategy So Simply Matters

In just a few pages, we introduced you to a handful of strategies available to any company. Appropriately and effectively pursuing any of these will serve a company well. Yet instead of such clarity, we often observe something that does not seem right.

Having participated in, led, and reviewed the outcome of numerous strategic planning efforts, Bruce notes that he rarely, if ever, has seen anything truly new or surprising arise from the planning efforts themselves. With the most diligent efforts often consuming months of elapsed time and countless hours of analysis, the outcome, at best, typically confirms what the most insightful would have guessed or, at worst, the result is contaminated by wishful thinking.

So how might we save some of the time and effort associated with an exhaustive effort? What questions can we discuss over coffee or lunch—after making our objectives crystal clear—to arrive at a first-pass strategy for an SMME, something to jump-start our thinking? We're not talking about abandoning a deep dive. We're just asking if we already have a pretty good idea as to how to proceed.

We suggest first returning to Porter's generic strategies—differentiation, low-cost, or focus—and asking which of these you are pursuing. We guarantee that almost no one will say that they are pursuing a low-cost and not a differentiation strategy. Most will say things such as "Our customers really like our products" and "We are the preferred supplier in our industry." Yet when confronted with a request to prove it, they often are hard-pressed to do so. If the company you own, advise, lead, or work for cannot honestly answer this question—and, yes, a number will be correct in providing these favorable responses; it's just that many are not—then you should pack it up. There is no point in going further if an honest, substantiated answer is not forthcoming.

But if it turns out that your company honestly concludes that it hasn't been differentiating, now the real work can begin. Now you can have hope. Now you can pursue strategic planning and differentiation—especially the kind of differentiation that comes from innovation—in an entirely new and authentic way with the opportunity for success.

INNOVATION AND VALUE COME IN MANY WAYS

In their book *Ten Types of Innovation*, Keeley, Pikkel, Quinn, and Walters recognize that innovation falls into three main categories: configuration, offering, and experience.[6] Our simple interpretation of their categories describes the three as follows:

- *Configuration*: This first category represents an internal view, including the business model or system and structure, the "backroom" operations. Configuration is how one makes money.
- *Offering*: The second category includes the product or service itself. Offering can take the form of individual product performance or the collective performance of a product portfolio, often based on a product platform.
- *Experience*: The third category of innovation is the purely experiential and emotional component and includes everything that directly interfaces with the customer, including brand and customer engagement.

In thinking about how one makes money, most of us recognize that the product or service (offering) delivered represents some value proposition. With this approach, margins should be determined on the basis of the value perceived by the customer. As an aside to those less experienced, this itself is an important point. Too many organizations still look only at manufacturing costs and simply apply a multiplier to set retail pricing. Using this approach, business performance will deteriorate with a race to the bottom, with the value proposition ignored. Instead, the total value—the complete value proposition—can fall into all three categories, each with its percentages and variabilities, and is most appropriately used to set prices.

A simple example of a company that pays attention to all three categories would be Apple. When you think about it, they have a remarkable business system, one in which they spend less than their industry average on R&D and solely rely on suppliers for all of their manufacturing. Thus they have concentrated on and optimized configuration. The second category of innovation, their core product offering, is based on a highly complex product when launched and presented to the end-user as the optimization of simplicity, with an easy-to-use interface. The third category of innovation is their experiential and emotional component. This includes everything from their brand to packaging to the out-of-the-box experience and includes the retail environment, which is nothing less than remarkable.

Digging deeper into this third category, think about the first time you walked into an Apple store. Where the heck was the checkout counter? And, of course, there wasn't one. What about all those tables loaded with products that you could just bang away on and, in fact, were invited to do so? And, hey, why not bring the kids along and let them mess about as well? The store itself is so innovative that it affords them patent protection based on the layout itself. This all falls under experience and is what makes one fall in love with the brand. Hitting home runs in all three arenas has given Apple the margins that most of us would die for. And again, these margins have absolutely nothing to do with some multiplier of manufacturing cost.

While we note that Apple falls into all three categories, one can be equally successful by picking and choosing one or two. Zara, the fashion manufacturer and retailer, known for high fashion at lower prices and rapidly changing styles, is an example of this approach. It would be easy to suggest that their internal systems are the standalone basis for their success. Yet Zara's name and the significant satisfaction generated by their business model are widely recognized and valued, and that by itself takes us into the realm of experience. It's a great brand.

We know them not because they spend lots of money on advertising, as they do not. They spend very little when compared with other high-end stores, all in high-end retail districts. The high-value brand they have developed results from charging less than competitors and with high-end current fashion products. They base their experiential component on effective and efficient customer loyalty and awareness generation through social media. As noted in *Business Horizons*, "customer satisfaction (of Zara) is the strongest determinant of loyalty."[7]

Harry's, the men's personal care manufacturer, is another brand worth considering to illustrate these ideas. They play a bit like Apple in possessing a unique business model (configuration) and a great product (offering). In addition, Harry's exhibits strong customer touchpoints (experience). We recognize Harry's as they began with their online offering only. Product cost was reasonable, with a very high-quality design coupled with precision blades secured through their purchase of a German blade company. Their ownership of the blade company allowed them to surpass other low-cost producers. It also allowed them to undercut larger corporate competitor's higher costs. Their configuration, based on vertical manufacturing, and an offering that required subscriptions, guaranteed them a potential customer for life. Similar to Zara's model, they developed a robust digital audience.

And of course, one can apply the same thinking in the service industry. An example is Southern New Hampshire University, a private nonprofit university. Southern New Hampshire University was similar to many other small schools in 2011, suffering from declining enrollment and many competitors in the same market category. What they did to ensure their success is what we should always be doing, recognize their audience. They accomplished this with a deep dive into their students' needs and recognized their students as dramatically different from the more classic traditional students. Southern New Hampshire University recognized that the preponderance of those applying or merely asking for information were coming from those already in the workforce, individuals who realized their need for a college education. Their candidates were not eighteen-year-olds wanting a college experience but instead were characterized by an overwhelming percentage of working adults requiring additional skills.

Their grasp of this opportunity allowed them to recognize they could configure their offering, online classes, with no additional expenditure and deliver it at a lower cost. They realized that their product, online education, could be a service that was not yet popular but was dedicated to addressing working students' needs, a college degree. They further explored the opportunity by engaging with potential major employers that this new online adult-educated user could serve.

To work at the level they needed, Southern New Hampshire University worked with the US Department of Education, which in 2013 accepted their online model for accreditation. In this case of higher education service, the product offering had to be of a sufficiently high caliber to secure and sustain accreditation. The service model also included the participation of employer partners who paid most of the tuition, which, for these students, was their only pathway to obtaining a degree.[8]

Being among the first in this space and spreading the word through local industry, the experiential component—the brand of Southern New Hampshire University—was being the "go to" institution dedicated to those who historically lacked the opportunity to earn a college degree.

To close this section, we note the importance of reviewing the totality of where innovation can and does occur, particularly as it expands our understanding of what innovation can entail. Once one accepts the significant value of Keeley and colleagues' configuration, offering, and experience view, the question then becomes, how does any size organization structure its planning to take the best advantage of this understanding? We consider this next.

OBJECTIVE-BASED PLANNING

Objective-based planning involves defining the organization's strategic objectives and restricting those objectives to some period of time and an associated budget. In this section, we discuss three objective-based planning methodologies, each of which addresses the needs of a specific type of company.

Prelude: Why Planning?

Without structure, we are playing a costly game of chance, and as noted elsewhere, product design and development is very much a game of chance: think "Vegas."

As we already discussed in both Chapters 2 (when considering design thinking) and 4 (when considering the phase-gate process), when we know very little, we make small bets; as we gain knowledge and confidence, the bet increases. Discovery-driven planning is a planning methodology particularly useful in situations in which significant up-front uncertainty exists.[9]

Similar to design thinking and phase-gate processes, discovery-driven planning tests assumptions by incrementally investing in innovation. Having already emphasized minimizing risk and investment by using such an approach with design thinking and phase-gate processes, we instead turn our attention to a second important benefit of planning, organizational alignment.

We need alignment within the organization for everyone to be on the same page. The lack of all players being aligned is an all too common root cause for poor performance and failure. Everyone has to know where we want to go, and they have to understand why. So the "why" becomes the critical motivator for the top talent involved and responsible for making the difference. Getting aligned on the primary objective clarifies assumptions that could undermine confidence and easily lead to discord. The basic approach also eliminates opinions that easily can be biased. To be a bit simplistic, we all need to be marching to the same drummer. The methodologies of objective-based planning provide us with means to achieve just such alignment.

Having structure allows for clarity and helps define executive-level leadership and the culture of your organization. When we review objective-based planning and the three defined structures used, we can readily appreciate and confirm that "all organizations are perfectly designed to get the results they get."[10]

All three structures we review here share a common form: the translation and cascading from the top of the organization down to the incremental components and ending up with the individual players. The variance of the three structures depends on the organization's complexity, culture, and focus. Each has its strengths and weaknesses, and there is no absolute, other than the recognition that objective-based planning must be in place to succeed. Your culture and your understanding of your organization will allow you to make the appropriate decision as to which methodology to use.

The Cascading Structure of Objective-Based Planning

Figure 6.2 illustrates the standard cascade structure of each objective-based planning methodology, starting at the top with the executive management team. The thread, as we discuss below, always begins with the organization's objectives.

Objective-Based Planning

Cascading Broad Objectives to Specific Responsibilities

(Objectives, Goals, Strategies, Measurements, Tactics)

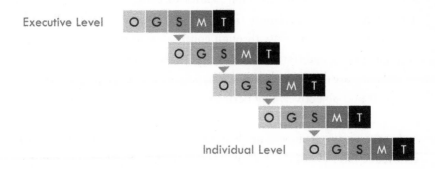

FIGURE 6.2. The standard cascade structure of each objective-based planning methodology.

Let's start by clarifying what we mean by the terms introduced across the top of Figure 6.2.

Objectives represent the highest-level organizational direction. They define an overarching vision for the company. They are stable, concise, and linked to the company mission. Objectives map to the right side of Figure 6.1 and typically include reference to both the nature of competitive advantage and financial success. A simple objective might read, "XYZ will be the preeminent company demonstrated by market share and profit margins worldwide."

Goals are stepping stones to achieving the higher-level objective. They are specific, measurable, achievable, and compatible. Goals also map to the right side of Figure 6.1, yet do so quantitatively, not merely qualitatively. Typically, they include a financial target, including specific dates when one should expect to meet them. A goals statement might read, "For 2023, our profit margins should be 75 percent and our market share 90 percent."

Strategies are the choices we make to achieve our objectives. They are where we choose to focus. Yet they need to remain sufficiently flexible to permit adaptation as the competitive environment shifts around your company. You may pursue multiple strategies in parallel. In general, strategies, as defined here, map to the middle of Figure 6.1—the portions depicted in *italics*.[11] Strategies might include, "Breakthrough products that are better than the competition while maintaining cost parity" (a differentiation market share strategy); or "Develop businesses, based on existing expertise, in new markets, with a focus on Germany" (a synergy strategy); or "Identify new products and concepts through continuous improvement based on customer needs" (a differentiation market share strategy).

Measures are the numerical benchmarks we use to track progress toward our goals and objectives. Key performance indicators are used as checkpoints to determine if our strategies are working. They are the ongoing reviews to ensure strategies are being met. Measures might read, "15 percent reduction in formula cost" or "Increase target shares in key countries by 10 percent."

Tactics are detailed actions taken to support the strategies. Tactics map to the left side of Figure 6.1, ultimately defining the day-to-day activities pursued in your company. Tactics could include, "Be first to market with leading-edge technologies" or "Standardize product platforms" or "Reduce stock-keeping unit complexity."

Again, the objectives, goals, strategies, measures, and tactics appearing across the top of Figure 6.2 and described above are established at the organization's highest level by the owners, board members, CEO, and president or GM and their leadership team. Then the departments at the next organizational level down take what is handed to them from the top level and develop their own objectives, goals, strategies, measures, and tactics. This appears as the second row down from the top in Figure 6.2. Notably, at this next level down, the objectives, goals, strategies, measures, and tactics are shifted to the right. It is precisely this shift down one level and to the right that we mean when we speak of the "cascading structure" of objective-based planning.

Now that we all appreciate the cascading requirement for successful alignment, we need to look at various methodologies with specific structures to identify the most suitable methodology for your organization.

Planning Option One: Objectives, Goals, Strategies, Measures, Tactics (OGSMT)

Using the graphic of Figure 6.2, we start with a structure well-suited for a larger, well-defined organization, consistent with that found in larger SMMEs. The basic structure is called OGSMT, representing the key elements objectives, goals, strategies, measures, and tactics. With this structure, one achieves clarity with a definition of what is to be accomplished and a methodology that will ensure success. Measurable goals are put in place followed by the specific strategies that will achieve them and supported by measurements of these accomplishments. OGSMT was first developed in the 1950s for large-scale challenges that organizations were facing, with Procter & Gamble a significant advocate of this methodology. Figure 6.3 illustrates an example of OGSMT.

What one needs to appreciate regarding OGSMT are the reasonable simplicity and the ease with which it can be implemented. While it might be comforting to have someone who has completed an OGSMT as either a leader or scribe, it is not at all necessary to have any background whatsoever. It is critical to have all of the key players in the room and ensure that they stay concentrated on the task. One can implement an OGSMT planning process on a whiteboard, with all of those present having a simple printout that looks a little bit like the graphic of Figure 6.3. Everyone needs to appreciate the definitions outlined in the previous section, as these guide the plan's construction.

What is critical in the basic OGSMT model is absolute concentration and adherence to what you seek to accomplish—companywide alignment. The objective level may also be the most difficult to determine, even though it should reflect the company's charter or mission statement.

A basic OGSMT example might begin with the highest, or business level as described in the previous section. Following the classic OGSMT structure shown in Figure 6.3, the business strategy will become the R&D unit's objectives. Thus, for the R&D unit, you may construct the following OGSMT:

Objectives: "Breakthrough products that are better and less expensive than the competition" or "Leverage global scale through simplification and standardization of formulas, packaging, and processes."

OGSMT

Cascading Broad Objectives to Specific Responsibilities

(Objectives, Goals, Strategies, Measurements, Tactics)

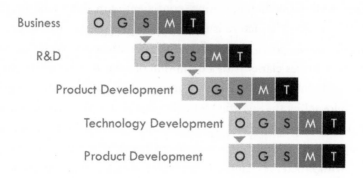

FIGURE 6.3. Generic OGSMT (objectives, goals, strategies, measures, tactics) planning structure.

Goals: "Achieve no less than 75 percent profit margin."

Strategies: "Focus on cost-efficient activities" or "Develop joint technology development programs with key suppliers" or "Introduce new efficient material packaging."

Measures: "Increase performance while maintaining the same or less formula cost" or "Reduce number of separate formula processes" or "Introduce new space-efficient packaging."

Tactics: "Standardize product platforms, packaging, processes" or "Reduce stock-keeping unit complexity."

Those R&D department strategies then become objectives for product development at the next level down. It is easy to see how clarity of objectives is the most critical component for achieving success. You can recognize from the start that the key tactics typically conclude three layers down within the organization. One can easily see the complexity at the group level. Having stated that, the OGSMT's value is that it is delivered as a simple one-page overview for each unit.

In large, diverse organizations, this OGSMT methodology can be extremely valuable in aligning groups, including product development, research, development, supply chain, sales, and marketing. The challenge, however, is the reality of a one-way street driven from the top that may minimize grassroots innovation.

Planning Option Two: Vision, Values, Methods, Obstacles, Measures (V2MOM)

Another methodology for objective-based planning is what is commonly known as V2MOM. This acronym represents vision, values, mission, obstacles, and measures. The methodology was developed by the founder of Salesforce, Marc Benioff, who stated succinctly, "While a company is growing fast, there is nothing more important than constant communication and complete alignment. We've been able to achieve both with the help of a secret management process that I developed a number of years ago."[12]

It obviously is working, as Salesforce was a startup in 1999 and twenty years later employed thirty thousand. More important, their growth came from a strong internal base of communication from the organization's very start. Their guiding principles and values have been critical in their growth. By their own definition, their principles reflect as the following, here including the detail that appeared in the company's very first V2MOM plan:[13]

Vision: Defines what you want to do or achieve

1. Rapidly create a world-class Internet company/site for sales force automation

Values: Principles and beliefs that help you pursue the vision

1. World-class organization
2. Time to market
3. Functional
4. Usability
5. Value-added partnerships

Methods: Actions and steps to take to get the job done

1. Hire the team
2. Finalize product specification and technical architecture
3. Rapidly develop the product specification to beta and production stages

4. Build partnerships with big e-commerce, content, and hosting companies

5. Build a launch plan

6. Develop exit strategy: IPO/acquisition

Obstacles: The challenges, problems, issues you have to overcome to achieve the vision

1. Developers

2. Product managers/business development person

Measures: Measurable results you aim to achieve

1. Prototype is state-of-the-art

2. High-quality functional system

3. Partnerships are online and integrated

4. Salesforce.com is regarded as leader and visionary

5. We are all rich"

Marc Benioff stated it all quite clearly when he noted, "The vision helped us define what we wanted to do. The values established what was most important about that vision; it set the principles and beliefs that guided it (in priority). The methods illustrated how we would get the job done by outlining the actions and the steps that everyone needed to take. The obstacles identified the challenges, problems, and issues we would have to overcome to achieve our vision. Finally, the measures specified the actual result we aimed to achieve; often this was defined as a numerical outcome."[14]

So while the V2MOM structure clearly is a bit different from OGSMT, it is easy to see the commonality. Let's visually see what this looks like in Figure 6.4.

The cascade effect here is similar to that found with the OGSMT approach. Everything starts at the highest, or business level. And while the C-suite, business level develops the primary company objectives, the V2MOM methodology supports a series of reviews and interviews with individuals within the organization. These individuals work collaboratively with their work partners, peers, and their manager to create their own V2MOM. As

V2MOM

Cascading Broad Objectives to Specific Responsibilities

(Vison, Values, Methods, Obstacles, and Measures)

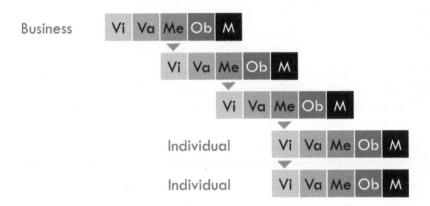

FIGURE 6.4. Generic V2MOM (vision, values, methods, obstacles, measures) planning structure.

a result, the V2MOM becomes more of a personal vision and values document tool using the corporate guide to establish its fit.

Filling in the boxes should be reasonably straightforward for all involved, and indeed everyone is or should be involved. The vision query is easy enough, as it begins with a simple question: "What is it you are trying to accomplish, and what is it you actually want?" Similarly, for values, anyone in the organization should be able to identify which values are most important. For the method question, a similar list, delineating the methods to achieve the vision should not be very complicated. In developing this V2MOM, then, all involved should be able to recognize the obstacles that the organization faces or will face. Again, this would typically generate a list. To complete the V2MOM planning process, the measurement component simply asks the question, "How will we know when we have accomplished this vision?"

V2MOM methodology is well designed for smaller, more agile organizations. Done correctly, everyone in the organization, including the youngest, least senior intern, should develop their own V2MOM and do it quarterly. That may be asking for a lot in a major, highly structured organization. Yet for small to mid-size companies that genuinely want to invest in innovation, the V2MOM planning option is proven to be highly effective. And while this methodology was developed specifically for Salesforce, one can easily see its value in almost every organizational issue that we all face, including down to the individual level. While you are reading this, take a quick stab at it, and see if you can't use the very simple vision, values, methods, obstacles, and measures in your life.

Planning Option Three: Objectives and Key Results (OKRs)

The third and final structure leads us into a specific key result planning methodology known as OKRs, or objectives and key results. OKRs share the same cascading structure and objectives that we have seen in OGSMT and V2MOM but are an even more straightforward approach.

One of the earliest investors in Google, John Doerr, introduced OKRs to Google as it was just getting started.[15] That was in 1999, and it has become a standard they have continued to use since inception. Their standard has always been that objectives have to be aggressive and ambitious. To ensure that feeling, it is strongly suggested within the Google culture that it feel a bit uncomfortable.[16] Key results are similar to goals, as defined in the first two structures, and are measurable. The measurements can be on any scale, but they should be relatively easy to grade. At Google, their scale ranges from zero to one.

Google has always gone out of its way to ensure that its OKRs are public for all to see within the organization. It also goes out of its way to let all appreciate there is no relevance to individual evaluations based on the grading of the OKRs. The purpose is solely to establish alignment within the organization as a means of achieving company goals.

Since Google demands ambitious reach, it should be no surprise that a standard grade within Google ranges from 0.6 to 0.7. And to strengthen that measurement, should any individual get consistent 1.0s, it is a signal to all that their OKRs are simply not sufficiently ambitious.

Google's products' market performance supports its success with OKRs. Consider Chrome and Android, each of which started with the ambitious goal of changing an industry in a very brief period of time.[17] As Google sees it, OKRs allow focus on essential goals and avoid distractions for less critical goals. All of them are big, none are incremental, and there is an understanding and acceptance that only some will succeed.[18]

For Google, their objectives

- "Express goals and intents;
- Are aggressive yet realistic;
- Must be tangible, objective, and unambiguous; should be obvious to a rational observer whether an objective has been achieved.
- The successful achievement of an objective must provide clear value for Google."[19]

Also for Google, key results

- "Express measurable milestones which, if achieved, will advance objective(s) in a useful manner to their constituents;
- Must describe outcomes, not activities. If your OKRs include words like "consult," "help," "analyze," or "participate," they describe activities. Instead, describe the end-use impact of these activities: "publish average and tail latency measurements from six Colossus cells by March 7," rather than "assess Colossus latency";
- Must include evidence of completion. This evidence must be available, credible, and easily discoverable. Examples of evidence include change lists, links to docs notes, and published metric reports."[20]

According to Google's implementation, recognizing that OKRs fall into either aspirational or committed variations, one needs to appreciate the difference from their perspective. If a team is committed, then delivery has to be made with a score of 1.0. If less than 1.0, then the question becomes, "Why?" On the other hand, if the OKRs are aspirational, the score would typically fall in the 0.6 to 0.7 range.

Let's see what OKRs look like, in Figure 6.5. The simplicity of OKRs is that only two boxes waterfall down to the next level.

OKRs
Cascading Broad Objectives to Specific Responsibilities
(Objectives and Key Results)

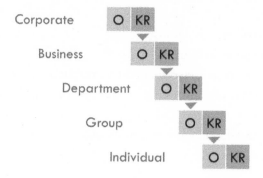

FIGURE 6.5. Generic OKRs (objectives and key results) planning structure.

Generalizing beyond Google's implementation, objectives need to be well thought through, and key results are your company's secret sauce. As with the two other methodologies, measurement is essential. If you can't measure it, you should not do it. Values, vision, and mission are defined separately and culturally driven. OKRs are a communication tool meant to be simple and highly scalable in the organization as it grows. Objectives should be ambitious and feel a bit uncomfortable, and they must delineate an unambiguous statement of a goal. Key results should make the objective achievable, as they are quantifiable and require objective grading.

So, now the "Why?" And the response is that the benefits of the OKRs methodology start with disciplined thinking and dedication to significant goals. They communicate accurately because everyone knows what is essential and what is not. They establish indicators for measuring progress, and they show how far along you are. They focus efforts and keep the organization in step. They are scalable from the individual to the enterprise, and they empower individuals to have an impact.

We must recognize that OKRs are negotiated at an individual level. Still, when moving them up to a staff level, they cannot be just a collection of individual OKRs. Therefore, some ladder up (in contrast to those that cascade down), and others simply may not. For Google, their goal is that 50 percent are bottom-up driven, which has enabled a percentage to elevate into the "moonshot" category for full development. Keep in mind that the CEO and the board still drive objectives. Since individuals propose their own OKRs, as long as they align to major critical corporate objectives, the individual's objective can become a preeminent corporate objective. It works for Google (Alphabet) as they are driven to the empowerment of teams for innovation.

A typical implementation cycle for using OKRs is quarterly. For example, at the first quarter's conclusion, key results are graded at a staff level, concurrent with the second quarter's start, when new OKRs are finalized. That cycle continues quarterly throughout the year. Annual OKRs should be communicated at the time of the first quarterly OKRs.

OKRs represent a great methodology tool for a highly agile company that demands swift movement and is fully supported from the top for individual initiatives.

Objective-Based Planning Summary

The keys to all three methodologies are communication, for leadership to ensure that the highest-level objectives are known and deemed essential, and empowerment, for leaders to provide the resources necessary to accomplish these objectives. Whether it is OGSMT, V2MOM, or OKRs, any of these three objective-based planning approaches will help enable innovation. The challenge is to ensure that you are choosing one of them: not selecting any is not allowed.

So Where Are We Regarding Innovation?

Now that we understand objective-based planning, it's time to go back and recall the three main areas in which innovation takes place: configuration, offering, and experience. What we just covered with objective-based planning is clearly in the configuration category, the internal back room.

Yet irrespective of all the methodologies we might use, innovation, by definition, requires reduction to practice in the marketplace. Do people want it, and are they willing to pay for the value they perceive? And it is impossible for us to identify a business that is not dependent on some end-user.

It's time for us to recognize the importance of focus, the kind of focus that objective-based planning gives to your innovation investments. For example, we should never confuse volume with value. So our advice to you is to understand your company's core competency. We admonish you to remember that you not only want to provide value to end-users by being better than anyone else in your space. You want them to *quake in their boots* if they even think about entering your arena of expertise. If you have achieved that, you have indeed established a strategic competitive advantage. Carry that thought with you forever. Without it, you might just find yourself in a race to the bottom.

A simple example may be Google's official mission statement: "Our company mission is to organize the world's information and make it universally accessible and useful."[21] That is one heck of a message. That draws a line in the sand and would make anyone quake in their shoes to think they can enter that space. While it's tempting to dismiss Google as an example, remember that they didn't exist just over two decades ago. They went from nothing to something remarkable in terms of size and scope. If you want to succeed, don't shy away from thinking big, beyond where you and your industry currently operate.

You should want to think about your core competency. It may be intellectual property. It may be your people, their expertise, and how they work together. It may just be inherent in your methodology. But regardless of what it is, if you have "it," shouldn't you want to use that for your strategy?

THE LEVERS OF STRATEGIC INNOVATION MANAGEMENT: CULTURE AND ORGANIZATION

Moving beyond the critical activities of defining strategies and developing plans based on them, senior executive leadership teams possess two means of driving innovation at the strategic level: defining organizational culture and establishing organizational structure. In this section, we consider the role of both in SMMEs.

The Need for a Renewal-Friendly Culture

Throughout this book, we have advocated for the kind of innovation that leads to renewal. We've done so because although your existing business may or may not be bad at the time, it's likely to be insufficient to survive and thrive over time. Therefore we argue for ambidextrous leadership and ambidextrous organizations, leaders and organizations that can both optimize the current business—at best pursuing incremental innovation within the existing paradigm, per Figure 1.2—and identify and develop new, innovative business opportunities—at best, pursuing new paradigms of competition and renewal through breakthrough innovation, per Figure 1.2.

As companies mature, the most successful appropriately develop great skill at optimizing the current business, especially the means of production. From a purely short-term economic perspective, this makes sense, as the current opportunity is the proverbial "bird in the hand." They develop a production-optimization (within the paradigm) culture characterized by the kind of descriptors listed in Table 6.1. They emphasize operational efficiency and a focus on tools such as six sigma and lean production. When they explore new business opportunities, at most they tread lightly, cautiously staying close to home, close to the products and markets that brought them the success they currently enjoy.

Unfortunately, as companies mature, they not only develop great skill at optimizing the current business, but—at the same time—they often wholly lose their ability to innovate in a meaningful way. Understand that we are *not* suggesting that your company necessarily should retain or assume a pure startup culture devoid of optimization (within the paradigm) expertise. What we are offering is that, for your company to succeed and survive over time, it must simultaneously embrace a renewal-friendly culture (see Table 6.1).

The challenge then is how to establish and maintain a healthy tension between the optimization (within the paradigm) culture required to sustain your current business and the innovation-friendly culture necessary to grow and renew it. Unfortunately, as we've witnessed time and again, it is easier and cleaner—but deadly—to not deal with this tension.

While never easy, we contend that, fortunately for you, it's easier to establish and maintain a new culture in an SMME than in a large mature company. We argue this in part because there are fewer places to "hide" in an SMME. If necessary, senior executive leadership can go right to the frontline employees to make a difference. There are so many management layers in larger companies that it becomes increasingly difficult to effect

TABLE 6.1. A comparison of optimization (within the paradigm) and renewal-friendly cultures.

Optimization (within the paradigm) Culture	Renewal-Friendly Culture
Heavy emphasis on cost reduction	Revenue growth
Risk minimized	Risk recognized
Failure punished	Learning rewarded
Predictability	Surprise and uncertainty
Stability	Volatility
Reliability	Agility
Highly structured	Individualism recognized
Simplistic	Complexity → Simplicity

change from the top. Also, it is typically easier to fire people in an SMME, as there are also fewer policies in place that are detached from the needs of the local environment. While this may seem harsh, it is an unfortunate reality if other approaches fail.

To our amusement, in the writing of this book, Bruce and Walter independently shared our enjoyment of the 2011 film *Moneyball*.[22] It tells a great—based on a true—story of innovation in an SMME. However, most important for this section is how the film depicts the cultural changes that Oakland A's general manager Billy Beane must navigate to ensure his team's competitive success. His actions in rebuilding the team's roster after losing key players ran counter to a hundred years of major league baseball culture.

Yet even this bold move was insufficient to succeed. So when the team's manager continued to field a player who did not fit Beane's new business model, Beane traded the player. And when the players continued as they always had, Beane and the Peter Brand composite character had to go into training facilities and the locker room to talk and work through the changes with them. None of this was easy, but it was the hard work necessary—when others scoffed at what Billy Beane was attempting—to establish what became a remarkably winning team culture.

So what kind of culture does your SMME have? What can you do, in your position, regardless of your organizational level, to establish and sustain a renewal-friendly culture? And will you do it as if your investment or job depended on it?

Organizing for Innovation Success

We contend that, with the right people, you can organize just about any way you'd like in an SMME.

There, we said it. Now, what do we mean by this?

By "any way you'd like," we're not suggesting any random organizational model. But we are saying that once you've narrowed your options down to a handful of reasonable possibilities, you likely won't go too wrong with any of them. And if you observe weaknesses or problems later, you can adapt to address and correct them.

So, what if you *don't* have the right people? What do we see you doing then?

Well, this is where the old joke about the man with the ill-fitting suit applies. In it, the man increasingly has to adapt his posture to fit his suit, rather than having the tailor make the proper alterations. In the end, a passerby who sees the man awkwardly accommodating the suit while walking down the street comments, "I don't know what's wrong with the fella, but don't the suit fit nice?"[23] The parallel we're suggesting is that not having the right people is a lot like the ill-fitting suit. If you must accommodate them too much by carefully crafting an organizational model, perhaps you're doing something wrong.

The gravest organizational mistake we've observed in SMMEs is to establish an entirely separate, dedicated "innovation lab" or some other similarly organized group. We're not talking about bringing people together to focus. But we are talking about separating people entirely—organizationally and often in a different location—from the core business.[24] And we're saying this despite Clayton Christensen's urging to do precisely what we are talking about.[25] By establishing a separate organization, company executive leadership is tacitly acknowledging that those optimizing the core business are *incapable* of working with those focused on the kind of innovation that leads to renewal. Christensen essentially made the same point. The company's executive core has given up on trying to establish a renewal-friendly culture. This means—if you're part of that core business—they've given up on *you* in the long term. Let that sink in for a minute. Once the core business goes away—and eventually, it will—you'll have to prove yourself worthy of being kept on because right now you are seen as a liability to renewal. With this in mind, how might this prompt you to change your behavior, to become more renewal-friendly, or to rethink your future with the company?

Like anything, there exists a range of organizational possibilities for any company. At one end, everyone is "perfect" in their breadth and depth of innovation skill and, collectively, they operate flexibly and ambidextrously as a remarkable whole, independently of how you organize. At the other end, if you have significant innovation expertise holes in your company, you may choose to "heroically" accommodate it, like the ill-fitting suit we just described. Yet what options exist between these two extremes?

One possibility is to employ the type of structural ambidexterity implemented in some large, mature companies. O'Connor, Corbett, and Peters advocate for establishing three distinct capabilities—discovery, incubation, and acceleration—as a means of addressing the problem of invention without successful commercialization.[26] They observe many large, mature companies excelling at the R&D part of discovery but lacking other essential aspects of discovery, such as developing the business models and markets, as well as the incubation expertise necessary to commercialize an idea and the acceleration required to grow it beyond launch.

At some level, such siloing can make a certain amount of sense in SMMEs, with it being more appropriate, at most, for larger SMMEs. As company size decreases, however, insufficient scale means that individuals must assume multiple roles so that, at times, people must be assigned one or more of these roles on a fractional basis. Further, regardless of company size, a holistic perspective of the business is reduced, if not lost, by partitioning roles in this manner.[27]

So where does this leave us? While a potentially helpful tool for SMMEs, structural ambidexterity is a less desirable situation than what you would find in a well-integrated, silo-free environment. Our recommendation for SMMEs then is to use such an organizational structure if required to accommodate a good but far-from-perfect workforce but not to rest or languish there. See it as a temporary fix along the way as you strive for a genuinely insight-filled, renewal-friendly, highly collaborative culture.

STRATEGIC INNOVATION MANAGEMENT: SOME CLOSING THOUGHTS

With this chapter, we complete our review of content necessary to help any SMME succeed with innovation. This chapter is somewhat unique among the rest in that it provides an executive-level perspective of innovation. Yet it does so in a way that "pulls back the curtain" for each of our audiences. So even if you are not in an executive-level role, this content should prove useful in that it will help you understand what those at the executive level are—or perhaps should be—doing.

For each member of our audience, keep in mind that we do *not* equate strategic innovation management with the long-term, significant, highly speculative investments often observed in large, mature companies. While we may have been less explicit in this chapter about our focus on SMMEs, this distinction is critical. Our emphasis has been on matters such as focus, clarity, and alignment. Make no mistake: in keeping with the rest of our book, this chapter stays the course on our major themes and insights for SMMEs—renewal to survive and thrive, manageable risk, reasonable cost, proven methods, personal courage, and people.

KEY POINTS AND TAKEAWAYS

- Strategy ties a company's vision, objectives, and goals to its everyday activities.
- Flying by the seat of one's pants and "hoping" is not a strategy. Instead, a simple, easily understood and implemented strategy typically involves identifying with one of three standard options: differentiation, low cost, or focus.
- Strategy can take on many forms, including but not limited to the basic business model, the backroom structure, the offering itself, or even its experiential and emotional component.
- Objective-based planning is a simple construct that involves defining the organization's strategic objectives, restricting those objectives to some time, and working within an associated budget.

- While a fully engaged innovation culture will enable the most and best innovation opportunities for investment, minimally, a renewal-friendly culture is necessary to succeed.
- While organizing for innovation is seen as necessary in large, mature companies, SMMEs have some latitude in organizing for innovation success. Such flexibility is based on an SMME's ability to avoid highly siloed structures and can be used to your company's advantage.

CHAPTER 7

Midtronics

AN EXEMPLAR OF SMME INNOVATION

> "Steve is playing the long game. He would much rather have a future than a stellar present."
>
> —Kevin Bertness, Midtronics CTO

PRELIMINARY QUESTIONS AND INTRODUCTORY THOUGHTS

- What does a genuinely innovative SMME look like?
- How does a genuinely innovative SMME succeed over time?
- What might I aspire to for my organization as we seek to succeed even beyond where our imaginations might take us?

Midtronics is an exemplar of SMME innovation. It has a proven track record of success, time and again not only surviving but also thriving as it renews itself and the battery management industry it leads. We share their story as this book's capstone, bringing together our major themes and insights—illustrating the application of the topics we cover—in one place for our audience to reflect on as a whole.

This is what it looks like when you "get it" when it comes to innovation that renews an SMME.

MIDTRONICS' STORY

Founded in 1984 by Steve McShane, Midtronics addresses the battery management needs of the transportation industry.[1] Its products range from handheld car battery testers of the type you may have seen used to determine remaining battery life during a recent oil change to larger diagnostic chargers of the kind found in service centers.[2] Two examples of Midtronics' products in their daily use environment appear in Figure 7.1. Midtronics works with vehicle manufacturers and dealers, battery manufacturers, and service centers, offering a product portfolio that addresses a wide range of customer needs for personal vehicles (internal combustion engine, hybrid electric, and plug-in electric), fleets, and trucks.

While the introductory paragraph describes what the company sells and whom it sells to, more so than at any company we know, employee behavior at Midtronics fully aligns with its stated purpose ("Advancing Battery Management") and values.[3] The Midtronics team has not given lip service to or "retired" these words on a plaque in a hallway or on a conference room wall; they live them.

As a consequence of this culture, Midtronics has been recognized variously for its contributions, including as a regular recipient of *MOTOR Magazine*'s "Top 20 Tools" award and *Professional Tool & Equipment News*'s Innovation Award. Further, Midtronics has been consistently ranked among the most innovative companies in the Chicago area, topping the list twice, as recognized by *Crain's Chicago Business*.

More important, their sought-after products, highly relational customer engagement, and deep and broad technical expertise place them as the global leader in battery management for the automotive market.

Prelude: Electric Vehicles, Car Batteries, and Car Battery Testers

While not common knowledge, at the outset of the automobile industry in the late 1800s, when no technology standard existed, electric vehicles represented one of the most common types of car, exceeding in numbers those powered by the internal combustion engine.[4] This preference was primarily because of the hazard associated with internal combustion engines, despite electric vehicles' limited range. Internal combustion engines' danger was due to the primitive way they were started, by a person using a hand crank

FIGURE 7.1. Two examples of Midtronics' products in their daily use environment, a battery tester (top) and a diagnostic charger (bottom). Reproduced with permission from Midtronics.

that could easily injure the "starter" if the crank did not disengage from the crankshaft after starting. It was only after manufacturers solved this problem, with an electric starter, and addressed other issues such as engine noise (reduced by adding a muffler) that cars powered by internal combustion engines emerged as the dominant technology.

While the internal combustion engine has dominated the automobile industry for decades, it relies on lead-acid batteries to have the energy available to power the electric starter. If the battery fails, the car will not start without a "jump" from some other source. Therefore, the car's battery requires testing to determine if it is reliable, that it holds sufficient charge to continue in its role and not leave the driver stranded at some entirely unforeseen time and place.

For decades, the industry standard for testing car batteries was the "load test." The load test is a cumbersome, complicated process that involves an individual placing a variable resistive load on the battery and then increasing the load resistance to maintain a constant current over a fifteen-second time interval. If the battery no longer holds a predetermined voltage after being drained in this manner, it is considered to have failed. Among several problems associated with this approach are that it is not repeatable, it requires a skilled technician to ensure accuracy, and it discharges the battery under test. Yet, while not ideal, it remained the standard well into the 1980s.

Midtronics Founding and Early History

Having worked at Motorola early in his career, Steve McShane kept in touch with his former colleagues after moving on. Through this network, in late 1985, he learned that Motorola sought to divest of its electronic battery tester business.

Motorola held a proprietary position with a then-revolutionary product, invented by Professor Keith Champlin of the University of Minnesota, based on measuring a battery's conductance. In contrast to the then standard load test, conductance testing generated neither sparks nor heat and required less skill to perform. Further, it uniquely enabled a technician to distinguish between two seemingly identical batteries if their measured voltages were the same but one carried sufficient charge to start a car and the other did not.

Despite these advantages, this product represented too small an opportunity for a company of Motorola's size and appetite for profit. After initial efforts to commercialize it, no internal champion existed for this product. Yet Steve saw potential where Motorola floundered. As a result, Steve negotiated an attractive deal, purchasing the entire business, including inventory, production equipment, and licenses to the proprietary technology, all for the book value of inventory. While perhaps not seeming significant at this stage, Steve's approach of assuming modest risk with a small investment as a means of probing a market will appear over and over again in this story.

Steve's suspicions about the business and his natural curiosity led him to try things that Motorola had not. Immediately after completing the acquisition, he began probing customer demand with this proprietary product at trade shows. As only an example, where Motorola feared that the product was overpriced and routinely sold it at a discount for $100 apiece, Steve instead tried raising its price, as his sales efforts focused on the value it could provide. To his satisfaction, he was able to raise prices significantly while gaining additional industry insight. Within the first few years, he nearly doubled the unit price and sold more than Motorola had in the process.

In direct dialog with current and potential customers, Steve continued to refine his relational approach with customers, understanding their needs, not just what they asked for. And in addition to his strong external focus on customers, he thought holistically, nurturing collaboration with Keith, working with him to modify products based on customer insight. Not only did Steve bring Keith into the discussion, he also brought him along to trade shows, adding further credibility to Midtronics' proprietary position.

In the process, Midtronics was small but successful. It grew organically, picking up customers one by one, with Steve funding growth from profits.

The Turning Point

Things might have easily continued like this, with Midtronics continuing as a small player for several years. Yet Midtronics succeeded where others failed. What happened?

In 1993, Steve began working with Ford, competing against the most sophisticated load tester ever made, the tool then used by Ford. Midtronics' initial engagement with Ford was not easy. For example, Ford's internal marketing group had approved the placement of Midtronics' battery tester in their dealer catalog along with their competitor's load tester. Yet when Ford's chief battery engineer realized this, he pulled Midtronics' product from the catalog.

Steve persisted, identifying the engineer within Ford who had challenged Midtronics' products, Karl Keckan. Karl was fully committed to solving Ford's battery problems and tenacious in the process. After carefully listening to Karl's concerns, Steve convinced him to give Midtronics' product a try. Karl began generating data using Midtronics' product and sharing it with Steve and Keith. In the process, Steve and Keith were able to modify the Midtronics product and convince Karl that it performed as well as or better than the sophisticated load tester. And it did all this while being easier to use. Steve had won over Karl, a tough, fair, highly professional customer. As Steve points out, Karl's actions contributed significantly to Ford's success in this area and, indirectly, to that of Midtronics, helping make the product better than it otherwise might have been.

Importantly, Steve began to realize that he was solving a much bigger problem for Ford than merely providing it with a tester. Midtronics was not "just" selling an advanced battery tester. Steve had reframed the challenge and was addressing Ford's battery warranty cost problem.

The result was that Midtronics' product went from challenging the established standard to becoming an "essential tool" that all US Ford dealers were required to buy and, most important, embraced. And customer demand was such that Midtronics could now charge a much higher price, which was related to the value to the customer.

With this, Midtronics renewed the basis of competition in the battery management industry.

All of this led Steve to begin asking two significant questions:

- How can we make a product that solves that problem better?
- What other problems can we solve?

For the first ten years, Steve had spent all his time convincing people that his product could effectively test a battery. By 1997, customers had stopped questioning whether Midtronics' conductance tester worked. Instead, they started asking what other problems Midtronics could solve. By the end of the 1990s, Midtronics was into nearly every car manufacturer selling in the United States and many in Europe.

Continuous Renewal

On the heels of Midtronics' success with Ford, Steve hired Kevin Bertness, an electrical engineer already working with Steve as a consultant, to convert Midtronics' then analog product to a digital format. The digital conversion was not just something nice to have, an incremental technological step. It enabled test automation, allowing service technicians to perform the test with the touch of a single button. Further, from the perspective of addressing Ford's warranty problem, it was huge. Over time, the digital conversion also allowed the inclusion of a unique warranty code for each battery, enabling Ford to document and verify whether and when a specific battery failed and thus, to Ford's financial benefit, whose responsibility it was.

What had been difficult to do with an analog load tester was now easy to do with Midtronics' digital conductance tester. This opened the door for Midtronics to replicate its initial success not only with the US Ford group, but now with Ford of Europe.

With this, Midtronics renewed the basis of competition in the battery management industry.

As the Ford opportunity emerged, Steve made additional critical hires in the mid- to late 1990s. These included people without industry experience who learned and carried on the culture of continuous innovation in all functional areas. Several have now assumed leadership roles in the company. Since then, this team has continued to probe, question, and understand the battery tester industry's significant unarticulated challenges.

For example, as recently as the late 1990s, customers with batteries suspected of failing under warranty had to leave their battery in the shop to charge overnight before testing. Service technicians routinely installed "loaner" batteries on a temporary basis, and the customer had to return to the shop the next day to find out whether their battery required replacement. While presenting a considerable inconvenience to both the customer and the shop technicians, this process was the unquestioned, accepted standard. In response, the Midtronics team created the "diagnostic charger," a product that improved customer experience by charging the battery in or out of the vehicle at the time of service, eliminating the need for an overnight delay and providing a decisive answer, either replace or return to service.

With this, Midtronics renewed the basis of competition in the battery management industry.

Soon afterward, Midtronics explored the need for electrical system analyzers, mainly a product to test alternators. At the time, the industry standard required accessing the alternator directly, an increasingly challenging test to perform, as car manufacturers began to place alternators in less accessible places. In response, Midtronics, understanding the need for a simple, reliable test, developed a way to test alternators using clips on the battery terminal rather than directly on the alternator.

With this, Midtronics renewed the basis of competition in the battery management industry.

Midtronics next began to consider the idea of preventative maintenance for batteries. At the time, preventive maintenance was the standard within the automotive industry for components such as brakes and tires but not batteries. Before Midtronics, it was not common knowledge that batteries failed gradually, as failure was defined as the battery being unable to start the car. Yet Midtronics' testers could determine something better, whether a battery was losing its capacity to start a car. With the ability to identify a failing battery before a road emergency, Midtronics' products could essentially direct business to the service provider performing a maintenance test rather than to whoever was closest to the location and available to sell a battery when and where a car battery "died." In this way, Midtronics simultaneously served both maintenance providers and their battery customers.

Still, success in the marketplace was not as easy as approaching their customers with a solution in hand, a solution to a problem that most of their customers at the time did not fully grasp. Fortunately, Midtronics had been in ongoing discussion with Dennis Brown, the insightful vice president of marketing at Interstate Battery, the industry leader in aftermarket batteries. Dennis had long desired to measure what he saw as the "marginal life" that remained in a battery before it could no longer start a car. He understood that if service providers could test every vehicle that came in for service, about 20 percent would have lost enough capacity to benefit from a new battery. He came up with a clever approach that worked in conjunction with a Midtronics conductance test. Midtronics had finally found a customer who understood the potential of the proactive testing they had been promoting for many years.

And with Interstate Battery embracing this approach, all of a sudden, many others in the industry became interested in this new-to-industry value proposition. Midtronics had created a whole new market for battery testers.

With this, Midtronics renewed the basis of competition in the battery management industry.

To be clear, Midtronics has not succeeded in every attempt at renewal. The company has, at times, failed to establish a sufficiently attractive value proposition for technologies that they invested in along the way. For example, at one time, they pursued the idea of placing a small battery monitor in every vehicle. They also explored the commodity charger business. For a while, they even incorporated a cellular radio into their testers as a means of collecting data and performing software updates; while the right solution in principle, the cellular radio was incredibly challenging to implement and was subsequently eclipsed by Wi-Fi connectivity. None of these bore fruit in the market.

Yet even these failures are not seen as wasted investments, as they helped Midtronics more deeply learn and embrace the importance of a unique value proposition to succeed.

With these, Midtronics more fully and profoundly grasped customer needs and restored its focus on finding unique solutions.

While Midtronics has failed at times, it also has chosen to exit businesses that, while performing reasonably well financially, ultimately were deemed to lack sufficient potential to justify the company operating outside its strategic focus.

Like so many other stories from Midtronics' history, its entry into battery management for the stationary power market, supporting the uptime needs of telecommunications and computing infrastructure applications, began with a call for help. In 1989, following a catastrophic power outage in the Ohio Bell system, Steve was asked if Midtronics could apply its expertise in the transportation market to the types of problems experienced in the stationary power market. While seemingly similar, the applications and potential solutions were anything but. Teaming with Keith and working closely with an Ohio Bell engineer, Midtronics solved their problem. And a subsequent success working with Pacific Bell positioned Midtronics as a go-to solution provider.

Following these initial successes, a highly respected industry expert, Dr. David Feder, who earlier led Bell Labs' Battery Development Department, publicly challenged the technology upon which Midtronics staked its stationary power market presence. As is Steve's style, he approached David to see if there was an appropriate way to address his concerns. They worked out a "deal" whereby, if Steve could convince a reputable, impartial third party to test Midtronics' product in competition with the method advocated by David, and if Midtronics' product performed as Steve suggested, then David would acknowledge the results in a paper presented at a major international conference. And this is precisely what happened: Steve's persistence and customer focus resulted in his winning over what had been an influential critic, just as he had with Karl at Ford.

Midtronics competed in the stationary power industry for nearly three decades, providing a financial return on its investment. Yet Todd Stukenberg, by then vice president and general manager of Midtronics' Stationary Power Division and a leading industry expert, compared his unit's potential in a crowded, stagnant industry to other emerging opportunities more closely aligned with the company's transportation business. He acknowledged that Midtronics' best course of action would be to sell the business, likely to a strategic buyer. Steve ultimately accepted Todd's recommendation, a tough decision after a sustained financial investment, multiple product generations, and an appreciation for the leader and team, which played key roles in this business's growth. Refocusing on the transportation business turned out to be the right decision, as Midtronics divested this business in 2018, allowing the company to focus entirely on the market where its innovation, leadership, and reputation were more promising, needed, and appreciated.

With this thirty-year story, Midtronics proved its ability to enter a new market and sustain success, as well as its ability to exit and refocus when it makes business sense to do so.

While openly acknowledging such "failures" and the resulting lessons learned, forays into other applications have performed significantly better. Having historically focused on lead-acid batteries used with conventional internal combustion engines, Midtronics has increased its attention to vehicle electrification. In 2001, they bought their first Prius to begin to understand how hybrid electric vehicles work. In 2008, they created a product to capture information about the condition of hybrid electric vehicle batteries. Interestingly, they learned that no one at that time really cared to know the batteries' conditions. Technologies and markets were still emerging, in a state of constant flux, and car manufacturers did not want to emphasize potential problems not obvious to the driver.

While this initial product did not sell well, it got Midtronics involved in and learning about electric vehicles. Importantly, it helped the company gain a foothold with those working on vehicle electrification within car manufacturers. So when Nissan, only six months before the launch of its plug-in electric Leaf, realized that it needed help with its service strategy, their engineers turned to Midtronics, with whom they already had a strong working relationship. The Midtronics team rolled up their sleeves to understand the nature of Nissan's problem and created the first electric vehicle module balancer, unique for Nissan, in time for their launch. While some might see this as easy, it was not, evidenced by the fact that nobody else could do it.

With this, Midtronics renewed the basis of competition in the battery management industry.

Not long after, with Midtronics having now proven itself in the electric vehicle industry, General Motors approached them with an emergency of their own. During testing conducted by the National Highway Traffic Safety Administration of the US Department of Transportation, a Chevy Volt, General Motors's first entrant in the electric vehicle market, burst into flames several weeks after crash testing, just before the Volt's planned launch. Suddenly, General Motors had a crisis, with the Volt launch in jeopardy, if anything, merely because of questions raised in potential customers' minds. With General Motors now keenly aware of their need to address this situation, Midtronics received an emergency call requesting their help. As is their approach, the Midtronics team listened carefully, grasping General Motors's real needs. Since Midtronics had already anticipated this need and was working on implementation, they were able to create a new product that solved several of General Motors's problems. This product not only balanced cells, like the earlier product for Nissan Leaf, but also provided emergency discharging to render the car safe at an accident scene quickly as well as rescue charging to enable a car to restart if it lost all power.

With this, Midtronics renewed the basis of competition in the battery management industry.

Later, as is their business model, Midtronics began to sell variations of this product to other electric vehicle original equipment manufacturers. In the process, always listening to customers, they learned that the product they developed for General Motors, while remarkable, had more features than what some other customers needed. Midtronics successfully adapted accordingly, separating the one all-inclusive product into three more-focused products, one each for balancing, emergency discharging, and rescue charging, more suitably addressing customer needs.

With this, Midtronics successfully pivoted, having listened to customers and understood their needs.

As Will Sampson, now Midtronics' president, reflects on the relentless renewal of the battery management industry pursued by Midtronics over time, he summarizes each cycle in three simple steps:

1. *Penetration*: What is the value proposition? Why will a customer buy the first one of any new concept? How can we turn everybody into our customers, making this a market?
2. *Reinvention*: Why might a customer buy a second one of this concept? Will additional features, such as larger display screens, improved user interfaces, the capability for software updates, or integrated printers, provide enough added value to induce customers to purchase an upgrade?
3. *Expansion*: What other problems can we solve for this product's customers?

With this approach, Will quickly emphasizes what each of those interviewed for this story acknowledged. The Midtronics team is not prone to try to "tell the future" but, instead, actively seeks new opportunities within a reasonable reach. It has been just this inclination that has reduced

Midtronics' risk and increased their likelihood of success, all while self-funding growth and renewal.

What's Next?

As part of a regrouping exercise in the late 2010s, Midtronics' leadership team formulated a well-considered yet straightforward strategy along with financial goals. In it, they specified three strategic objectives:

1. Grow the current business supporting the battery management needs of internal-combustion-engine powered vehicles.
2. Grow new business in specific geographic regions.
3. Grow new business beyond currently addressed applications, including but not limited to vehicle electrification.

Shortly afterward, Jason Ruban took on responsibility for the third strategic objective by assuming a newly formed "Vice President of Business Innovation" position. Consistent with Steve's fund-as-you-go approach, only Jason was dedicated full time at first to the strategic innovation objective.

As Jason initially reviewed existing innovation opportunities and processes, he realized the need for an innovation management system. The then current approach was ad hoc, which worked when the company was smaller. Yet as Midtronics grew, many ideas were lost. For example, on the drive back to the airport and while waiting for a flight home after a customer visit, countless ideas would spontaneously emerge in lively conversation among the sales, marketing, and technical team members. While some ideas would fly, Jason realized that many others were just forgotten "in the bottom of a beer glass at the airport." Midtronics experienced an embarrassment of riches, one of the "hazards" of working with insightful, curious, creative colleagues. It wasn't that they were bad ideas. There just were not always the time or resources to pursue them as suggested.

In response, Jason established an internal phase-gate-like process—separate from, but feeding Midtronics' existing new product development and business development phase-gate processes—to capture the large flow of innovative ideas.

The process comprises two phases. The first phase is to capture and document every idea. Easy to implement, submissions take the form of an email, with just a sentence or two addressing each of three topics:

- Describe the idea or application.
- What is the impact on the customer or market?
- What is the impact on Midtronics?

While simple in form, this approach requires those submitting proposals to give thought to impact. This is a low but essential bar, a hurdle that challenges and develops anyone submitting an idea to give it more than passing thought.

The second phase is to explore ideas. Teams review proposals, perhaps grouping some that have merit. Next, an individual or small group is assigned to develop a simple business case addressing three topics:

- Is it feasible?
- Can we sell it?
- Is there a market for it?

Those ideas that pass this gate feed Midtronics' new product development phase-gate process, converting ideas into products and products into new business.

Equally important as its value to capture and vet ideas is that Jason established this process to identify potential customer needs, not only current customer problems. While a change for Midtronics, it is well justified by the volatile, uncertain, complex, and ambiguous nature of the emergent industries they serve. Midtronics is not getting out over its skis, getting ahead of itself. Instead, it is willing to judiciously take on some risk now to be prepared to strike when clear customer needs appear later.

The core team that collaborated so successfully over the past few decades, now joined by an emerging next generation of innovation leaders, today even more intentionally works together to move Midtronics into new business opportunities. While not disclosing currently confidential company information about specific customer needs and Midtronics' response, the team continues to pursue, embrace, understand, and solve customer problems precisely as depicted in the stories shared earlier. Midtronics relentlessly renews its industry and the basis of competition, all the while pivoting as new opportunities dictate.

The Unmistakable Patterns

So, what patterns emerge in these stories? Let's explore them in the context of this book's logical flow and critical teachings.

Midtronics grasps The Case for Innovation (Chapter 1).

As demonstrated by the numerous stories shared here, Midtronics has a proven track record of innovation investment and success, not only surviving but thriving as it renews its business and industry. Midtronics proves that an ambidextrous view of business management, focusing on both operations and innovation, the present and the future, can be embraced with considerable financial success.

Midtronics employs Design Thinking (Chapter 2) naturally.

In each story, we see that Midtronics is customer-focused, not a product-centric company. Marketing and customer service represent core company strengths, with a robust engineering capability insightfully addressing customer needs. When a customer asks, "Can you help us?" Kevin instinctively replies, "What can you tell us about your problem?" rather than "What do you want?" While anybody can ask customers what they want, the Midtronics team spends considerable time deeply understanding their underlying needs. Such curiosity is further illustrated by Jason, who encourages engineers and software developers to "go and hang out at a nearby customer's service area to experience it." They gain significant insight from such informal engagement as well as meaning in their work.

Further, the Midtronics team generates ideas, many of them, as they probe customer demand. And as part of this effort, they create prototypes for customers to interact with. As Steve points out, Kevin can quickly prototype something to show a customer, creatively using what's commonly available to make a working device. Engaging in this way provides insight as to how customers react to and interact with new ideas. Steve sees this approach of trying out ideas and constantly iterating as orders of magnitude more valuable than only having something to talk about with customers.

Finally, the team accepts the kind of risk characteristic of design thinking. Not unnecessary risk. Not foolish risk. But the appropriate risk necessary to innovate.

Design thinking is part of Midtronics' DNA.

Midtronics understands and pursues Emotional Design (Chapter 3).
Midtronics' products are intentionally designed with the shop technician in mind, giving them a product with a look and feel, in addition to performance, that technicians are proud to use. The product designers seek a truly "pleasurable" experience for end-users.

Midtronics has been most successful when both attentive to customer needs and solving customers' problems with proprietary, revolutionary products. Midtronics communicates this excellence by bringing its technical expertise and experts to the forefront, where others regularly leave engineers and software developers behind.

Further, the partnerships that Midtronics establishes with customers are remarkable, adding to their emotional experience. When Midtronics makes mistakes, they make things right. And if a customer asks for something that is not in their best interest, the Midtronics team has talked companies out of buying what they asked for. It isn't every day that you experience the kind of integrity they demonstrate and the respect they offer.

Midtronics effectively deploys multiple Innovation Processes and Tools (Chapter 4).
The Midtronics team relies on effective processes and tools, developing those individuals who are new to innovation as well as refreshing their experts' memories.

They employ simple, easy-to-implement phase-gate processes to capture and evaluate new ideas, develop new products, and create new business.

They have practiced open innovation from the start, basing their initial business on proprietary technology developed at a university and continuing to collaborate with the inventor for many years.

They use lean innovation, working with "lead customers" like Karl, Dennis, and David, as they develop new products. The team gets close to these people to encourage them to discuss their problems, allowing Midtronics to solve those problems. Steve readily acknowledges the benefit of working with such individuals. As he notes, "There is no champion like a convert, your toughest challenger, as they are the ones who care."

Finally, they create roadmaps to guide and communicate their plans for the future.

Midtronics employs The Innovators and Those Who Manage Them (Chapter 5).

Kevin is a proven Serial Innovator. He comfortably collaborates with Jason and others to flexibly team as he seeks to solve customer problems. Further, Steve and now Will "manage" him with insight, partnering rather than dictating, providing him with significant problems to work on and the resources necessary to innovate. They allow him to try things, encouraging his burning curiosity. As Steve says about Kevin, "If I can get you interested in something, you can do it." And they also give him "permission to fail." As Kevin puts it, he often learns by trying things, things that might catastrophically fail in the lab. But he does so realizing that one has to "break a few eggs to make an omelet." This free yet profoundly insightful and focused exploration enables him and the entire team to discover the best path forward.

Consistent with Midtronics "playing the long game," Kevin actively develops others' innovative skills, creating a pipeline of those with the expertise to maintain Midtronics' innovative capability.

Finally, Midtronics practices Strategic Innovation Management (Chapter 6).

Midtronics employs a planning structure appropriate for its industry and market, most closely aligned with the objectives, goals, strategies, measures, tactics (OGSMT) option described in Chapter 6. At the highest level, it takes the following general form:

- *Objective*: Midtronics will lead the way in improving how the world manages batteries.
- *Goals*: Multiyear financial goals are established and reviewed annually.
- *Strategies*: These take the form of the three discussed earlier (grow the current business, grow new business in specific geographic regions, grow new business beyond currently addressed applications).
- *Measures*: Standard financial measures are used to evaluate performance.
- *Tactic*: Deeply understand customer needs to renew the industry with new-to-market solutions.

And just like these planning strategies, Midtronics keeps its innovation strategy simple and straightforward. Yet in some respects, it is precisely this intentional simplicity that makes Midtronics culture so challenging for competitors to copy.

WHAT MIDTRONICS' STORY COULD MEAN FOR YOU

As a final entry in the Midtronics story, we share Steve McShane's Founding Philosophy in Table 7.1. Steve began reflecting on the philosophies that formed the basis for Midtronics' growth and success in the 2010 time frame. He prepared and released this document at the time of Midtronics' thirty-fifth anniversary as a company in 2019.

Steve's Founding Philosophy represents both a reflection on and a reminder of what brought Midtronics successfully to that point in time and a charge for the future. Compared to many companies' rather generic mission, vision, or value statements, the Founding Philosophy is both real and embraced, as we hope you have observed in their story.

At several points throughout this book, we ask you, our readers, direct questions along the lines of, What would you do? We typically pose these questions in the context of industry renewal, challenges, or opportunities brought on through breakthrough innovation.

TABLE 7.1. Steve McShane's Founding Philosophy that formed the basis for Midtronics' growth and success. Reproduced with permission from Stephen McShane, CEO of Midtronics.

Build trust, collaboration, and teamwork	A competent team is far more important than a product. A great team that operates on the basis of trust and respect can respond to challenges, can invent new products, and will continue to uncover strategic opportunities.
Create customer value with our innovative technologies and exceptional service	From early on we determined that we will never succeed by merely taking orders for commoditized products. We need to continually use our curiosity, our technologies, our base of knowledge, and customer relationships to find ways to add value to our customers by satisfying their needs.
Put quality before profits	It is our obligation to provide our customers with products that satisfy their needs for performance, durability, and quality. This requires careful planning and flawless execution by the entire organization. Sustaining a strong business relationship or partnership built on integrity and quality is far more important than any short-term profit we may gain by cutting corners.
Invest in people and the future of our business	From the beginning, we plowed our profits back into the company. We hire talented people with great attitudes, values, and a desire to be part of a winning team. We invest in new technologies and markets, allowing us to be more responsive than competing companies, thus sustaining our leadership position in the industry.

Here, we take a slightly different approach. Keeping in mind that we address this to all of our audiences—SMME owners, board members, CEOs, presidents or GMs and their leadership teams, innovators, and all other employees—our questions to you now are

- If you compare your company's culture and practices honestly to Midtronics' practiced Founding Philosophy, what do you see? Where do you align? What are the gaps?
- Suppose you pursued a culture and practices similar to those described in Midtronics' story and summarized in their Founding

Philosophy, appropriately tailored to what your industry could become if it led the way forward. What could and would it mean for your company and for you personally?

KEY POINTS AND TAKEAWAYS

- SMMEs that succeed at innovation renew to survive and thrive.
- SMMEs that succeed at innovation effectively manage risk.
- SMMEs that succeed at innovation do so at a reasonable cost because they place small bets early on, increasing their investment only as justified.
- SMMEs that succeed at innovation employ proven methods, such as design thinking and phase-gate processes.
- SMMEs that succeed at innovation are led by and consist of individuals who possess innovative insight and exhibit personal courage in the face of volatility, uncertainty, complexity, and ambiguity.

CHAPTER 8

A Call to Action

"Fate leads the willing and drags along the reluctant."
—Lucius Annaeus Seneca, first-century CE Roman
philosopher, statesman, orator, and tragedian[1]

By now, we hope that—through story and reason—we've convinced you of the need for renewal to survive and thrive. If we've failed, stop reading. There's nothing more we can do for you.

But if you've taken our message to heart, we next hope that you've also understood what is possible and what it takes. Our goal has been to help you see that the type of innovation that leads to renewal is possible with manageable risk and reasonable cost—and that proven methods are available to those with the personal courage and skill necessary to employ them.

This is it, our message in a nutshell. It's all a bit like the children's game of "musical chairs." Will you be ready when the music stops?

With Seneca, in the quote that leads this chapter, we say that fate leads the willing (*those who pursue innovation*) and drags along the reluctant (*those who ignore or reject it*).

So what does this mean for each of our audiences? What is our "call to action" for each?

In the following sections, we first address each of our audiences separately with a message tailored to its role, responsibilities, and potential. Knowing that not all will heed the call, we include words of caution, laying out the dangers and implications of reluctance. Yet, in hope, we encourage each one of you in a way most appropriate for you.

We then close with a message to our entire audience.

OUR MESSAGE TO OWNERS, BOARD MEMBERS, AND CEOS

The question for you is as simple as it was at the beginning of this book: invest in innovation that leads to renewal or not?

If you choose to invest, now you can—*must* (if you hope to succeed)—do so with the low-investment, low-risk, high-value methodologies described herein, led by those you can trust with this critical investment. And here's a great way to start: perform the assessment of Appendix 2, "Assessing Your Company's Innovation Capability"—it's a gap analysis that will help you see what you're doing well and where you need to improve. We're excited for you and your SMME, wishing you the very best in this endeavor as you seek to satisfy investment goals, fulfill customer needs, and create and sustain jobs.

If you choose not to invest or merely to put on a show, you have to accept the consequences. A race to the bottom is never a good strategy. If you want to run that race, you certainly are welcome to do so, all the while hoping that someone else doesn't have an even lower price.[2] It is a strategy, and the volume you might secure in the process helps your costing; there is no doubt you can sell a lot more at a lower price. But keep in mind that many in your SMME will see your actions for what they are.[3] They will know that you're milking the business. They will realize that the clock is ticking; the music is still playing . . . for now. With this knowledge, they will make informed personal decisions about whether to stay or go somewhere else, somewhere with better long-term prospects. You risk losing your next generation of employees—especially potential leaders, as they are the most mobile—before the music stops due to renewal brought about by a competitor. And for each of the next generation that you retain, it will become increasingly expensive as you buy their temporary participation, but not loyalty, out of the ever-smaller margins you generate.

For the sake of all involved, including yourselves, we hope that you choose wisely, neither ignoring innovation nor investing randomly or recklessly. Now the choice is yours.

Respectfully,

Bruce and Walter

OUR MESSAGE TO PRESIDENTS OR GMS AND THEIR LEADERSHIP TEAMS

Yours is a challenging position yet one that is full of opportunity.

Bounded on one side by your SMME's owners, board, and CEO—and on the other side by the company's employees—you are tasked with bridging the two, taking strategic, directional guidance from one and translating it into successful action of the other.

After reading this book, your first act should be to determine whether these two groups independently believe in the potential of the kind of innovation that leads to renewal and continued growth. If so, you're in luck. While the path forward may be challenging, it won't be because you're pushing on immovable objects. So go have fun as you seek to grow the business.

Unfortunately, there are three more-challenging scenarios. Opposition to innovation—either active or passive—may come from either one or both groups. If internal resistance is present and you don't have an existing, agreed-upon plan to work through it, you should wonder why you missed this earlier. Perhaps you only now see the value of the kind of innovation we describe here. Maybe it's a result of insufficient due diligence or wishful thinking on your part during the hiring process. Regardless, you need to consider your options carefully because your time is limited.

If you cannot secure buy-in for innovation, at least at first from the owners, board members, and CEO, your options are few. Perhaps you're at a stage in life where you want to ride it out, hoping that the industry your SMME competes in will survive "long enough" for you to reach retirement. Not entirely satisfying, perhaps, but it's something to consider seriously. However, if you start down that path and you're blindsided by someone else who's chosen to renew the industry . . . well, good luck. Not only will you likely be left out in the economic cold—that is, unless you prenegotiated a "golden parachute"—but you will also have doomed your employees to that fate. And the thought of this should be even less satisfying.

If you succeed in receiving enough of a green light from the owners, their board, and the CEO to explore the kind of innovation we describe here, there is hope. While turning around an organization that doesn't get it when it comes to renewal requires courage, it can be done, at least to the benefit of those who are able and willing to join you down this path. In this book, we've provided you with what you need to move in this direction.

Now, there's one more scenario that we must address. What about the case when *you* do not buy into the idea of investing in the kind of innovation that leads to renewal? This is particularly sad, as it is to no one's benefit. But we will let you in on a little "secret." Our message to those who are skilled and inclined toward innovating (immediately following this note to you) encourages them to *at least take some critical, initial steps* on the path toward the kind of high-value innovation that leads to renewal. As you will see in that note, we do not encourage wasting time or resources. We want what is right for all. Now, before you and your SMME's owner, board members, and CEO think that we're suggesting you abuse their good nature by severely restricting resources for innovation, our message to you is simple: "Don't even think about it." We encourage your company's proven and aspiring innovators to pursue innovation despite your lack of commitment. And if they chose to do what we suggest, they are exhibiting a level of courage and selflessness that you are not. We hope that, by demonstrating some viable paths to renewal, they can convince you that such innovation is worth your time and resources—to the benefit of all.

For the sake of all involved, including yourselves, we hope that you navigate these challenges well. You are in the driver's seat and have been handed the keys. Now, take this company to places not previously thought possible, doing so with the hope of one who enjoys being part of a winner and believes in a new, better future for everyone involved.

In anticipation of great success,

Bruce and Walter

OUR MESSAGE TO THOSE WHO ARE SKILLED
AND INCLINED TOWARD INNOVATING

If you are a proven innovator—one who has successfully renewed the basis of competition for your company and industry, exhibiting some or all of the patterns described here—we hope this book helps others understand and work with you even more effectively than before. If you aspire to innovate on the level we describe in this book, we hope this book helps you identify gaps in your performance that can be remedied with the guidance we provide. For each of you in this audience who is operating with proper company support for innovation, we say, "Go do it! Enjoy and be grateful for the opportunity you have received; make the most of it."

But for those of you lacking company support for innovation, we have a special message: you or a small group of you still just might be able to pull off something big for your SMME. As we've illustrated throughout, there are relatively low-investment, low-risk methodologies that you can employ to *at least take some critical, initial steps* on the path toward the kind of high-value innovation that leads to renewal. Make no mistake; we are not suggesting that you go off and "play" while not fulfilling your work commitments. We do not want anyone to believe that what we are saying here is a license to ignore the expectations of those who pay your salary or to whom you report. But what we are suggesting is that—at times and in ways that do not violate the terms and spirit of your employment—you dig deeper, seek to understand customer needs more intimately, question unarticulated assumptions, consider alternatives, generate ideas, and try out some ideas. If you're getting your job done, accomplishing what is expected of you, then here's your chance. This is *precisely* what Griffin, Price, and Vojak observed from Serial Innovators in countless companies.[4] The Serial Innovators often operated as something of an *informal* skunkworks, exploring and trying out ideas until they were sufficiently developed and validated to bring forward, to see the light of day. And there's absolutely no reason why you can't do it where you are. That is unless you choose not to do so. And how satisfying will that be?

We guarantee that none of you proven and aspiring innovators will regret trying. You will have given it your best. And if you identify truly viable, potentially high-impact opportunities that your employer fails to act on, realize at that moment that your company may never embrace real innovation, eventually placing its existence and your job at risk. If your employer is averse to or incapable of exploring or succeeding at renewal, knowing so will help you consider your career options before the inevitable occurs.

For the sake of all involved, including yourselves, we hope that you accept these challenges. You can make things happen that others cannot. Do so assertively, yet humbly, knowing that you are a servant to all.

In anticipation of hearing exciting stories of your success,
Bruce and Walter

OUR MESSAGE TO THOSE WHO ARE SKILLED AND INCLINED TOWARD OPTIMIZING THE EXISTING BUSINESS

Yours are important roles, just as important as those of anyone else in the SMME. With your skill and buy-in, the company can succeed. Without it, either you or the company will fail.

Hopefully, you've seen in our book how to implement innovation in SMMEs successfully. Regardless of whether you are in production, design, engineering, finance, sales, marketing, human resources, or some other function, it should help you understand and collaborate most effectively with those around you who make innovation happen. Doing so will increase the likelihood of your company and your job surviving and thriving through difficult times.

Unfortunately, while many in your roles embrace and contribute significantly to the kind of innovation that leads to renewal, we often find three types of people who do not: the unable, the inflexible, and the unwilling. Someone can help those in the first two categories. They can do nothing for those in the third once the unwilling have made up their mind to resist.

The unable lack either the aptitude or skill to contribute. To the extent that training or mentorship are available, they can be suitable investments, if time permits, to help the unable come up to speed.

The inflexible are typically very good at what they do, often expert. Yet they strictly apply the tenets of their trade, even at times when it is inappropriate to do so. The production engineer needing to work out all the details before the new product concept is defined is just one example. Earnest? Yes. But helpful at the time when you are probing the market and exploring options? Often not. Fortunately, the inflexible can be helped. Such wisdom can be developed, but it takes the time and attention of those who know better to guide in this direction.

Finally, the unwilling block progress either actively or passively. At times, they are the ones who raise countless objections in meetings, stalling discussion, and are never satisfied with the answers received. Others are those who just never seem to get around to doing what's necessary to help advance innovation investments. While it may take some time to recognize the unwilling—and we encourage patience before declaring anyone as unwilling—they and those like them are pernicious to an organization seeking renewal. We cannot emphasize enough that the unwilling are the ones who are best removed from an organization, and quickly once seen for their unwillingness. For everyone's sake, including their own, the unwilling are best suited somewhere else where they can most appropriately contribute. Anything less is a costly mistake.

For the sake of all those with skill and buy-in who are involved, including yourselves, we hope that you accept your essential yet often unrecognized role. You can help make things happen that others cannot. Do so in a way such that everyone wins.

Know that—while unheralded—your role is just as important as those of the others,

Bruce and Walter

OUR CLOSING MESSAGE TO ALL

Either you embrace the kind of innovation we've described, or you do not. One of the great features of the free market is that it's your choice. We desire that you choose wisely.

We hope you've found that we not only made your options clear and the opportunity made available by innovation compelling but also provided you with what you need to succeed.

We've pulled no punches and hope you understand. Holding back would only sugarcoat the significance of what each one of you faces. We know because we've been there.

Our best wishes to all for what can be an exciting, fulfilling, hopeful opportunity for those who make no excuses and heed this call.

With great hope for your and your SMME's future,

Bruce and Walter

Herbst and Herbst Design Thinking Phase-Gate Process

To help our audience understand how to implement the design thinking methodology and a simple phase-gate process, in this appendix we provide additional detail behind the Herbst and Herbst Design Thinking Phase-Gate Process appearing as Figure 2.1 and summarized in Table 4.1.

PHASE 0: RESEARCH

Summary: Synthesize end-user and competitor insights.

Description: The starting point for every project requires not only an understanding of those you are designing for but an understanding of what the competition is doing. This effort is directed at the end-user "needs," not at the client "wants," where the client is the sponsor of the project but not the user. Clients are just that—those individuals who direct the development. The product requirements document becomes the contractual agreement between the client and the creative team ensuring an understanding, from a user perspective, of what they would like rather than developing any preliminary specifications, as those come later. The design team then creates a series of statements noting what a product "should have" and/or "should be," but not as a specification. The team uses this end-user information to define the parameters of the program.

Output: Product requirement document

PHASE 1: VISIONING

Summary: Generate insights by looking to external trends and inspiration, as well as technical architecture.

Description: Visioning is defined as visually supporting images that surround the design team, to ensure adherence to the end-users' aspirational images of themselves and/or their surroundings. In other words, the design team attempts to capture the end-users' feelings of who they think themselves to be. They may not live in a luxury New York apartment, but they believe they "should" or "could" and thus deserve a certain level of design sophistication in the item they will be purchasing, if one is dealing with something related to the home. This visioning keeps the creative team on the emotional edge to ensure that their final effort reflects the emotional feelings of the end-user. For ultimate success, this activity includes a broad spectrum overall, of colors, finishes, and materials supporting an appropriate aesthetic. To capture the basic DNA of the end-user, the team will create and surround themselves with visuals to ensure constant attention to the final direction.

Output: Framed problem

PHASE 2: CONCEPTS

Summary: Brainstorm, breadboard, and develop concepts.

Description: Preliminary ideations are developed as concept sketches based on team brainstorming to ensure full exploration of the subject. Concept sketches are normally done using computer-generated programs and represent various options that should be tested and/or reviewed. Complementing the sketch concepts, the team will develop preliminary physical mockups to confirm the final iterations will be workable.

Output: Product concept 1.0 (the first iteration of the product)

PHASE 3: REVIEW

Summary: Refine product concept 1.0 iteratively, develop product image or story.

Description: An internal review with the core team of developers to include the marketing team will direct continued development of multiple concepts and directions. Supporting that, continued development of end-user personas will be included to ensure absolute targeting.

Output: Product concept 2.0 (the second iteration of the product)

PHASE 4: RESEARCH

Summary: Test and validate product concept 2.0.

Description: Multiple directions chosen by the total team will be presented to viable candidates. Viable candidates are those who have purchased this category of goods and/or will be purchasing within this category. Those candidates will include gatekeepers and end-users to ensure validation of a final selected direction.

Output: Product concept 3.0 based on end-user response.

PHASE 4B: CONFIRM CHANNEL

Summary: Test and validate product concept 3.0 proposed distribution channel.

Description: One should always appreciate the channel of distribution for success. This channel can be based on existing channels and or new channels, whether they be online or through brick and mortar. Once it is understood who the retailers should be, to include online, it is always wise to confirm at the highest level possible the actual future commitment. This confirmation ensures success in distribution and gives final confirmation to your channel and the retailer. Minor modifications may be required for ultimate success, to include packaging and/or color modifications to differentiate stock-keeping units between retailers.

Output: Confirmed distribution channel

PHASE 5: DEVELOP

Summary: Complete engineering release "Alpha" to commercialize product concept 3.0.

Description: Final engineering documentation will culminate in a one-off "looks like/works like" Alpha prototype to confirm final engineering. The one-off Alpha replicates every component and allows for preliminary testing and ensuring of final engineering. While the Alpha allows for production release, it is not unusual that initial production release will run "Betas," which by definition are based on single cavity tooling—providing quick, inexpensive turnaround—prior to full production runs.

Output: Alpha product release

PHASE 6: RESEARCH RELEASE

Summary: Confirm with targeted market.

Description: Prior to full tooling release, final end-user research needs to be completed to ensure capital costs will net out with profitable results. This final end-user research confirms that no changes have occurred in the market and that the final product will meet the anticipated demand.

Output: Commercialized product

APPENDIX 2
Assessing Your Company's Innovation Capability

To support our audiences' innovation efforts, we provide a comprehensive assessment tool designed to be implemented by anyone possessing reasonably good insight regarding the SMME under consideration. Ideally, this tool will be applied periodically by those most senior in the organization—owners, board members, CEO, and president or GM and their leadership team—as a means of identifying and closing capability gaps. It can also serve a useful purpose when conducted, typically informally, by someone deeper within the company to bring to light gaps that have been dismissed or ignored, which must be addressed to succeed at innovation.

The comprehensive assessment tool comprises eight individual assessments, as follows:

1. Strategy
2. Financing
3. Design thinking and emotional design
4. Innovation processes and tools
5. People

6. Culture
7. Organization
8. Results

STRATEGY ASSESSMENT

To assess your company's innovation strategy, you need to consider both companywide and innovation-specific strategies.

For your companywide and innovation-specific strategies, it is helpful to begin by describing what you have in place for both. And if there are multiple strategies, identify and describe each. Digging deeper, you will want to identify what policies and processes are in place to develop your companywide and innovation strategies, including commenting on how closely they are followed. In particular, you will want to know who establishes these strategies and how and when they are established in practice. You also will want to know who approves these strategies and how and when they are approved in practice. Finally, it is critical to understand the extent to which your innovation strategies align with and cascade from your companywide strategies, as discussed in Chapter 6.

By reflecting on responses to these questions and how uniformly everyone answers them, you will gain insight into whether your company possesses strategic clarity and alignment relative to innovation.

FINANCING ASSESSMENT

Two organizational levels of innovation investment are appropriately considered when assessing your company's innovation capability: companywide annual innovation investment and investment at the specific innovation project level.

Questions should be asked regarding how *companywide annual innovation investment objectives and budgets are set.* For the companywide innovation objectives, these questions should include identifying the overall financial objective for innovation, being explicit in terms of financial metrics such as revenue growth, profitability, return on investment, and so on; any nonfinancial objectives, again being explicit; who sets the objectives and how they are set; who must be made aware of these objectives; and how the objectives are communicated. For the companywide annual innovation budgets, these questions can include identifying who sets these budgets, how they are set, and what investment portfolio you seek in terms of balancing risk and reward. Collectively, these questions help you see whether you have rationally considered your annual innovation investment budgeting process and established means to implement it.

Similar questions should be raised about how *specific innovation project financial hurdles are set and investment decisions are made*. For specific innovation project financial hurdles, these questions should include identifying the policies and processes in place to support specific innovation project investment decision making, how closely are they followed, and how specific innovation project investment decisions are made and who has authority to make them. Collectively, these questions help you see whether you have rationally considered your specific innovation project investments and established means to implement them.

DESIGN THINKING AND EMOTIONAL DESIGN ASSESSMENT

A good place to start when assessing your company's capabilities associated with methodologies such as design thinking and emotional design is to conduct simple assessments regarding both the extent that your company employs them and how effectively your company employs them. After a careful rereading of Chapters 2 and 3, these can be scored to ensure a firm grasp on the concepts by applying a simple seven-level Likert scale to the descriptions provided in those chapters. Then, to the extent that your company does not score a "7" on these questions, you need to probe the gap deeply, asking such questions as, "Why is this the case?" "Is everyone satisfied with this situation?" "Why are some, but not others satisfied?" and "How do you plan to eliminate the gap?" One of the more critical assessments should include the questions, "Using that same Likert scale, does management recognize that failures are acceptable as long as there are learnings?" and "Are post-mortems standard operating procedures?"

INNOVATION PROCESSES AND TOOLS ASSESSMENT

Similar to assessing your company's capabilities associated with methodologies, it is crucial to evaluate your company's capabilities related to innovation processes and tools, such as phase-gate process, lean innovation, open innovation,

2x2 matrices, and product and technology roadmaps. Again, it is appropriate to conduct simple assessments regarding the extent that your company employs them and how effectively your company employs them. After a careful re-reading of Chapter 4, these can also be scored to ensure a firm grasp of the concepts by applying a seven-level Likert scale to each of the descriptions provided in that chapter. As before, to the extent that you do not score your company with a "7" on these questions, you need to probe the gap more deeply, asking, "Why is this the case?" "Is everyone satisfied with this situation?" "Why are some, but not others satisfied?" and "How do you plan to eliminate the gap?"

PEOPLE ASSESSMENT

The skill and attitudes of four categories of people should be assessed to ensure both capability and alignment:

- Owners, board members, and CEO
- President or GM and their leadership team
- Those who are skilled and inclined toward innovating (including those who aspire to be skilled innovators)
- Those who are skilled and inclined toward optimizing the existing business

As a reminder, these four categories of those working in or with SMMEs comprise our primary audiences.

While questions raised with and about the *owners, board members, and CEO* are essentially identical to those to be raised with and about the *presidents or GMs and their leadership teams*, these two groups should be assessed separately to evaluate the strength of and alignment between them. Each individual should share their personal perspective relative to innovation (their role, strategy, priorities, expectations, and appropriate investment levels). Each should address whether, or to what extent, they support investment in innovation that leads to renewal. Assessment involves considering whether or not individuals in each group possess similar understanding and perspectives as others in this group and whether the two groups hold a shared overall view. Gaps in innovation-related insight may also be revealed in this portion of the assessment.

For *those who are skilled and inclined toward innovating*, begin by listing and describing all *past innovations* for which they were a key contributor or had primary responsibility, from ideation through production, that resulted in successful commercialization or great learnings. Address questions such as, "What is the "story"?" "How did their innovation have an impact on the industry and the company?" "What has been the financial impact for the company?" and "Would we classify this as incremental innovation, working within the existing paradigm, or breakthrough innovation, renewing the basis of competition in the industry?"

It is critical to be painfully honest with all responses, as answers to these questions often do not align with behavior and results associated with the high standard of a proven innovator that we share in this book. This is no time to be inappropriately generous in your assessment, as the sustained livelihood of all is at stake.

Next, and again for *those who are skilled and inclined toward innovating*, list and describe all *current innovation investment projects* for which they are recognized as a key contributor or having primary responsibility. As before, address questions such as, "How do we expect this innovation investment to have an impact on the industry and the company?" "What strategic competitive advantage might we gain if this innovation investment is successful?" "How well protected with resulting intellectual property might our advantage be if this innovation investment is successful?" "What do we expect will be the financial impact for the company?" and "Would we classify this as an incremental innovation project, working within the existing paradigm, or as breakthrough innovation, renewing the basis of competition in the industry?"

With these questions, we seek to determine whether the allocation of people and resources is appropriate for what those at the executive level seek to accomplish in their objective-based planning exercise. As depicted in the far right column of Table A2.1 (Strong Renew), a solid portfolio might comprise 10 percent of your innovation expertise and investment addressing potential breakthrough innovation, with 30 percent addressing new platform innovation, and 60 percent improving the existing business with incremental innovation. Unfortunately, too often this is not the case. Instead, 100 percent of the innovation expertise and investment is applied to prop up the existing, mature business continuously (middle column of Table A2.1, Extend), optimizing within the paradigm, or, at best, a portion is diverted to create new platforms (column to the right of center in Table A2.1, Renew).

Further, using this portion of the overall assessment, you must ask whether the right people are tasked with platform or breakthrough innovation opportunities. No one is served if those assigned to these opportunities are incapable of delivering. Again, difficult questions must be asked and answered. To help answer these questions, you can assess individuals on the basis of the Serial Innovator characteristics discussed in Chapter 5, how effectively they engage with problems, projects, business, and people. You can score these by applying the same seven-level Likert scale described earlier in this assessment. To the extent that gaps in innovation expertise are revealed, appropriate development plans may be developed and implemented.

For *those inclined toward innovating but who are not yet skilled or proven*—those who aspire to be innovators from whom you've observed potential—their performance should be carefully tracked over time to ensure that they are on the path to proving themselves with repeated, increasingly significant commercial success. For each aspiring innovator, conduct simple assessments regarding how effectively they engage with problems, projects, business, and people as described in Chapter 5. Again, this can be performed by applying the same simple seven-level Likert scale to their effectiveness. Finally, for those aspiring innovators, this part of your assessment can conclude with an evaluation of how satisfied you are with your portfolio of innovators today and how you are preparing a future portfolio of innovators by developing a pipeline. In addition to the expertise defined previously, you might also look at their role as innovators. Are they creators of a new future, or continuous improvers, problem preventers, or problem solvers?[1] All are important, but knowing their role is equally critical for an innovation strategy. To the extent that these analyses expose gaps, plans should be developed to eliminate them. To the extent possible and appropriate, match proven innovators with aspiring innovators to guide their personal development.

Turning to *those who are skilled and inclined toward optimizing the existing business*, it is again helpful to determine their individual perspectives

TABLE A2.1. The four core capabilities and the five SMME categories of competitiveness, originally appearing as Table 1.1, used to illustrate what a solid innovation investment portfolio might look like (Strong Renew) in contrast to less effective options (Extend and Renew).

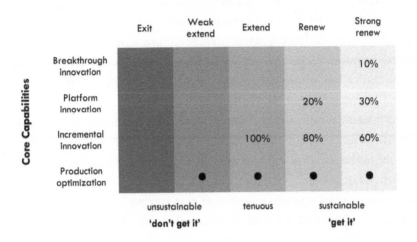

relative to innovation (their role, strategy, priorities, expectations, appropriate investment) and the extent that they support investment in innovation that leads to renewal. Often this is anecdotal, on the basis of observed behavior. For example, for each individual identified as part of this group, it is helpful to describe specific situations when their behavior either supported or impeded innovation investments. Impeding an innovation investment includes any actions that slow progress toward commercialization. Then, for those behaviors that supported innovation investments, ask yourself what has or can be done to reinforce such behavior. And for those behaviors that impeded innovation investments, ask yourself what has or can be done to discourage such behavior.

Finally, for our discussion of people, it is essential to accept that, at times, extensive change is necessary to ensure success. While rarely easy, those in any role who do not accept or, worse, either actively or passively impede innovation investment that leads to renewal may best be removed from the organization. Similarly, if you assess the behaviors of owners, board members, CEO, and president or GM and their leadership team and find them lacking sufficient commitment to the kind of renewal that leads a company to survive and thrive, you may be best served looking elsewhere for work.

CULTURE ASSESSMENT

The focus of your culture assessment is to determine how well the company manages the tension between an optimization (within the current paradigm) culture and a renewal-friendly culture, as depicted in Table 6.1. Here the question is less one of "Where are you on the spectrum between an optimization (within the current paradigm) and a renewal-friendly culture?" and more one of "How effectively can all functions within the company operate at each end of the spectrum?" This distinction is significant because there truly are times when portions of your business must focus on one or the other yet still be able to pivot quickly to the opposite position as necessary.

When conducting this assessment, you can perform it on functional groups or individuals, or both. For example, those in manufacturing operations require great discipline to ensure the lowest-cost, most reliable, most reproducible, highest-quality output. Yet when tasked with ramping production on a new-to-industry product—one that the company intends to use to renew the basis of competition—these same people must be poised to act quickly, assume risk, and be open to learning that just might arise through at least temporary failure. While large companies may have the luxury to establish separate operations, SMMEs often do not. That said, the great satisfaction gained by successfully navigating a challenge such as this can make working in an SMME a rewarding and exhilarating experience.

ORGANIZATION ASSESSMENT

For this portion of the overall assessment, you want to ask questions about where innovation is organizationally located within the company and why it has been placed there.

If the innovation investment is segregated from the current business, you should probe the reasoning behind it. Since such a decision is usually motivated by the existing, core business's inability to work seamlessly with those implementing an innovation investment, it is worth pursuing other options. These other approaches should include addressing weaknesses in the current business.

To the extent that the units tasked with implementing the company's innovation investment possess responsibility without authority, this should be noted in the assessment. A not unusual example of this is to assign responsibility for innovation to engineering organizations, yet to have sales and marketing organizations retain control of customer engagement. Inevitably, those in engineering find their access to customers limited, at best. While those inexperienced in overseeing innovation investments often do not identify this as an organizational barrier, it can block any opportunity for success, resulting in significant wasted time and resources.

RESULTS ASSESSMENT

We end this comprehensive assessment with a deep dive into the results you have experienced in your company to date. Following is a simple yet powerful list of questions:

- What quantitative metrics does your company use to measure innovation success?
- What are the measurable results to date?
- Can you provide a qualitative discussion of the results of your innovation investment?
- What has worked?
- What hasn't worked?
- Are you satisfied with these quantitative and qualitative results?
- If yes, how do you plan to improve on and reinforce them?
- If not, then—based on what you have observed in the other assessments—what changes do you need to make, and how do you plan to implement those?

Glossary

Ambidextrous leadership: Leaders capable of simultaneously optimizing the current business and identifying and developing new, innovative business opportunities.

Ambidextrous organization: Organizations capable of simultaneously optimizing the current business and identifying and developing new, innovative business opportunities.

Ansoff growth options matrix: A 2x2 strategy matrix that depicts four primary growth options (displayed as quadrants) available to any company focusing on new markets and new products: further penetrating existing markets with existing products, developing new markets with current products, creating new products to address existing markets, and diversifying by developing new products to address new markets.

Back end: The shortened form for the back end of innovation.

Back end of innovation: The implementation, idea-developing and -commercializing second of two major, sequential steps of any new product or process development activity. It immediately follows the front end of innovation.

BCG growth-share matrix: A 2x2 strategy matrix that depicts the state of a portfolio of strategic business units on the S-curve. The four quadrants of this 2x2 matric map are high-growth leaders that run the risk of being overtaken (Stars), high-growth followers that run the risk of being left behind (Question Marks), low-growth leaders that are relatively entrenched as they generate cash for a time (Cash Cows), and low-growth followers that are best divested (Dogs).

Breakthrough innovation: An innovation so unique, commercially attractive, and financially successful that it redefines and renews the nature and basis of competition in an industry. Breakthrough innovation moves those working in an industry from one paradigm to another new, unexpected one.

Core competency: A set of capabilities that, collectively, differentiate a company from its competition—broadly and coherently across many or all of its businesses or product offerings—in such a way that it provides a strategic advantage.

Design thinking: A methodology for innovation. Design thinking includes exploring multiple solutions, understanding what drives your customers, understanding and assuming appropriate risk, testing ideas with end-users, and constantly iterating.

Differentiation: One of Porter's three generic strategies. Differentiation involves defining a highly desirable product distinct from that of the competition, yet often proximate in price to competitive products.

Early adopter: Lead customer.

Emergence: The first of three S-curve phases, characterized by the emergence of a product, service, or business in the marketplace. While not limited to entrepreneurial startups, it often is associated with them.

Emotional design: Design that seeks to tap into a customer's simple gut reaction to a product. Emotional design addresses the totality of a product or service, not just the aesthetic of style. It includes but is not limited to ease of use and ease of understanding. It can undoubtedly include "the back room" operations and their impact on customer experience.

Empathy: For innovation, empathy involves profoundly understanding what drives your customers, not just what they say drives them.

End-User: The actual user of the product or service as distinguished from the "buyer" who may be the "gatekeeper" or "customer" sponsoring the item or service. The clarification is critical as only the end-user is qualified for the final judgment that is measured as success or failure in the market.

Exit: One of three strategic options available to a company that reaches maturity. Pursuing this option involves "milking" the business financially while making the minimum investment necessary to sustain it. It ends with either the shutdown or sale of the company or its assets.

Extend maturity: One of three strategic options available to a company that reaches maturity. Pursuing this option involves optimizing production while the most capable also invest in incremental product innovation.

Focus: One of Porter's three generic strategies. Pursuing a focus strategy involves seeking to dominate an otherwise unaddressed niche.

Front end: The shortened form for the front end of innovation.

Front end of innovation: The creative, opportunity-recognizing first of two major, sequential steps of any new product or process development activity.

Fuzzy front end: A significant component of the front end of innovation that deals explicitly with only three variables: the business opportunity plan, which includes a market and financial analysis, a pretechnical evaluation, and competitive research. Such a "fuzzy" view acknowledges the intuitive, creative aspects of innovation and seeks to not overcontrol it. It is also "fuzzy" due to the initial lack of absolute product definition, which emerges over time.

Gate: A point in a phase-gate process at which a decision is made whether to proceed with the product development process.

Growth: The second of three S-curve phases, characterized by the rapid increase in revenue of a product, service, or business. In this phase, a company standardizes and expands operations to meet growing demand.

Incremental innovation: An innovation that extends, as opposed to renews, a company's product portfolio. Incremental innovation occurs within the existing paradigm, the basis for competition within an industry. Examples include launching slightly different new products in existing markets or existing products in new markets.

Industrial design: The practice of designing products and services with the concentration of useability, functionality, manufacturability, and overall aesthetics.

Innovation: The commercialization or actual productive use, based on creativity, of products, processes, services, or business models—commercial use with financial or social impact. It is the reduction to practice of creativity. If it's not in the market or public use, it is not innovation addressing a user's needs.

Innovation funnel: A graphical depiction of innovation that conveys the sense that a relatively large number of untested ideas are winnowed down over time to a manageable and proven set, ready for commercialization.

Lead customer: Customers most likely to engage with the startup early on. Early adopter.

Lean innovation: An approach to reduce waste in the pursuit of innovation. This book introduces lean innovation from two perspectives: the quality community and the entrepreneurial community.

Lean product development: A methodology directed to optimization in reducing time of development, while addressing value and customer needs.

Lean production: A systematic approach to reduce waste in the manufacture of goods.

Lean startup: A concept emerging from the new-business-development aspects of entrepreneurial practice. It emphasizes customer-based wants over speculative product development.

Lean thinking: The application of lean production concepts broadly across various enterprise functions in a company.

Likert scale: A multiple-level analog scale used as part of a qualitative questionnaire. While qualitative, the spacing between individual levels is assumed to be essentially equal. A familiar (seven-level) Likert scale is one in which responses to a question might take the form strongly disagree, disagree, somewhat disagree, neither disagree nor agree, somewhat agree, agree, strongly agree.

Low cost: One of Porter's three generic strategies. Pursuing a low-cost strategy involves competing on the basis of price with a product whose performance is proximate to other competitive products.

Market segmentation: The dividing of a market into subsets of customers sharing common buyer behavior. This could include geography, demographics, psychographics, and behavior.

Mature company: A company that has passed, as recognized in hindsight, an inflection point in the S-curve—upon which revenue growth begins to slow.

Mature enterprise: See mature company.

Maturity: The third of three S-curve phases, characterized by a plateauing of revenue of a product, service, or business. It is recognized in hindsight as being beyond an inflection point in the S-curve—upon which revenue growth begins to slow.

Minimum viable product: The simplest form of a product, possessing the essential features for "lead" customers or early adopters.

Muda: Wasteful activities in a process that neither add value for the customer nor necessarily support those that add value for the customer. Muda is one of the three categories of wasteful practices addressed by lean production.

Mura: A wasteful unevenness of production flow. Mura is one of the three categories of wasteful practices addressed by lean production.

Muri: The wasteful practice of unreasonable work expectations. Muri is one of the three categories of wasteful practices addressed by lean production.

New product and process development process: The general term for any process used to manage and guide the development of new products or processes from idea conception to commercialization. A phase-gate process is an example of such a process.

Objective-based planning: A process used to align the work of everyone in an organization strategically. The alignment occurs by cascading, for example, an objective, goals, strategies, measures, and tactics from the highest level of the company to each group and, in some cases, individual employees.

OGSMT: An objective-based planning option in which objectives, goals, strategies, measures, and tactics are aligned throughout the organization.

OKRs: An objective-based planning option in which objectives and key results are aligned throughout the organization.

Open innovation: A concept that encourages innovators and forward-thinking companies to look outside the company and shed a "not invented here" attitude regarding new ideas and insights.

Paradigm: A standard, shared way of perceiving something. For this book's purposes, it is a standard, shared way in which all those in an industry view a product or the basis of competition. Incremental innovations occur within an existing paradigm, the current basis of competition, while breakthrough innovations move an industry from one paradigm to a new, unexpected one.

Phase: One of a series of increasing investments and activities separated by decisions on whether or not to continue (gates) in a phase-gate process.

Phase-gate process: A "master tool" of innovation, providing discipline when it might otherwise be lacking. In its most basic form, a phase-gate process is a series of increasing investments and activities (phases) separated by decisions on whether or not to continue (gates).

Picket fence: An intellectual property strategy by which a company generates a competitive barrier of multiple patents covering the innovator's inventions. Such a picket fence can be strengthened by protecting both products and processes, even if only products are offered for sale.

Platform innovation: An innovation more impactful on the company and its industry than a single incremental innovation based on the expectation of an ecosystem of continued yet standalone products. It typically involves establishing a defensible base that enables rapid conversion and growth into multiple spinoff products.

Porter's generic strategies: Three distinct, foundational strategies, identified by Harvard Business School professor Michael Porter, used to pursue economies of scale: differentiation, low cost, and focus.

Product and technology roadmaps: A mapping tool that takes the form of a set of concurrent timelines and provides a clear, concise visual summary of and the link between customer requirements and company product and technology development plans over time.

Product development manager: An individual possessing the authority and resources to oversee the development of a new product for some or all of the way from idea conception to commercialization. Product development managers typically serve as project managers who guide the activity through a phase-gate process.

Product requirement document: A document that serves as an internal-to-company contract. The requirements allow all to understand what that product or service should do.

Project portfolio mapping: The use of a 2x2 matrix to visualize and communicate investment allocations over time as well as potentially varying technologies. Those using such a map can determine whether their investments are appropriately balanced and aligned with company strategy.

Renew or renewal: One of three strategic options available to a company that reaches maturity. Succeeding at this option results in redefining the basis of competition in your industry. It restarts S-curve growth and competitively sets apart those who prevail.

S-curve: The typical shape of the revenue versus time curve for a product, service, or business—from emergence, through growth, to maturity.

Serial Innovator: A cutting-edge thinker who repeatedly creates and delivers breakthrough innovations in a large, mature organization.

Small- and medium-sized mature enterprise (SMME): A company small- to medium-sized due to it having annual revenue up to several hundred million dollars and mature due to it having passed, as recognized in hindsight, an inflection point in the S-curve—upon which revenue growth begins to slow.

SMME: Abbreviation for small- and medium-sized mature enterprise.

Stage: Terminology used for a (phase-gate process) phase in a Stage-Gate process.

Stage-Gate process: A type of phase-gate process introduced and developed by Robert Cooper.

Strategy: A broad philosophy followed while attempting to accomplish those objectives and goals. Strategy ties a company's vision, objectives, and goals to its day-to-day activities.

2x2 matrices: Simple schematics used variously in strategic planning to visualize, communicate, and stimulate discussion on the most salient and critical issues under consideration. They reduce a problem to two questions, resulting in four quadrants, each depicting a very different strategic scenario.

Visceral: Relating to the internal feelings one experiences in response to an external stimulus.

V2MOM: An objective-based planning option in which a vision, values, methods, obstacles, and measures are aligned throughout the organization.

White space mapping: The use of a 2x2 matrix to map unaddressed yet potentially desirable product price-performance characteristics. Companies can often recognize a new product opportunity by locating competing products on a map of feature desirability versus price.

Notes

FRONTMATTER

1. Samuel Johnson, *The Rambler*, no. 178, Saturday, November 30, 1751. https://www.johnsonessays.com/the-rambler/no-178-many-advantages-not-to-be-enjoyed-together/.

PREFACE AND ACKNOWLEDGMENTS

1. Craig Calcaterra, "Opening Day 2019: 'Everybody Has a Plan Until They Get Punched in the Mouth,'" NBC Sports, March 28, 2019, https://mlb.nbcsports.com/2019/03/28/opening-day-2019-everybody-has-a-plan-until-they-get-punched-in-the-mouth/. Tyson drew on a similar saying by Joe Louis as a nod when he offered this response to a reporter's question about his fight plan for Evander Holyfield; it is widely recognized as one of Tyson's most famous quotes.

2. "#26 Oakland Athletics," *Forbes*, accessed March 1, 2021, https://www.forbes.com/teams/oakland-athletics/?sh=4894df3626ac.

3. Michael Lewis, *Moneyball: The Art of Winning an Unfair Game* (New York: W. W. Norton, 2003).

INTRODUCTION

1. William J. Baumol, *Good Capitalism, Bad Capitalism, and the Economics of Growth and Prosperity* (New Haven, CT: Yale University Press, 2007), 228.

2. "Your Automation Advantage," Wes-Tech Automation Solutions, accessed March 1, 2021, https://wes-tech.com/.

3. The Wes-Tech story was developed through a series of private communications with John Veleris, George Garifalis, and Jason Arends between 2016 and 2021. Providing leadership in factory automation since 1976, Wes-Tech designs, builds, and implements innovative automation solutions across a wide variety of industries. For full disclosure, Bruce serves on JVA Partners' advisory board. JVA Partners owns Wes-Tech.

4. The term *VUCA* is widely attributed to the United States Army. For additional information about its meaning, see Nathan Bennet and G. James Lemoine, "What VUCA Really Means for You," *Harvard Business Review* (January–February 2014): 27–37; and Jeroen Kraaijenbrink, "What Does VUCA Really Mean?" *Forbes*, December 19, 2018, accessed March 1, 2021, https://www.forbes.com/sites/jeroenkraaijenbrink/2018/12/19/what-does-vuca-really-mean/.

5. "Creating Value," JVA Partners, accessed March 1, 2021, https://jvapartners.com/. Founded in 1998, metro-Chicago-based JVA Partners is an operationally focused private investment firm. For full disclosure, Bruce serves on JVA Partners's board of directors.

CHAPTER 1

1. "We Believe in a Better Way," OXO, accessed March 1, 2021, https://www.oxo.com/aboutus.

2. Roberto A. Ferdman, "Baby Carrots Are Not Baby Carrots," *The Washington Post*, January 13, 2016, https://www.washingtonpost.com/news/wonk/wp/2016/01/13/no-one-understands-baby-carrots/.

3. Charles A. O'Reilly III and Michael L. Tushman, "The Ambidextrous Organization," *Harvard Business Review* (April 2004): 74–81.

4. Michael L. Tushman, Wendy K. Smith, and Andy Binns, "The Ambidextrous CEO," *Harvard Business Review* (June 2011): 74–80.

CHAPTER 2

1. Daniel H. Pink, *A Whole New Mind: Why Right-Brainers Will Rule the Future* (New York: Riverhead Books, 2005), 1.

2. Herbert A. Simon, *The Sciences of the Artificial* (Cambridge, MA: The MIT Press, 1969), 20.

3. Jeanne Liedtka, "Why Design Thinking Works," *Harvard Business Review* (September–October 2018): 72–79.

4. Marne Levine, "The No-Filter Leadership Style of Instagram COO Marne Levine," *Fast Company*, November 17, 2017, https://www.fastcompany.com/40491509/the-no-filter-leadership-style-of-instagram-coo-marne-levine.

5. Oregon State University Libraries Special Collections & Archives Research Center, "Clarifying Three Widespread Quotes," *The Pauling Blog*, October 8, 2008, https://paulingblog.wordpress.com/2008/10/28/clarifying-three-widespread-quotes/.

6. Adam Grant, *Originals: How Non-Conformists Move the World* (New York: Viking, 2016), 34.

7. Jon Kolko, "Design Thinking Comes of Age," *Harvard Business Review* (September 2015): 66–71.

8. Shahram Heshmat, "What Is Confirmation Bias?" *Psychology Today*, April 23, 2015, https://www.psychologytoday.com/us/blog/science-choice/201504/what-is-confirmation-bias.

9. *Encyclopaedia Britannica*, s.v. "Dean Kamen: American Inventor," accessed March 1, 2021, https://www.britannica.com/biography/Dean-Kamen.

10. Randall S. Wright, "Connecting to the Counterculture: The Interview Guide," *Research-Technology Management* 60, no. 5 (September–October 2017): 52–54.

11. David Dunning, Chip Heath, and Jerry M. Suls, "Flawed Self-Assessment: Implications for Health, Education and the Workplace," *Psychological Science in the Public Interest* 5, no. 3 (2004): 69–106.

12. Grant, *Originals*, 42.

13. Robert I. Sutton, "If You're the Boss, Start Killing More Good Ideas," *Harvard Business Review*, August 27, 2010, https://hbr.org/2010/08/if-youre-the-boss-start-killin.

14. Justin Berg, "Balancing on the Creative Highwire: Forecasting the Success of Novel Ideas in Organizations," *Administrative Science Quarterly* 61, no. 3 (2016): 433–468.

15. Slice, "About Slice," accessed March 1, 2021, https://www.sliceproducts.com/content/about-slice.

16. Cory Levins, "Box Cutter Safety Tips to Follow," Air Sea Containers, October 15, 2017, https://www.airseacontainers.com/blog/box-cutter-safety-tips/.

17. TJ Scimone, private conversation, September 2020.

18. For further information on the "voice of the customer," see Abbie Griffin and John R. Hauser, "The Voice of the Customer," *Marketing Science* 12, no. 3 (1993): 1–27; and Steven P. Gaskin et al., "Voice of the Customer," *Wiley International Encyclopedia of Marketing*, December 15, 2010, https://doi.org/10.1002/9781444316568.wiem05020.

19. Agile Alliance, "Manifesto for Agile Software Development," accessed November 19, 2021, https://agilemanifesto.org/.

CHAPTER 3

1. Alissa L. Russ et al., "The Science of Human Factors: Separating Fact from Fiction," *BMJ Quality and Safety* 22, no. 10 (2013): 802–808, http://dx.doi.org/10.1136/bmjqs-2012-001450.

2. "Royal ROY 1062—Peeler, Stainless Steel," JES Restaurant Equipment, accessed March 1, 2021, https://www.jesrestaurantequipment.com/royal-roy1062.html.

3. "Swivel Peeler," OXO, accessed March 1, 2021, https://www.oxo.com/swivel-peeler.html.

4. "OXO Swivel Peeler," Target, accessed March 1, 2021, https://www.target.com/p/oxo-swivel-peeler/-/A-13567836.

5. Braun, "Braun History: In Depth," December 2014, https://www.braun.de/assets/de-de/pdf/braun-history.pdf. Braun's story was developed from material found in this white paper.

6. Company Histories, "Braun GmbH," accessed March 1, 2021, https://www.company-histories.com/Braun-GmbH-Company-History.html.

7. Michael Sliwinski, "10 Design Principles by Dieter Rams," accessed March 1, 2021, https://sliwinski.com/designed/.

8. *Objectified*, directed by Gary Hustwit (Brooklyn, NY: Plexi Productions, 2009).

9. Walter Isaacson, *Steve Jobs* (New York: Simon & Schuster, 2011), 387.

10. Amrutha Gayathri, "Steve Jobs' Personal Life: His Idiosyncrasies, Likes and Dislikes," *International Business Times*, October 8, 2011, https://www.ibtimes.com/steve-jobs-personal-life-his-idiosyncrasies-likes-dislikes-322098.

11. Rob Walker, "The Guts of a New Machine," *New York Times*, November 30, 2003, https://www.nytimes.com/2003/11/30/magazine/the-guts-of-a-new-machine.html.

12. David Derbyshire, "His Goal Was to Make It Simple to Use and a Joy to Look At. He Succeeded. The Result Was the iPod," *The Telegraph*, November 19, 2005, https://www.telegraph.co.uk/news/uknews/1503379/His-goal-was-to-make-it-simple-to-use-and-a-joy-to-look-at.-He-succeeded.-The-result-was-the-iPod.html.

13. Jonny Evans, "Ive Talks Design," *Macworld*, March 4, 2008. https://www.macworld.co.uk/opinion/ive-talks-design-3484673/.

14. "Black+Decker Model TO1373SSD," JC Penny, accessed November 28, 2021, https://www.jcpenney.com/p/blackdecker-4-slice-countertop-toaster-oven/ppr5007211650?pTmplType=regular&catId=SearchResults&searchTerm=TO1373SSD&productGridView=medium&badge=collection.

15. "Cuisinart Model TOB-40N," JC Penny, accessed November 28, 2021, https://www.jcpenney.com/p/cuisinart-custom-classic-toaster-oven-broiler/ppr5007163451?pTmplType=regular&catId=SearchResults&searchTerm=cuisinart+toaster&productGridView=medium&urlState=brand%3Dcuisinart%26product_type%3Dtoasters%2B%252B%2Bovens&badge=fewleft.

16. "Adult Toothbrush," Save Rite Medical, accessed March 1, 2021, https://www.saveritemedical.com/products/adult-toothbrush.

17. "Alessi Kettle, 9093," Williams Sonoma, accessed March 1, 2021, https://www.williams-sonoma.com/products/alessi-9093-kettle.

18. "Mr. Coffee Carterton Stainless Steel Whistling Tea Kettle, 1.5-Quart, Mirror Polish," Amazon, accessed March 1, 2021, https://www.amazon.com/Mr-Coffee-91408-02-Carterton-Stainless/dp/B00F9U0O20.

19. "How Product Design Decisions Can Make or Break Your Cost Model," *Manufacturing Hub*, accessed March 1, 2021, https://www.manufacturinghub.io/product-design/how-product-design-decisions-can-make-or-break-your-cost-model/.

20. Melissa Dalrymple, Sam Pickover, and Benedict Sheppard, "Are You Asking Enough from Your Design Leaders?" *McKinsey Quarterly*, February 19, 2020, https://www.mckinsey.com/business-functions/mckinsey-design/our-insights/are-you-asking-enough-from-your-design-leaders.

21. Benedict Sheppard et al., "The Business Value of Design," *McKinsey Quarterly*, October 25, 2018, https://www.mckinsey.com/business-functions/mckinsey-design/our-insights/the-business-value-of-design.

22. Abigail Stevenson, "T-Mobile CEO to Cramer: 'Shut Up and Listen,'" Mad Money, April 29, 2015, https://www.cnbc.com/2015/04/28/t-mobile-ceo-to-cramer-shut-up-and-listen.html.

23. IKEA, "Inter IKEA Group Financial Summary FY17," accessed March 1, 2021, https://preview.thenewsmarket.com/Previews/IKEA/DocumentAssets/493700.pdf.

CHAPTER 4

1. W. Edwards Deming, *Out of the Crisis* (Cambridge, MA: The MIT Press, 1986), 87.

2. For further information on the phase-gate process, see Karl T. Ulrich, Steven D. Eppinger, and Maria C. Yang, "Chapter 2: Product Development Process and Organization," in *Product Design and Development, Seventh Edition* (New York: McGraw Hill, 2020), 11–33; and Robert G. Cooper, "Chapter 4: The Stage-Gate® Idea-to-Launch System," in *Winning at New Products: Creating Value Through Innovation, Fifth Edition* (New York: Basic Books, 2017), 99–146.

3. Anil Khurana and Stephen R. Rosenthal, "Integrating the Fuzzy Front End of New Product Development," *Sloan Management Review* 38, no. 2 (Winter 1997): 190–191.

4. For each phase, roles are best defined by including whether the role is responsible for conducting the activity, accountable for the activity, consulted during the activity, or informed about the activity.

5. For each gate, roles are best defined by including whether the role is responsible for conducting the activity, accountable for the activity, consulted during the activity, or informed about the activity.

6. For further information on lean production, see James P. Womack, Daniel T. Jones, and Daniel Roos, *The Machine That Changed the World* (New York: Scribner, 1990).

7. For further information on lean thinking as it applies more broadly to the enterprise, see James P. Womack and Daniel T. Jones, *Lean Thinking, Second Edition* (New York: The Free Press, 1996).

8. See, for example, Deming, *Out of the Crisis*, 88.

9. For further information on lean product development, see Allan C. Ward and Durward K. Sobeck II, *Lean Product and Process Development, Second Edition* (Cambridge, MA: Lean Enterprise Institute, 2014); James M. Morgan and Jeffrey K. Liker, *The Toyota Product Development System* (New York: Productivity Press, 2006); Michael N. Kennedy, *Product Development for the Lean Enterprise* (Richmond, VA: The Oaklea Press, 2003); and Barry L. Cross, *Lean Innovation: Understanding What's Next in Today's Economy* (Boca Raton, FL: CRC Press, 2003).

10. For further information on the lean startup, see Steve Blank, *The Four Steps to the Epiphany: Successful Strategies for Products That Win* (Palo Alto, CA: K&S Ranch Press, 2005); and Eric Ries, *The Lean Startup* (New York: Crown Business, 2011).

11. For further information on open innovation, see Henry Chesbrough, *Open Innovation* (Boston: Harvard Business School Press, 2003); and Charles H. Noble, Serdar S. Durmusoglu, and Abbie Griffin, eds., *Open Innovation: New Product Development Essentials from the PDMA* (Hoboken, NJ: John Wiley & Sons, 2014).

12. For further information on open innovation in SMMEs, see Wim Vanhaverbeke, *Managing Open Innovation in SMEs* (Cambridge, UK: Cambridge University Press, 2017); Manuel Fernández-Esquinas, Madelon van Oostrom, Hugo Pinto, eds., *Innovation in SMEs and Micro Firms: Culture, Entrepreneurial Dynamics and Regional Development* (New York: Routledge, 2018); and Claudine Gay and Berangere L. Szostak, *Innovation and Creativity in SMEs: Challenges, Evolutions and Prospects* (Hoboken, NJ: John Wiley & Sons, 2019).

13. For information on Michael Porter's generic strategies, see Michael E. Porter, *Competitive Strategy: Techniques for Analyzing Industries and Competitors* (New York: The Free Press, 1980); and Roger L. Martin, "There Are Still Only Two Ways to Compete," *Harvard Business Review*, April 21, 2015, https://hbr.org/2015/04/there-are-still-only-two-ways-to-compete.

14. Steven C. Wheelwright and Kim B. Clark, "Creating Project Plans to Focus Product Development," *Harvard Business Review* (March–April 1992): 70–82.

CHAPTER 5

1. Abbie Griffin, Raymond L. Price, and Bruce A. Vojak, *Serial Innovators: How Individuals Create and Deliver Breakthrough Innovations in Mature Firms* (Stanford, CA: Stanford University Press, 2012).

2. See, for example, portions of the following in which entrepreneurs are profiled: Adam Grant, *Originals: How Non-Conformists Move the World* (New York: Viking, 2016); and Melissa A. Schilling, *Quirky: The Remarkable Story of the Traits, Foibles, and Genius of Breakthrough Innovators Who Changed the World* (New York: PublicAffairs, 2018).

3. See John Carreyrou, *Bad Blood: Secrets and Lies in a Silicon Valley Startup* (New York: Alfred A. Knopf, 2018).

4. See Frederick Winslow Taylor, *The Principles of Scientific Management* (New York: Harper & Brothers, 1911).

5. Griffin, Price, and Vojak, *Serial Innovators*.

6. Nancy Dawes's story was developed through a series of private communications with her during 2020 and 2021.

7. Tom's story is shared in the "Introduction" of Griffin, Price, and Vojak, *Serial Innovators*, 3–9.

8. "Chapter 6: Identifying and Developing Serial Innovators," in Griffin, Price, and Vojak, *Serial Innovators*, 135–151.

9. "Chapter 2: The Processes by Which Serial Innovators Innovate," in Griffin, Price, and Vojak, *Serial Innovators*, 36–69.

10. Joshua Wolf Shenk, *Powers of Two: Finding the Essence of Innovation in Creative Pairs* (New York: Houghton Mifflin Harcourt, 2014).

11. David E. Goldberg, "The Importance of Pairwork in Interdisciplinary and Educational Initiatives," *Proceedings of the 39th ASEE/IEEE Frontiers in Education Conference* (2009).

12. See John M. Hebda, Bruce A. Vojak, Abbie Griffin, and Raymond L. Price, "Motivating Technical Visionaries in Large American Companies," *IEEE Transactions on Engineering Management* 54 (2007): 433–444; Hebda, Vojak, Griffin, and Price, "Motivating and Demotivating Technical Visionaries in Large Corporations: A Comparison of Perspectives," *R&D Management* 42 (2012): 101–119; and "Chapter 7: Managing Serial Innovators for Impact," in Griffin, Price, and Vojak, *Serial Innovators*, 152–182.

13. W. Edwards Deming, *Out of the Crisis* (Cambridge, MA: The MIT Press, 1986), 88.

14. Examples include the six sigma DMAIC (Define, Measure, Analyze, Improve, Control) Process or the more strategic OODA (Observe, Orient, Decide, Act) Loop.

15. See Eric O'Donnell, "Clark Terry's 3 Steps to Learning Improvisation," Jazz Advice, published on June 9, 2011, video, 1:07, https://www.jazzadvice.com/clark-terrys-3-steps-to-learning-improvisation/; and Clark Terry, "Clark Terry, NYPL Jazz Oral History," The New York Public Library, published on September 16, 2008, interviewed on September 15, 1993, YouTube video, 0:20, https://www.youtube.com/watch?v=Gs7scf4nymU&feature=emb_logo.

CHAPTER 6

1. Dorie Clark, "If Strategy Is So Important, Why Don't We Make Time for It?" *Harvard Business Review*, June 21, 2018, https://hbr.org/2018/06/if-strategy-is-so-important-why-dont-we-make-time-for-it.

2. Robert A. Pitts and Charles C. Snow, *Strategies for Competitive Success* (New York: Wiley, 1986).

3. Pitts and Snow, "Chapter 2: Achieving Competitive Advantage Through Market Share," in *Strategies for Competitive Success*, 7–23.

4. Pitts and Snow, "Chapter 4: Achieving Competitive Advantage through Synergy," in *Strategies for Competitive Success*, 47–62.

5. For information on Michael Porter's generic strategies, see Michael E. Porter, *Competitive Strategy: Techniques for Analyzing Industries and Competitors* (New York: The Free Press, 1980); and Roger L. Martin, "There Are Still Only Two Ways to Compete," *Harvard Business Review*, April 21, 2015, https://hbr.org/2015/04/there-are-still-only-two-ways-to-compete.

6. Larry Keeley, Ryan Pikkel, Brian Quinn, and Helen Walters, *Ten Types of Innovation: The Discipline of Building Breakthroughs* (Hoboken, NJ: John Wiley & Sons, 2013), 16–17.

7. Ana Margarida Gamboa and Helena Martins Gonçalves, "Customer Loyalty Through Social Networks: Lessons from Zara on Facebook," *Business Horizons* 57, no. 6 (November–December 2014): 709–717.

8. Brian Fleming, "Challenging the Traditional Higher Education Model: College for America at Southern New Hampshire University," in *Taking Action: Positioning Low Income Workers to Succeed in a Changing Economy*, The Hatcher Group, 2019, https://www.aecf.org/resources/taking-action/.

9. Rita Gunther McGrath and Ian MacMillan, "Discovery-Driven Planning," *Harvard Business Review*, (July–August 1995): 4–12.

10. Earl Conway and Paul Batalden, "Like Magic? ('Every System Is Perfectly Designed . .')," Institute for Healthcare Improvement, August 21, 2015, http://www.ihi.org/communities/blogs/origin-of-every-system-is-perfectly-designed-quote.

11. Note that while we could easily omit "market share → economies of scale" and "synergies → economies of scope" in Figure 6.1 for this discussion, we included them in that earlier section to help guide the reader with additional detail.

12. Matt Preuss, "V2MOM: The Salesforce Secret to Company Alignment," accessed March 1, 2021, https://visible.vc/blog/v2mom-salesforce/.

13. Preuss, "V2MOM."

14. Preuss, "V2MOM."

15. John Doerr, "When John Doerr Brought a 'Gift' to Google's Founders" (an excerpt from his book, *Measure What Matters*), *Wired*, April

24, 2018, accessed November 30, 2021, https://www.wired.com/story/when-john-doerr-brought-a-gift-to-googles-founders/.

16. Rick Klau, "How Google Sets Goals," October 25, 2012, https://library.gv.com/how-google-sets-goals-okrs-a1f69b0b72c7.

17. While Android was acquired, not founded, by Google, the purchase was completed early on in Android's life, well before it rose to the prominence it enjoys at the time of writing.

18. Google, "Google's OKR Playbook," What Matters, accessed March 1, 2021, https://www.whatmatters.com/resources/google-okr-playbook/.

19. Google, "Google's OKR Playbook."

20. Google, "Google's OKR Playbook."

21. Google, "Our Approach to Search," accessed March 1, 2021, https://www.google.com/search/howsearchworks/mission/.

22. *Moneyball*, directed by Bennett Miller (Culver City, CA: Columbia Pictures, 2011).

23. Calvada Productions, "Don't the Suit Fit Nice," excerpt from "The Sleeping Brother," season 1, episode 27 of *The Dick Van Dyke Show*, March 28, 1962, YouTube video clip, 1:09, https://www.youtube.com/watch?v=gpWLwp6GR9Q.

24. A striking statement to this effect appeared in an exchange on LinkedIn. In response to the prompt, "Most think that innovation labs fail because of _____, when they really fail because of _____ ." an insightful, experienced, outspoken individual shared, "Forget that. Innovation fails as soon as you have the lab." Nicholas Partridge, "Most Think That...," LinkedIn, March 13, 2021, https://www.linkedin.com/posts/npartridge_most-think-that-innovation-labs-fail-because-activity-6776513711566938112-ZRAg.

25. Clayton Christensen, *The Innovator's Dilemma* (Boston: Harvard Business Review Press, 1997).

26. See, for example, Gina Colarelli O'Connor, Andrew C. Corbett, and Lois S. Peters, *Beyond the Champion: Institutionalizing Innovation Through People* (Stanford, CA: Stanford University Press, 2018); and Gina O'Connor, "Real Innovation Requires More Than an R&D Budget," *Harvard Business Review*, December 19, 2019, https://hbr.org/2019/12/real-innovation-requires-more-than-an-rd-budget.

27. Justin Bariso, "Why Intelligent Minds Like Elon Musk and Steve Jobs Embrace the 'No Silo Rule,'" *Inc.com*, October 28, 2020, https://www.inc.com/justin-bariso/why-intelligent-minds-like-elon-musk-steve-jobs-embrace-no-silo-rule.html.

CHAPTER 7

1. The Midtronics story was developed through a series of private communications with Steve McShane, Will Sampson, Kevin Bertness, and Jason Ruban in late 2020. For full disclosure, Bruce serves on Midtronics' advisory board.

2. Midtronics, "We Are Midtronics," accessed March 1, 2020, https://www.midtronics.com/.

3. For a list of Midtronics' values, see https://www.midtronics.com/about-midtronics/.

4. Kevin A. Wilson, "Worth the Watt: A Brief History of the Electric Car, 1830 to Present," *Car and Driver*, March 15, 2018, https://www.caranddriver.com/features/g15378765/worth-the-watt-a-brief-history-of-the-electric-car-1830-to-present/.

CHAPTER 8

1. "Ducunt volentem fata, nolentem trahunt." From Seneca, *Epistulae Morales ad Lucilium*, 107.11, *Encyclopaedia Britannica*, s.v. "Seneca: Roman Philosopher and Statesman [4 BCE – 65 CE]," accessed March 1, 2021, https://www.britannica.com/biography/Lucius-Annaeus-Seneca-Roman-philosopher-and-statesman.

2. If you want a glimpse of what happens to an entire community when most, if not all of the employers, engage in a race to the bottom, see the following: Brian Alexander, "Where Progress Stopped," *MIT Technology Review*, (March/April 2021), 58–63.

3. And as an aside, any savvy supplier or customer will already have noticed your behavior and eventually will act accordingly.

4. Abbie Griffin, Raymond L. Price, and Bruce A. Vojak, *Serial Innovators: How Individuals Create and Deliver Breakthrough Innovations in Mature Firms* (Stanford, CA: Stanford University Press, 2012).

APPENDIX 2

1. Andrew Bolwell, "What Type of Innovator Are You?" September 24, 2014. https://andrewbolwell.com/2014/09/24/what-type-of-innovator-are-you/.

Bibliography

Agile Alliance. "Manifesto for Agile Software Development." Accessed November 19, 2021. https://agilemanifesto.org/.

Alexander, Brian. "Where Progress Stopped." *MIT Technology Review* (March/April 2021): 58–63.

Bariso, Justin. "Why Intelligent Minds Like Elon Musk and Steve Jobs Embrace the 'No Silo Rule.'" *Inc.com*, October 28, 2020. https://www.inc.com/justin-bariso/why-intelligent-minds-like-elon-musk-steve-jobs-embrace-no-silo-rule.html.

Baumol, William J. *Good Capitalism, Bad Capitalism, and the Economics of Growth and Prosperity.* New Haven, CT: Yale University Press, 2007.

Bennet, Nathan, and G. James Lemoine. "What VUCA Really Means for You." *Harvard Business Review* (January–February 2014).

Berg, Justin. "Balancing on the Creative Highwire: Forecasting the Success of Novel Ideas in Organizations." *Administrative Science Quarterly* 61, no. 3 (2016): 433–468.

Blank, Steve. *The Four Steps to the Epiphany: Successful Strategies for Products That Win.* Palo Alto, CA: K&S Ranch Press, 2005.

Bolwell, Andrew. "What Type of Innovator Are You?" September 24, 2014. https://andrewbolwell.com/2014/09/24/what-type-of-innovator-are-you/.

Braun. "Braun History: In Depth." December 2014. https://www.braun.de/assets/de-de/pdf/braun-history.pdf.

Calcaterra, Craig. "Opening Day 2019: 'Everybody Has a Plan Until They Get Punched in the Mouth.'" NBC Sports. March 28, 2019. https://mlb.nbcsports.com/2019/03/28/opening-day-2019-everybody-has-a-plan-until-they-get-punched-in-the-mouth/.

Calvada Productions. "Don't the Suit Fit Nice." Excerpt from "The Sleeping Brother." Season 1, episode 27. *The Dick Van Dyke Show*. March 28, 1962. YouTube video clip, 1:09. https://www.youtube.com/watch?v=gpWLwp6GR9Q.

Carreyrou, John. *Bad Blood: Secrets and Lies in a Silicon Valley Startup*. New York: Alfred A. Knopf, 2018.

Chesbrough, Henry. *Open Innovation*. Boston: Harvard Business School Press, 2003.

Christensen, Clayton. *The Innovator's Dilemma*. Boston: Harvard Business Review Press, 1997.

Clark, Dorie. "If Strategy Is So Important, Why Don't We Make Time for It?" *Harvard Business Review*, June 21, 2018. https://hbr.org/2018/06/if-strategy-is-so-important-why-dont-we-make-time-for-it.

Company Histories. "Braun GmbH." Accessed March 1, 2021. https://www.company-histories.com/Braun-GmbH-Company-History.html.

Conway, Earl, and Paul Batalden. "Like Magic? ('Every System Is Perfectly Designed . .')." Institute for Healthcare Improvement. August 21, 2015. http://www.ihi.org/communities/blogs/origin-of-every-system-is-perfectly-designed-quote.

Cooper, Robert G. "Chapter 4: The Stage-Gate® Idea-to Launch System." In *Winning at New Products: Creating Value Through Innovation, Fifth Edition*. New York: Basic Books, 2017.

Cross, Barry L. *Lean Innovation: Understanding What's Next in Today's Economy*. Boca Raton, FL: CRC Press, 2003.

Dalrymple, Melissa, Sam Pickover, and Benedict Sheppard. "Are You Asking Enough rom Your Design Leaders?" *McKinsey Quarterly*, February 19, 2020. https://www.mckinsey.com/business-functions/mckinsey-design/our-insights/are-you-asking-enough-from-your-design-leaders.

Deming, W. Edwards. *Out of the Crisis*. Cambridge, MA: The MIT Press, 1986.

Derbyshire, David. "His Goal Was to Make It Simple to Use and a Joy to Look At. He Succeeded. The Result Was the iPod." *The Telegraph*, November 19, 2005. https://www.telegraph.co.uk/news/uknews/1503379/His-goal-was-to-make-it-simple-to-use-and-a-joy-to-look-at.-He-succeeded.-The-result-was-the-iPod.html.

Doerr, John. "When John Doerr Brought a 'Gift' to Google's Founders" (an excerpt from his book, *Measure What Matters*). *Wired*, April 24, 2018. https://www.wired.com/story/when-john-doerr-brought-a-gift-to-googles-founders/.

Dunning, David, Chip Heath, and Jerry M. Suls. "Flawed Self-Assessment: Implications for Health, Education and the Workplace." *Psychological Science in the Public Interest* 5, no. 3 (2004): 69–106.

Evans, Jonny. "Ive Talks Design." *Macworld*, March 4, 2008. https://www.macworld.co.uk/opinion/ive-talks-design-3484673/.

Ferdman, Roberto A. "Baby Carrots Are Not Baby Carrots." *The Washington Post*, January 13, 2016. https://www.washingtonpost.com/news/wonk/wp/2016/01/13/no-one-understands-baby-carrots/.

Fernández-Esquinas, Manuel, Madelon van Oostrom, and Hugo Pinto, eds. *Innovation in SMEs and Micro Firms: Culture, Entrepreneurial Dynamics and Regional Development*. New York: Routledge, 2018.

Fleming, Brian. "Challenging the Traditional Higher Education Model: College for America at Southern New Hampshire University." In *Taking Action: Positioning Low Income Workers to Succeed in a Changing Economy*. The Hatcher Group, 2019. https://www.aecf.org/resources/taking-action/.

Gamboa, Ana Margarida, and Helena Martins Gonçalves. "Customer Loyalty Through Social Networks: Lessons from Zara on Facebook." *Business Horizons* 57, no. 6 (November–December 2014): 709–717.

Gaskin, Steven P., Abbie Griffin, John R. Hauser, Gerald M. Katz, and Robert L. Klein. "Voice of the Customer." *Wiley International Encyclopedia of Marketing*. December 15, 2010. https://doi.org/10.1002/9781444316568.wiem05020.

Gay, Claudine, and Berangere L. Szostak. *Innovation and Creativity in SMEs: Challenges, Evolutions and Prospects*. Hoboken, NJ: John Wiley & Sons, 2019.

Gayathri, Amrutha. "Steve Jobs' Personal Life: His Idiosyncrasies, Likes and Dislikes." *International Business Times*, October 8, 2011. https://www.ibtimes.com/steve-jobs-personal-life-his-idiosyncrasies-likes-dislikes-322098.

Goldberg, David E. "The Importance of Pairwork in Interdisciplinary and Educational Initiatives." *Proceedings of the 39th ASEE/IEEE Frontiers in Education Conference* (2009).

Google. "Google's OKR Playbook." What Matters. Accessed March 1, 2021. https://www.whatmatters.com/resources/google-okr-playbook/.

———. "Our Approach to Search." Accessed March 1, 2021. https://www.google.com/search/howsearchworks/mission/.

Grant, Adam. *Originals: How Non-Conformists Move the World*. New York: Viking, 2016.

Griffin, Abbie, and John R. Hauser. "The Voice of the Customer." *Marketing Science* 12, no. 3 (1993): 1–27.

Griffin, Abbie, Raymond L. Price, and Bruce A. Vojak. *Serial Innovators: How Individuals Create and Deliver Breakthrough Innovations in Mature Firms.* Stanford, CA: Stanford University Press, 2012.

Hebda, John M., Bruce A. Vojak, Abbie Griffin, and Raymond L. Price. "Motivating Technical Visionaries in Large American Companies." *IEEE Transactions on Engineering Management* 54 (2007): 433–444.

———. "Motivating and Demotivating Technical Visionaries in Large Corporations: A Comparison of Perspectives." *R&D Management* 42 (2012): 101–119.

Heshmat, Shahram. "What Is Confirmation Bias?" *Psychology Today*, April 23, 2015. https://www.psychologytoday.com/us/blog/science-choice/201504/what-is-confirmation-bias.

"How Product Design Decisions Can Make or Break Your Cost Model." *Manufacturing Hub.* Accessed March 1, 2021. https://www.manufacturinghub.io/product-design/how-product-design-decisions-can-make-or-break-your-cost-model/.

IKEA. "Inter IKEA Group Financial Summary FY17." Accessed March 1, 2021. https://www.ikea.com/ms/en_CA/pdf/yearly_summary/IKEA_Group_Summary_2017.pdf.

Isaacson, Walter. *Steve Jobs.* New York: Simon & Schuster, 2011.

Johnson, Samuel. *The Rambler*, no. 178, Saturday, November 30, 1751. https://www.johnsonessays.com/the-rambler/no-178-many-advantages-not-to-be-enjoyed-together/.

JVA Partners. "Creating Value." Accessed March 1, 2021. https://jvapartners.com/.

Keeley, Larry, Ryan Pikkel, Brian Quinn, and Helen Walters. *Ten Types of Innovation: The Discipline of Building Breakthroughs.* Hoboken, NJ: John Wiley & Sons, 2013.

Kennedy, Michael N. *Product Development for the Lean Enterprise.* Richmond, VA: The Oaklea Press, 2003.

Khurana, Anil, and Stephen R. Rosenthal. "Integrating the Fuzzy Front End of New Product Development." *Sloan Management Review* 38, no. 2 (Winter 1997): 190–191. https://doi.org/10.1016/s0737-6782(98)90098-4.

Klau, Rick. "How Google Sets Goals." October 25, 2012. https://library.gv.com/how-google-sets-goals-okrs-a1f69b0b72c7.

Kolko, Jon. "Design Thinking Comes of Age." *Harvard Business Review* (September 2015).

Kraaijenbrink, Jeroen. "What Does VUCA Really Mean?" *Forbes*, December 19, 2018.

Levine, Marne. "The No-Filter Leadership Style of Instagram COO Marne Levine." *Fast Company*, November 17, 2017. https://www.fastcompany.com/40491509/the-no-filter-leadership-style-of-instagram-coo-marne-levine.

Levins, Cory. "Box Cutter Safety Tips to Follow." Air Sea Containers. October 15, 2017. https://www.airseacontainers.com/blog/box-cutter-safety-tips/.

Lewis, Michael. *Moneyball: The Art of Winning an Unfair Game.* New York: W. W. Norton, 2003.

Liedtka, Jeanne. "Why Design Thinking Works." *Harvard Business Review* (September–October 2018).

Martin, Roger L. "There Are Still Only Two Ways to Compete." *Harvard Business Review*, April 21, 2015. https://hbr.org/2015/04/there-are-still-only-two-ways-to-compete.

McGrath, Rita Gunther, and Ian MacMillan. "Discovery-Driven Planning." *Harvard Business Review* (July–August 1995).

Midtronics. "We Are Midtronics." Accessed March 1, 2020. https://www.midtronics.com/.

Moneyball. Directed by Bennett Miller. Culver City, CA: Columbia Pictures, 2011.

Morgan, James M., and Jeffrey K. Liker. *The Toyota Product Development System.* New York: Productivity Press, 2006.

Noble, Charles H., Serdar S. Durmusoglu, and Abbie Griffin, eds. *Open Innovation: New Product Development Essentials from the PDMA.* Hoboken, NJ: John Wiley & Sons, 2014.

"#26 Oakland Athletics." *Forbes.* Accessed March 1, 2021. https://www.forbes.com/teams/oakland-athletics/?sh=4894df3626ac.

Objectified. Directed by Gary Hustwit. Brooklyn, NY: Plexi Productions, 2009.

O'Connor, Gina. "Real Innovation Requires More Than an R&D Budget." *Harvard Business Review*, December 19, 2019. https://hbr.org/2019/12/real-innovation-requires-more-than-an-rd-budget.

O'Connor, Gina Colarelli, Andrew C. Corbett, and Lois S. Peters. *Beyond the Champion: Institutionalizing Innovation Through People.* Stanford, CA: Stanford University Press, 2018.

O'Donnell, Eric. "Clark Terry's 3 Steps to Learning Improvisation." Jazz Advice. Published on June 9, 2011. Video, 1:07. https://www.jazzadvice.com/clark-terrys-3-steps-to-learning-improvisation/.

Oregon State University Libraries Special Collections & Archives Research Center. "Clarifying Three Widespread Quotes." *The Pauling Blog.* October 8, 2008. https://paulingblog.wordpress.com/2008/10/28/clarifying-three-widespread-quotes/.

O'Reilly III, Charles A., and Michael L. Tushman. "The Ambidextrous Organization." *Harvard Business Review* (April 2004).

OXO. "We Believe in a Better Way." Accessed March 1, 2021. https://www.oxo.com/aboutus.

Partridge, Nicholas. "Most Think That Innovation Labs Fail Because of _____ , When They Really Fail Because of _____." LinkedIn. March 13, 2021. https://www.linkedin.com/posts/npartridge_most-think-that-innovation-labs-fail-because-activity-6776513711566938112-ZRAg.

Pink, Daniel H. *A Whole New Mind: Why Right-Brainers Will Rule the Future.* New York: Riverhead Books, 2005.

Pitts, Robert A., and Charles C. Snow. *Strategies for Competitive Success.* New York: Wiley, 1986.

Porter, Michael E. *Competitive Strategy: Techniques for Analyzing Industries and Competitors.* New York: The Free Press, 1980.

Preuss, Matt. "V2MOM: The Salesforce Secret to Company Alignment." Accessed March 1, 2021. https://visible.vc/blog/v2mom-salesforce/.

Ries, Eric. *The Lean Startup.* New York: Crown Business, 2011.

Russ, Alissa L., Rollin J. Fairbanks, Ben-Tzion Karsh, Laura G. Militello, Jason J. Saleem, and Robert L. Wears. "The Science of Human Factors: Separating Fact from Fiction." *BMJ Quality and Safety* 22, no. 10 (2013): 802–808. http://dx.doi.org/10.1136/bmjqs-2012-001450.

Schilling, Melissa A. *Quirky: The Remarkable Story of the Traits, Foibles, and Genius of Breakthrough Innovators Who Changed the World.* New York: PublicAffairs, 2018.

Seneca. *Epistulae Morales ad Lucilium,* 107.11.

Shenk, Joshua Wolf. *Powers of Two: Finding the Essence of Innovation in Creative Pairs.* New York: Houghton Mifflin Harcourt, 2014.

Sheppard, Benedict, Hugo Sarrazin, Garen Kouyoumjian, and Fabricio Dore. "The Business Value of Design." *McKinsey Quarterly,* October 25, 2018. https://www.mckinsey.com/business-functions/mckinsey-design/our-insights/the-business-value-of-design.

Simon, Herbert A. *The Sciences of the Artificial.* Cambridge, MA: The MIT Press, 1969.

Slice. "About Slice." Accessed March 1, 2021. https://www.sliceproducts.com/content/about-slice.

Sliwinski, Michael. "10 Design Principles by Dieter Rams." Accessed March 1, 2021. https://sliwinski.com/designed/.

Stevenson, Abigail. "T-Mobile CEO to Cramer: 'Shut Up and Listen.'" Mad Money, April 29, 2015. https://www.cnbc.com/2015/04/28/t-mobile-ceo-to-cramer-shut-up-and-listen.html.

Sutton, Robert I. "If You're the Boss, Start Killing More Good Ideas." *Harvard Business Review*, August 27, 2010. https://hbr.org/2010/08/if-youre-the-boss-start-killin.

Taylor, Frederick Winslow. *The Principles of Scientific Management*. New York: Harper & Brothers, 1911.

Terry, Clark. "Clark Terry, NYPL Jazz Oral History." The New York Public Library. Published on September 16, 2008. Interviewed on September 15, 1993. YouTube video, 0:20. https://www.youtube.com/watch?v=Gs7scf4nymU&feature=emb_logo.

Tushman, Michael L., Wendy K. Smith, and Andy Binns. "The Ambidextrous CEO." *Harvard Business Review* (June 2011).

Ulrich, Karl T., Steven D. Eppinger, and Maria C. Yang. "Chapter 2: Product Development Process and Organization." In *Product Design and Development, Seventh Edition*. New York: McGraw Hill, 2020.

Vanhaverbeke, Wim. *Managing Open Innovation in SMEs*. Cambridge, UK: Cambridge University Press, 2017.

Walker, Rob. "The Guts of a New Machine." *New York Times*, November 30, 2003. https://www.nytimes.com/2003/11/30/magazine/the-guts-of-a-new-machine.html.

Ward, Allan C., and Durward K. Sobeck II. *Lean Product and Process Development, Second Edition*. Cambridge, MA: Lean Enterprise Institute, 2014.

Wes-Tech Automation Solutions. "Your Automation Advantage." Accessed March 1, 2021. https://wes-tech.com/.

Wheelwright, Steven C., and Kim B. Clark. "Creating Project Plans to Focus Product Development." *Harvard Business Review* (March–April 1992).

Wilson, Kevin A. "Worth the Watt: A Brief History of the Electric Car, 1830 to Present." *Car and Driver*, March 15, 2018. https://www.caranddriver.com/features/g15378765/worth-the-watt-a-brief-history-of-the-electric-car-1830-to-present/.

Womack, James P., and Daniel T. Jones. *Lean Thinking, Second Edition*. New York: The Free Press, 1996.

Womack, James P., Daniel T. Jones, and Daniel Roos. *The Machine That Changed the World*. New York: Scribner, 1990.

Wright, Randall S. "Connecting to the Counterculture: The Interview Guide." *Research-Technology Management* 60, no. 5 (September–October 2017): 52–54.

Index